Mound Builders and Monument Makers of the Northern Great Lakes, 1200–1600

Mound Builders and Monument Makers of the Northern Great Lakes, 1200–1600

Meghan C. L. Howey

University of Oklahoma Press | Norman

Library of Congress Cataloging-in-Publication Data

Howey, Meghan C. L., 1978–
   Mound builders and monument makers of the northern Great Lakes, 1200–1600 / Meghan C. L. Howey.
       p. cm.
   Includes bibliographical references and index.
   ISBN 978-0-8061-4288-3 (hardcover : alk. paper) 1. Mound-builders—Great Lakes Region (North America) 2. Mounds—Great Lakes Region (North America) 3. Great Lakes Region (North America)—Antiquities. I. Title.
   E78.G7H69 2012
   977—dc23
                          2012014111

Interior layout and composition: Alcorn Publication Design

Contents

Illustrations

Tables

Acknowledgments

At the heart of this book is the past captured in the archaeological landscape of northern Michigan. Studying this landscape has allowed me to learn new things about the depth and complexity of human societies. This volume represents my effort to share what I have learned with others. While this book is about the past, it would not have been possible without the help of countless people in the present. I want to take this opportunity to express my deep gratitude to those who have helped me in this journey.

Since first deciding to pursue anthropological archaeology as an undergraduate, I have been the lucky beneficiary of extensive mentoring and support from senior scholars. Many have taken time to help me along the way and foster my intellectual growth. Their generosity makes me proud and grateful to be part of this discipline.

First, I thank the faculty at the University of Michigan for an exciting graduate education and continued guidance today. John O'Shea deserves primary mention for the support he has given me throughout the research process behind this book, which began as my dissertation and developed into a larger, ongoing program. By always challenging me to push my work and interpretations further, John has helped me become a better scholar. His support has never wavered, even in moments when I have, and this has meant the world to me. He is a mentor in the best sense of the word. This work has benefited immensely from the critical feedback provided by Carla Sinopoli, Robert Whallon, and Gregory Dowd. I also want to extend deep gratitude to Joyce Marcus for her steadfast encouragement to publish this book.

I want to thank my undergraduate mentors, Karen Rosenberg and Thomas Rocek, at the University of Delaware. I turn to them continuously for advice and am grateful that they are always there to offer it. I want to acknowledge the archaeology faculty at Michigan State University, especially Bill Lovis, Jodie O'Gorman, Lynne Goldstein, and John Norder, who shared their knowledge so readily, provided me easy access to their collections, and supported my work in ways far beyond my expectations. Timothy Pauketat of the University of Illinois also has gone above and beyond in supporting my development as an archaeologist as well as the publication of this book. His work inspires me to think in new ways, and his help is a much appreciated gift. I am deeply grateful to my many University of New Hampshire colleagues who have helped me. In particular, I want to thank my chair, Joe Lugalla, for his great support of junior faculty and Siobhan Senier for mentoring me.

The field research presented in this book relied on the generosity of landowners, the labor of others, and funding from the James B. Griffin Fellowship and the Halsey Fund at the University of Michigan Museum of Anthropology (UMMA). George Masters allowed me to work at the Cut River Mounds site (20RO1) and gave me free reign to do my research on his land. Hiroko Cook granted me permission to work at the Chief White Bird site (20RO50) and became a real friend as we worked in her yard. The University of Michigan granted me permission to work on the Missaukee Earthworks (20MA11–12) and the Michigan Department of Natural Resources (DNR) gave me permits to work at the Meade's Bridge site (20RO5). Numerous UMMA field school students participated in excavations at sites central to this project. My thanks go to all the field school students as well as all of the other students and friends who helped me do my field research. I especially want to thank Margaret Wilson, Dan Pugh, Allison Davis, Mary Smith, Eli Adam, Amy Roache, Steph Salwen, Brad Krueger, Kyle Stock, Alice Yao, and Bethany Dykstra. Amy Nicodemus did all faunal analysis, and Katie Parker did all of the floral analysis; this project has benefited tremendously from their expertise.

A Junior Faculty Fellowship from the University of New Hampshire Center for the Humanities provided invaluable time to finish the manuscript. The University of New Hampshire Department of Anthropology and College of Liberal Arts Dean's Office provided funding for copyediting and indexing of the book. Special thanks to Kathy Lewis and Susan Kennedy, who did wonderful jobs copyediting. Alessandra Jacobi Tamulevich and Emily Jerman at the University of Oklahoma Press have been generous in helping me through the process of publishing.

Finally, this book would not have been possible without the love and support of family and friends. As a professor, my mother, Jacquelyn, showed me the power and importance of knowledge and education in the world. She taught me to be committed and driven, to follow my dreams wherever they led, but also to remember to laugh along the way. While she is no longer here, she remains in everything I do. I want to thank my dad, Michael, for being there every step of the way; he has been my fan club, my sounding board, and my friend. Thank you to my dad and my sister Cora for being unfailingly proud of me. My deepest gratitude goes to Melissa, my partner, my best friend, and at the end of the day my biggest supporter. She has been truly selfless in supporting my dreams without hesitation. The depth of my gratitude is hard to put into words. While finishing this book, I became a new parent of our beautiful boy, Jack. The past, the present, and the future are connected in him in ways I never saw before. In finishing this work, I look forward to the new chapters of learning that lie ahead of me.

MOUND BUILDERS AND MONUMENT MAKERS OF THE NORTHERN GREAT LAKES, 1200–1600

Introduction

In the summer of 1924 F. M. Vreeland, an avocational archaeologist, went on a site-finding trip in northern Michigan. While in Houghton Lake, a town on Michigan's largest inland lake, Vreeland heard stories of "mounds." He went searching and found three burial mounds near the Mound Hotel, on the north side of the lake at the confluence of the Cut River and Houghton Lake. From people who had been living around the lake for some time, Vreeland (1924) heard the following story (from his personal records):

> A great Indian battle had once been fought on the lake . . . between the Chippewas who resided on the south side of the lake and the Ottawas on the north side. There was a quarrel over the fishing rights of the lake, and a battle ensued and both sides were well-nigh exterminated and the dead of one tribe were buried sitting up in the mounds on the north side of the lake.

Why begin this book with a story recorded by someone who tended to see archaeology as something of a treasure hunt and used exaggerated views of historic American Indian tribes to describe the archaeology of Houghton Lake? Because the facts and fallacies of this story provide a marvelous opportunity to introduce the reader to major themes considered here.

First, the story that Vreeland heard highlights our persistent fascination with mounds—what was their function, and how were they constructed by American Indians? As pioneers pushed west from the original colonies and encountered the thousands of mounds and earthworks spread across the heart of the continent, they developed theories about these structures that were intimately intertwined with the colonial project of building America. The legacies of these incorrect theories are problems that archaeologists must grapple with today.

In this book I focus on a series of mounds and earthworks in northern Michigan that date to circa A.D. 1200–1600. I review past interpretations and present new data to support our current understanding of these impressive mounds and earthworks as part of an actively constructed regional ritual landscape. Cut River Mounds (20RO1), the site mentioned in Vreeland's story, is discussed in detail (see chapter 4). Three important elements of this site are alluded to in his story. First, the "great" battle suggests that the Cut River confluence was a key resource zone for the area's inhabitants, so essential that the rights to it had to be claimed and defined. Second, this natural landmark was imbued with sacred qualities, as evidenced by one group using it to bury its dead. Third, the story of this ancient place was still being told in the 1920s, which indicates that the locale was worthy of legend-making and remembering. Indeed, today's residents of Houghton Lake continue to tell numerous (sometimes similarly speculative) tales about the site.

One goal of this book is to demonstrate how egalitarian societies incorporate ceremonial monuments into their social and ritual behaviors. The elements of the Cut River Mounds outlined above touch on aspects important for understanding how groups formed ties to their territory, resources, sacred places, and community and how memory and cultural commemoration are important to people who have no permanent political hierarchies. While I am not the first scholar to suggest that egalitarian societies construct monuments, such constructions carry a legacy in archaeology. Archaeologists have often believed that they must have been the product of complex and hierarchical societies. This connection is still axiomatic in much archaeological thinking (Randall and Sassaman 2010). I hope that this book contributes to the important and ongoing work of developing models of how past societies used monuments that avoid overemphasizing the idea that this necessarily entailed climbing to a higher evolutionary rung including hereditary and permanent inequality.

I argue that during Late Prehistory (ca. A.D. 1200–1600) the indigenous communities of the northern Great Lakes used mounds and earthworks as ceremonial monuments that formed a "symbolically interactive, topographically bounded, aesthetically effective, and meaningfully holistic landscape" (Dillehay 2007: 318). These egalitarian tribal communities practiced monumentalism by constructing and modifying landscapes in sophisticated ways to coordinate regional developments.

The story from Vreeland also shows how some earlier scholars used postcontact groups to explain precontact history. Vreeland accepts stories about a battle between "the Chippewas" and "the Ottawas" as a reasonable explanation for an archaeological site. Many archaeologies of North America have moved away from using colonially recorded (and often colonially imposed) indigenous groupings as prototypes for the past. Yet this remains a recurring and limiting issue in the Great Lakes, where a static paradigm (which maps historic tribes onto prehistory) has driven the archaeology of Late Prehistory for decades.

A second goal of this book is to find ways to avoid overreliance on simplified views of historic American Indian communities of the northern Great Lakes as prototypes for the past. This kind of simplification hinders our ability to understand the actual dynamic interaction involving precontact communities, postcontact communities, and the way in which both are presented in the textual and material record. I aim to demonstrate how historic and contemporary indigenous stories and beliefs can be weighted and contrasted with archaeological data to develop richer histories overall.

The Mound Builder Myth, the "Savage Slot," and Legacies in North American Archaeology

Two key aspects for Euro-Americans during the colonial era and the establishment of the Republic of the United States were the presence of American Indians and the troubling evidence that they had legitimate claims to the land. This evidence included the thousands of mounds and earthworks spread throughout much of middle and eastern North America. As postrevolutionary "new" Americans pushed west from the original colonies, these earthworks not only inspired awe but also created confusion. How could displacing American Indians from their land be reconciled with this evidence of their long tenure?

The American Indian held a central position in forging the identity of the new Republic of the United States. The Revolution in 1776 had envisioned a radical break from the past, the formation of a political system different from that of dynastic England. Because it was conceived as a break from the metropole, the Revolution left America seeking an "American" identity (Anderson 2006 [1983]: 191–93). Because American Indians were distinctly non-European, their otherness became central to this identity building. "Playing Indian," in the words of Phillip J. Deloria (1998: 63), "allowed rebellious Americans to cross and confound boundaries of national identity."

While people "played Indian" to imagine a new American national identity, a conflict always existed between real Indians and these idealized Indians who let Americans be savage and rebellious yet civilized and orderly (Deloria 1998). The existence of real Indians had long been fascinating and mysterious to European colonists, but by the start of the nineteenth century they viewed Indians as hindrances to America's geopolitical expansion. The new patriots considered Indians to be enemies of the nation (Conn 2004; Deloria 1998). As a consequence, the nineteenth century saw a "rapid naturalizing of the epistemology of racial difference in regard to Native peoples" (Konkle 2004: 39).

At the heart of the nationalist and racially polarized discourse over this "Indian problem" was the question of the origin of real Indians and whether they had indeed built the thousands of earthen constructions throughout North America. The existence of Native American peoples and the evidence that they had legitimate claim to the land had to be explained away (Konkle 2004: 5).

The advance of print capitalism, with newspapers and books booming in postrevolutionary America, was enabling people to relate to others in profoundly new ways and to imagine themselves as part of an American Republic (Anderson 2006 [1983]: 36). Ideas about the geographic and ethnic origins of Native Americans had circulated since the earliest history of colonization. The increase in print capitalism in the late eighteenth and early nineteenth centuries allowed these views to be widely disseminated and consumed by the public and politicians alike.

Questions about the origins and past activities of American Indians formed a major part of political, social, and intellectual discussions during the critical development of the United States from the end of the Revolution through the close of the nineteenth century. The territorial dispossession of Indian lands was a priority, so most U.S. citizens did not want to believe that Indians had a long history. Furthermore, many Euro-Americans did not want to believe that all those impressive mounds had been built by American Indians. It was a lot easier to take land from "savages" who had not been there long and had never used the land "properly" than from people who were capable of the level of culture implied by the great mounds and earthworks (Blakeslee 1987: 789).

A myth emerged in the waning years of the eighteenth century that these mounds had been constructed by an unknown white people that the Indians had destroyed.

Belief in such a "Mound Builder race" offered a way to justify the grabbing of Indian lands (Mallam 1976), so the myth blossomed in the nineteenth century (McGuire 1997: 69).

The Mound Builder myth circulated through the mainstream print media and "won broad acceptance by scholars and the American public" (Thomas 2000: 128). The colonial justifications emerging from the myth are obvious: if Indians had destroyed the white Mound Builders, white Americans were justified in killing Indians and removing them from their lands. The myth offered colonists a palatable way to reconcile the desire to remove American Indians with the evidence that Indians had built settlements and thus had a legitimate claim to the land (Mann 2003). These political ramifications helped the myth circulate and ascend in popularity. Settlers on the frontier, eager to fulfill America's Manifest Destiny, particularly endorsed this myth, because they stood to gain economically from the removal of Indians (Silverberg 1968).

The ultimate political application of this myth came from President Andrew Jackson when he argued for passage of the Indian Removal Act of 1830. In his First Annual Message to Congress on December 8, 1830, Jackson stated:

> Humanity has often wept over the fate of the aborigines of this country, and Philanthropy has been long busily employed in devising means to avert it, but its progress has never for a moment been arrested, and one by one have many powerful tribes disappeared from the earth. To follow to the tomb the last of his race and to tread on the graves of extinct nations excite melancholy reflections. But true philanthropy reconciles the mind to these vicissitudes as it does to the extinction of one generation to make room for another. *In the monuments and fortresses of an unknown people, spread over the extensive regions of the West, we behold the memorials of a once powerful race, which was exterminated or has disappeared to make room for the existing savage tribes.*[1]

The Mound Builder myth, which undermined American Indians' connection to their lands, helped propagate hateful and racist ideas. It was used to justify the physical removal of Indians from their lands, one of the essential components of the colonial project of building America (Miller 2008). The myth allowed the removal of tribes from their homelands to be recast and envisioned as appropriate vengeance "on behalf of that great and martyred ancient culture" (Silverberg 1968: 58).

Thus these ideas about Native American origins and who should be credited with building the mounds shaped America's colonial policies and affected the lives of Indians in the nineteenth century. The Mound Builder myth, so wildly popular in the nineteenth century, was not dismissed by the scholarly community until anthropologist Cyrus Thomas, on an expedition sponsored by the Smithsonian Institution, demonstrated that American Indians had built the mounds (Thomas 1894). Although this deconstruction of the myth was a necessary and important development, it came only after massive land removals already had been accomplished, treaty making had stopped, and the Dawes Act and other policies of assimilation were in full swing. The acknowledgment that the American Indians built the mounds was not made until they were no longer a threat to the country's "progress."

Thomas's 1894 work ended the debate among archaeologists; they now know that the ancestors of living American Indians built the mounds. But acknowledging that the American Indians built the mounds does not free us from the negative impact of the Mound Builder myth.

Scholarly debunking of the myth hardly affected the theory's popularity with the public. Similar ideas continue to circulate today. A simple Google search reveals the prominence of the idea that North American mounds were not built by Indians. Credit is given to Atlantis, to the lost tribes of Israel, and to aliens but not to American Indians. Sadly, these ideas are more widely circulated than scientific studies and must be combated by archaeologists.

Moreover, legacies of the Mound Builder myth lurk in the dark or unconscious corners of academic archaeology (Pauketat 2004: 3). Historical narratives, of which the Mound Builder myth is a powerful (and national) example, can structure our ways of thinking about the past even long after their original circulation (Mann 2005: 2). North American archaeologists have inherited an interpretive conservatism from the nineteenth century that can lead us to downplay the cultural achievements and dynamism of American Indians in pre-Columbian times. Timothy R. Pauketat (2004: 3) challenges readers with the question of what we would call the great site of Cahokia if its monuments were made of stone or constructed in the Near East rather than made of earth in North America. Would we call them pyramids, not mounds; call Cahokia a city, not a town and mound center; consider it the heart of a civilization, not a chiefdom? Stephen Lekson (2010) makes a similar argument about Chaco Canyon. While it is legitimate to debate these questions, discomfort with the idea that a pre-Columbian site in North America could be a city highlights the persistence of views and terms that "downsize" pre-Columbian North American achievements. But being a paramount chiefdom is *not* demeaning. Labels can mask meaningful patterns and behaviors, so we must choose and define them carefully.

Archaeologists must remember and challenge this colonial legacy and continue to move discourse about the pre-Columbian history of North America away from such insidious ideas. Archaeology must show that American Indian history did not begin with Christopher Columbus and did not end with removal (DuVal 2006: 248).

As anthropology crystallized as a discipline in the nineteenth century, it filled the "Savage slot," becoming almost by default a discipline aimed at exposing Westerners to the lives and mores of the Other (Trouillot 2003: 19). In recent decades cultural anthropology has attempted to deconstruct this slot and reorient understandings of the emergence of the world system after A.D. 1492. Anthropologists have demonstrated that the "savages" or Others were actually active agents in change and not simply its recipients (see Said 2003 [1978]; Wolf 1997 [1982]). As cultural anthropology has taken aim at destabilizing the "Savage slot" (Trouillot 2003: 28), misconceptions of a static pre-Columbian world may be replacing it. Christopher Cobb (2005) warns that the increasing understanding that the "world became global in the sixteenth century" (Trouillot 2003: 29) presumes, whether intentionally or not, a static pre-Columbian Other, using it as a foil for the dynamism of the postcontact world. America before the arrival of Columbus risks becoming a land that time forgot: Indians are cast as pristine primitives, the "people without history," used by various publics and scholars both to understand and to criticize modernity (Wolf 1997 [1982]).

This homogeneous view of precontact Native North America obscures the reality of its enormous diversity (see, for example, Alt [ed.] 2010; Cobb 2005; DuVal 2006; Ethridge 2003; Gallivan 2003, 2007; Galloway 2002; Lekson 2009; Mills 2000; Milner 2004; Pauketat 2004; Peregrine and Lekson 2006; Schroeder 2004a; Silliman 2009; Wesson 2008). Systematic investigations of the archaeological record, which holds the material evidence of rich histories stretching back centuries before Columbus arrived in America, offer the opportunity to keep the precontact world from slipping into this stagnant "Savage slot" (Cobb 2005).

The histories captured in mounds and earthworks are particularly powerful in illustrating the dynamism of pre-Columbian North America. Having survived decades of destruction in the name of American "progress," these structures stand as testaments to indigenous dynamics and ingenuity. The earthen constructions in northern Michigan, the focus of this book, hold the deep histories of the ancestral Anishinaabeg peoples who planned and built them, used them, revered them, and modified and maintained them for centuries. These constructions are embedded in the cultural landscape and social, economic, and ideological context of the Late Prehistoric period (ca. A.D. 1200–1600). Documenting them and reexamining the regional and social processes that produced them will help us to understand the centuries before European contact.

Ceremonial Monuments and Egalitarian Societies

Just as we should not be too conservative in understanding how complex the large-scale societies of North American prehistory were, we must also acknowledge and develop an appreciation for how complicated the small-scale societies were. Not only complex indigenous North American societies had the ability to construct earthen mounds and earthworks. The continent has a spectacular trajectory, from Watson Brake (Middle Archaic, ca. 3350–3000 B.C.) to Poverty Point (Late Archaic, ca. 1500–1300 B.C.) to Adena constructions (Early Woodland, ca. 1000 B.C. to 100 B.C.) to Hopewellian earthworks (Middle Woodland, ca. A.D. 1–500). These structures indicate egalitarian communities built magnificent monuments throughout North America for millennia (see Bernardini 2004; Carr and Case [eds.] 2005; Clay 1987, 1998, 2009; Gibson 2007; Kidder 2002; Lepper 2004; Milner 2004; Milner and Jefferies 1998; Sassaman 2005; Saunders and Allen 1994; Saunders et al. 2005; Sherwood and Kidder 2011). Conducting contextualized studies of these earthen constructions demonstrates just how dynamic egalitarian societies were, showing conclusively that American Indian history did not begin with Columbus. We can also extend anthropological frameworks for understanding the diversity of egalitarian societies through these studies.

Recent decades have seen archaeologists engage in an intense "unpacking of the evolutionary portmanteau" as applied to social organization (McIntosh 1999: 4). Time and again, this has called into question traditional typologies that rely on a suite of "bipolar traits" to categorize what a society *is* (Feinman and Neitzel 1984; O'Shea and Barker 1996). In moving away from the constraints of static types and trait lists, archaeologists have begun to focus not on what societies are but on what societies (and actors in them) *do*, as ethnologists have been doing for more than a century (see Yoffee 2005). Much of the work in this unpacking has been done by scholars studying complex societies or societies with permanent hierarchical leadership and ascribed inequality (Arnold 2000: 17). This research has produced critical insights into social complexity, including deeper appreciations for the array of trajectories toward complexity (Chapman 2003) and the multiple sources of power and authority used to construct and maintain permanent inequalities (Blanton et al. 1996; Feinman et al. 2000; Yoffee 2005).

But a tendency to see institutionalized hierarchy as a major investment with a correlated major sociopolitical payoff still exists. Avoiding permanent hierarchy may actually require more investment (leveling mechanisms and strategies to smooth over differences before they take hold). Constant maintenance is demanded to prevent the rise of asymmetrical relations (either through intentional actions or as the consequence of unintended stochastic processes). Nonhierarchical societies may actually hold greater social rewards, such as sharing and buffering risk as a group. Thus scholars interested in complex societies face the challenge of understanding the processes involved in the eventual destruction of powerful and elaborate behavioral patterns that maintain equality in small-scale societies (Trigger 1990a: 145).

While nonhierarchical societies have frequently been conceptualized from a passive perspective as by-products of organizational simplicity, my work seeks to position them as emerging from complicated institutions and ideologies that conferred advantages on participating communities (Wiessner 2002: 235). By considering the cultural processes of egalitarian social systems and the critical role played by ritual, I explore the ways in which communities construct and use ceremonial monuments to navigate these processes.

While most activities occur at the household level, both suprahousehold and regional intersocietal interaction offer critical economic and social advantages to egalitarian communities (see Ewers 1988; Ford 1972; Fortier 2001; Fowles 2002; Halstead and O'Shea 1989; Junker 1996; Meyer and Thistle 1995; Peterson 1975; Spielmann 1983; Spielmann and Eder 1994; Trigger 1987; Vehik 2002). To maintain internal and external interaction, people must rely on social bridges between their immediate households and larger social groupings. Building these bridges requires securing economic and social reciprocity between people whose daily lives have little to do with these levels of interaction. These reciprocal exchanges provide contexts where participants could easily deceive others to manipulate exchanges or to aggrandize themselves rather than to forge social connections. This has the potential to transform the nonhierarchical social order (Watanabe 2007).

What keeps actors from seeking material or social advantage in these situations? I suggest that through participating in liturgy (public and communal ritual) actors consent to follow these commitments (Rappaport 1999). Making allies that can be relied on later is essential.

When people participate in liturgy, they enact their public acceptance of the social order, regardless of their private beliefs, thereby perpetuating their social systems. I argue that ceremonial monuments are one effective means of ensuring tribal cultural processes because they give material form to the immaterial ideas of social and moral order that liturgy expresses (Keane 2007: 109). In this context we can understand how small-scale societies use ceremonial monuments to cement their egalitarian ethos. Monumentalism, the use of monuments to anchor a "symbolically interactive, topographically bounded, aesthetically effective, and meaningfully holistic landscape" (Dillehay 2007: 318), is a straightforward and effective means of furthering egalitarian social organization. Groups can develop and maintain monumental landscapes in interesting ways without ascending some kind of ladder toward social and hierarchical complexity.

Modeling Late Prehistory in Northern Michigan

Another theme of this book (for which the Vreeland story provides an entry point) is questioning the reliance on overly simplified views of historic Great Lakes Native American communities as accurate prototypes of the past. Given that Vreeland was working more than eighty years ago, his wholesale acceptance of a battle between "the Chippewas" and "the Ottawas" as the explanation for an archaeological site seems to be an intellectual artifact of his time. While not nearly as simplistic, the long-standing model of Late Prehistory in Michigan unfortunately also emphasizes a one-to-one relationship between historic tribes and precontact communities (Fitting and Cleland 1969).

In brief, this model rests on two assumptions: (1) that historic tribes are discrete, homogeneous, and static entities (such as "the Ojibwas" or "the Potawatomis") and (2) that the patterns of Native American peoples during the postcontact period can be projected backward in time to understand precontact cultures of the Great Lakes. Recent ethnohistoric research shows the pitfalls and limitations of this view of historic tribal groups in eastern North America (cf. Axtell 1997; DuVal 2006; Ethridge 2003; Ethridge and Hudson [eds.] 2002; Galloway 1995, 2002; Merrell 1989; O'Brien 1997; White 1991; Witgen 2007). New ethnohistoric research highlights the fluid nature of early historic Indian communities in the Great Lakes and illustrates how the French Empire worked to carve out discrete tribes from mobile, multiethnic Algonquian groups who could take on different ethnic and social identities when necessary (Witgen 2007: 642). If homogeneous historic tribal groups were an imagined colonial ideal, how much should these inventions impact our interpretation of the past? While archaeologists working in other parts of North America have shed such static paradigms, they remain a powerful shaping force in the interpretation of Great Lakes archaeology and thus warrant serious consideration and evaluation here.

In examining Great Lakes Late Prehistory, we must remember that the archaeological record does not owe its existence to historical sources or to colonial Europeans, so it makes little sense for its interpretation to be driven by these sources. The archaeological record holds the direct evidence of decisions and actions by people during the centuries before contact and should be treated as an independent line of evidence to reconstruct the dynamics of this time. Giving greater priority to postcontact sources can lead to the devaluation of American Indian life before Europeans. Indeed, recent work in Michigan is modifying this long-standing model every time the material evidence from site survey, excavation, and carbon dating is published, revealing discrepancies between the archaeological record and historically observed cultural activities/adaptations (e.g., Dunham 2009; Howey and O'Shea 2006; Milner 1998; O'Gorman 2007; O'Gorman and Lovis 2006; O'Shea 2003; O'Shea and Milner 2002).

To continue to move our investigations of Late Prehistory forward, we need to keep material evidence as a data set that is complementary and parallel to historic sources. Privileging historic data sources generates inaccurately static views of the past and keeps the pre-Columbian world populated by people without their own history. I do not mean to suggest that we approach Late Prehistory without recognizing any connections among ethnohistory, archaeological sites, and living tribal communities. After colonial encounter, shifting relations of violence remade America (Blackhawk 2006:6). As American Indian groups attempted to deal with "forces that threatened their existence" (Angel 2002: 74), they used cultural systems that were in place prior to contact to deal with these new forces. The challenge before us is to consider the organizing principles—including territory, kinship, social roles, religious practices, and economic structures—that retained meaning and efficacy from the precontact to postcontact worlds. By building a picture of the dynamic developments of Late Prehistory on its terms, rather than imposing expectations from history, archaeology can provide a critical foundation for understanding the extent and impact of the colonial encounter in the Great Lakes as well as the active responses and decisions that Indian communities made during this period.

In addition to these considerations, we should incorporate broader anthropological understandings of the ways in which members of nonhierarchical societies use ritual practices at ceremonial monuments to give material form to cultural processes (e.g., Bradley 1998; Buikstra and Charles 1999; Chapman 1995; Johansen 2004; Randall and Sassaman 2010; Sassaman 2005; Sherratt 1990; Wright 2007). Accordingly, I use this kind of model to contextualize the dynamic choices that Anishinaabeg communities made in Late Prehistory.

While there are different interpretations of specific developments in Late Prehistory in the northern Great Lakes, it is widely agreed that a dramatic shift after A.D. 1000/1100 brought an end to a long-established socioeconomic system based on high mobility, fluid social boundaries, and procurement activities across resource zones. Evidence indicates that these significant developments of Late Prehistory (A.D. 1200–1600) were largely related to resource transformations. After about A.D. 1200 communities living along Lake Michigan and Lake Huron developed more specialized subsistence economies that involved a marked increase in maize horticulture as well as targeted exploitation of fall- and spring-spawning Great Lakes fish species. Both of these activities benefited from an increasing focus on shoreline and coastal settlements. Increasing sedentism improved prospects for successful maize horticulture in the region's highly variable climate (O'Shea 2003) and allowed groups to secure access to key fishing locations (Holman and Lovis 2008).

The decrease in mobility caused more intensive interactions between local groups and led people to strengthen claims to resource zones. As social interaction became increasingly important in the new economic and social setting, coastal horticulturalists settled into more permanent villages on the coasts of Lake Michigan and Lake Huron. They also developed corporate social identities, demarcated exclusive territories, and barred others from these socioeconomic advances. The emergence of distinctive new ceramic styles along the shores of the Great Lakes during Late Prehistory reflects this process of coastal group identity formation. I argue that inland groups, living outside of the "lake-effect" coastal farming and fishing zones, were confined to the interior and had less access to the developments in the lakeshore communities. Inland communities found their access to coastal resources increasingly limited by alliances that excluded them.

With increasing territorialism and heightening social difference or alterity (see Taussig 1993) between the coasts and inland, what had been a long-established foraging and freely mobile system was no longer sustainable. The milieu of Late Prehistory (A.D. 1200–1600) demanded creative new social, economic, and ideological strategies. Through my research program focused on two types of sites with monumental constructions in northern Michigan, burial mounds and earthwork enclosures, I found that communities created multiple social alliances and new relationships during ritual events at suprahousehold and regional monumental locales. Before my research, these constructed features were seen as disarticulated sites scattered across space. By situating these sites in their broader context, the monumentalism practiced by the communities of the region during Late Prehistory becomes apparent: constructed places were used to anchor a regional ritual system based on competing social demands. This system operated for hundreds of years before it was interrupted by European contact circa A.D. 1600.

The Organization of This Book

Chapter 1 develops a theoretically informed framework of the ways in which egalitarian societies employ monumentalism, using monuments or the "built environment" to create and anchor meaningful regional landscapes (Dillehay 2007). Some suggest that the unpacking of neo-evolution in archaeology has raised a need for a total "excision" of the cultural-form concept from our work (Yoffee 2005: 6), but it is more productive to use process-based understandings of cultural forms: studying what people do while also maintaining an awareness that they do it within a cultural form that mediates their social worlds (see Wolf 1997 [1982]). Hence I focus on how the social processes of tribal societies can be inscribed in and facilitated by monuments. Drawing inspiration from contemporary scholarship on ritual and monumentality in North Atlantic and North American archaeology, I develop a framework of the ways in which tribal societies can create and use monuments—or, more broadly, monumental landscapes—to further egalitarian social organization.

Chapter 2 offers an overview of Michigan prehistory with particular emphasis on the traditional model for explaining the developments of Late Prehistory in the region, which I refer to as the Biotic/Historic Model. An examination of recent archaeological findings and details of colonial encounter in the Northeast and Great Lakes region exposes this model's shortcomings, particularly how it prevents us from holding archaeological and ethnohistoric data in a parallel rather than dependent relation. I consider the need for fresh models of this period.

Chapter 3 lays out a model of regional ritual organization in northern Michigan circa A.D. 1200–1600 informed by theoretical understandings of the ways in which tribal societies use monuments. During Late Prehistory, as groups navigated new and heightening territorialism in the region, people used monumentalism as the means of creating and sustaining essential networks of social, economic, and ideological interaction.

Drawing on spatial modeling of mound sites across the northern Lower Peninsula, I propose that American Indian communities used burial mounds to stake territorial resource claims and provide contexts for panresidential interaction to increase internal cohesion. Chapter 4 presents the results of my research at the Cut River

Mounds site (20RO1). My findings allow us to consider the ways in which communities transformed local resource zones into panresidential, intratribal, ceremonial monument centers during Late Prehistory.

Mounds were not the only ceremonial constructions anchoring the regional landscape; a multilayered monumental landscape also existed. I propose that large earthwork enclosures were purposefully constructed in contrasting positions to mounds to serve a distinct role as regional interaction centers accessible (both physically but also symbolically) to multiple communities. Chapter 5 explores the series of earthwork enclosures spread across northern Michigan. Larger than any other sites in the area, these enclosures have long been assumed to be fortifications. New excavations at a pair of these enclosures (the Missaukee Earthworks, 20MA11–12) show definitively that they were not fortifications. Instead, data indicate that this site was constructed as a regional ritual precinct meant to draw together inland foragers and coastal horticulturalist-fishers. Exchange between coastal and inland groups would have been mutually beneficial, as people were all living in environments with considerable subsistence risk.

Chapter 5 also presents my ethnohistoric research on Anishinaabeg ritual practices, specifically the Midewiwin. The importance of this ceremonial complex among the Algonquin-speaking people of the Great Lakes Region was frequently noted throughout the historical era (cf. Copway 1980 [1851]; Densmore 1929; Hoffman 1891; Landes 1968; Warren 1984 [1885]). The historical Midewiwin was "more than just another ceremony, for it provided an institutional setting for the teaching of the world view (religious beliefs) of the Ojibwa people" (Angel 2002: 48). I found a clear connection between this prehistoric monument and Bear's Journey (Howey and O'Shea 2006). Bear was the servitor who delivered the secrets of the Midé rites to the Anishinaabeg in a journey between two earths. I suggest that the two enclosures at Missaukee are monumental renditions of these earths. Connecting the primordial delivery of the most important ritual system among historic and contemporary Great Lakes tribes and these earthworks suggests that the intertribal ritual here played a profoundly fundamental role in structuring Late Prehistoric regional organization.

The research program at the Missaukee Earthworks for the first time provides a reliable comparative base from which to situate the rest of the series of northern Late Prehistoric earthworks, which are the focus of chapter 6. Comparing landscape position and design features reveals numerous similarities across these structures, which suggest that these sites shared a blueprint as precincts based on pairs of enclosures. Finding so many shared aspects is particularly striking given the scarcity of extant data available from other enclosure sites. Bear's Journey between the two earths seems to have been repeated in monumental form across the region. By assessing the only other available ceramic assemblages from northern enclosures, I confirm that two more enclosure sites likewise had a regional or intertribal character, drawing inland and coastal groups to them.

In chapter 6 I present my macroregional spatial analysis of the accessibility of these sites conducted through multicriteria cost surface analysis in Geographic Information Systems (GIS). This modeling demonstrates that enclosures were positioned to be uniquely accessible by multiple communities but that their use was arranged geographically. These enclosures formed monumental anchors of a macroregionally imbricated ceremonial circuit.

Chapter 7 begins with a summary of how the Anishinaabeg of the northern Great Lakes, the "Spontaneous People," inscribed and ensured their worlds with multiple monuments across the landscape, sustaining a complicated if not complex regional organization for centuries (A.D. 1200–1600). By combining anthropological perspectives on monumentalism in egalitarian societies, excavations in a previously uninvestigated part of the northern Great Lakes, a contextualized incorporation of ethnohistory, and regional spatial modeling, I show the great dynamism present before the colonial encounter that heretofore has gone un(der)appreciated. I conclude by emphasizing how this study offers an important perspective (beyond the specific cases) on the ways in which archaeology can continue to counter the colonial legacies of our discipline and keep the pre-Columbian past from filling anthropology's static "Savage slot."

CHAPTER 1

Creating Ritual and Constructing Monuments

PERSPECTIVES ON EGALITARIAN SOCIETIES

With a GPS (Global Positioning System) in our cars, cell phones, and computers, we live in a mapped world. The space around us is diagramed, distinguished, and ordered. What our maps never show us, however, is that we do not actually live in these neatly abstracted spaces. We inhabit a world made of culturally contextualized places that we endow with attachment. Archaeologists can never recover the strong emotive ties that people had to their places; but through artifacts they can understand events and activities occurring at places and assess their social significance.

Places and their meanings are anchored to features on the landscape and are "continually woven into the fabric of social life" (Basso 1996: 110). Landscapes are constituted by the pattern of activities that collapse into their features (Ingold 1993: 162). These features become symbols of and for a way of living. Landscapes contain the material remains, and the physical and material reality of landscapes constrains and directs ways of living (Basso 1996: 63). Individuals and landscapes have a dialectical relationship: individuals inhabit landscape, and it inhabits them (Basso 1996: 102).

This dialectical inhabitation creates a continuum of human-material intervention that we can expect to find in ancient landscapes (Ashmore and Knapp 1999: 10). People create, move between, and conduct practices at constructed features in the landscape, from obviously marked places like monuments to daily spaces like villages and more subtle alterations like shrines (see Fowles 2009). People likewise engage with natural features that they invest with powerful religious, artistic, or other meanings (Ashmore and Knapp 1999: 11; see Basso 1996; Bradley 2000; Norder 2003; Smith 2001; Tacon 1999). This moving and practicing at monuments, shrines, rock art, sacred natural features, villages, and homes defines networks, both local and regional, of social interaction; these elements serve as reference nodes in time and space for communities (Dillehay 2007: 153). The cultural landscape organized and sustained past social dynamics.

This book explores the social processes responsible for and embedded within the construction of monuments in past landscapes. Drawing on a concept from Tom D. Dillehay (2007: 318), I examine how egalitarian communities use monuments to anchor a "symbolically interactive, topographically bounded, aesthetically effective, and meaningfully holistic landscape."

Monuments are material constructions erected to mark and commemorate places, events, and persons. These structures are typically built at a larger, more permanent, and more elaborate scale than other constructions, involving more labor (often a great deal more) than a single individual can do (Lekson 1999b; Trigger 1990b). Monuments are durable: their construction permanently alters the landscape (Johansen et al. 2004). Individuals and groups have repeated chances to experience monuments in various ways (Tilley 1994). Monuments also serve as distinct referents, symbolizing something specific for the individuals who build and use them (Bernardini 2004: 333). They develop a legitimizing and attractive quality and make a statement that is understood across space and time. As symbolically charged places, they attract individuals. Thus monuments are constructions with an active life (Bradley 2002: 137). More than passive memorials, they were a shaping force in the lives of the people who built them (and those who followed). Once monuments are engaged in public ritual, they organize people's responses and patterns of interaction (Dillehay 2007: 5).

Monuments provide archaeologists with an explicit and materially accessible entry point into past social, economic, and ideological developments. As noted in the introduction, it is still common for social complexity and monumentalism to be linked in some archaeological thinking (or to be axiomatic: see Randall and Sassaman 2010). Monuments have long been perceived as resulting from and being indicative of "complex" societies: for example, V. Gordon Childe (1950) included monumental architecture in his criteria for urban civilization. This coupling of monuments and complexity, in addition to being so long established, follows a coherent line of reasoning that can be fruitful in looking at some, but not all, settings.

Constructing monumental architecture requires the corralling of a substantial labor force while at the same time meeting the day-to-day subsistence needs of the society. This suggests to many that a relatively high level of social complexity and political power must be in place (Dillehay 2007: 1; Sherwood and Kidder 2011). Timothy Earle (1997: 156–57) states that "monumental constructions require leadership, coordination, and finance. They are inherently expensive in terms of a group's resources, requiring many individuals to work together for long hours. Monumental construction is not found in egalitarian societies." Bruce G. Trigger (1990b: 120) offers a similar view, noting that while some egalitarian societies may "construct large multi-family dwellings, men's houses, lineage shrines, and tribal forts, monumental architecture is generally present on a modest scale, if at all." Given both this long-standing view and the logical reasoning process that supports it, it is not surprising that influential scholars have cast monuments as an "important index of social complexity" (Sherratt 1990: 147).

Recent research, however, has begun to move beyond the idea that monuments are the "consequence of social complexity" (Sherratt 1990: 165). This research includes studies of prehistoric landscapes and monuments on the North Atlantic coast of Europe (e.g., Barrett 1994; Bender and Aitken 1998; Bradley 1998, 2002; Edmonds 1999; Hodder 1984; Johansen et al. 2004; Parker Pearson et al. 2006; Pollard 2008; Scarre [ed.] 2002; Sherratt 1990; Thomas 1999; Tilley 1994) and in the Americas (e.g., Adler and Wilshusen 1990; Bernardini 2004; Buikstra and Charles 1999; Carr and Case [eds.] 2005; Clay 1987, 1998, 2009; Dillehay 1990, 2007; Gibson 2007; Heckenberger 2005; Kidder 2002; Lepper 2004; Mahoney 2001; Milner 2004; Milner and Jefferies 1998; Sassaman 2005; Saunders 1994; Saunders et al. 2005; Van Dyke 2008; Wallis 2008). These researchers have shown that noncomplex societies constructed, utilized, maintained, negotiated, and renegotiated the meanings and roles of monuments across vast spaces and long periods. Thus, although logical reasoning may suggest a connection between monuments and complexity, the argument is not as tight as it appears. Many noncomplex societies satisfied the requirements for monument construction (large amounts of labor, organization, and resources) without an institutionalized hierarchy.

This knowledge has clearly opened the door to a discussion of monumentality in the absence of centralized political control and coerced labor in archaeology. Here I offer one framework for understanding the power that tribal societies have to accomplish substantial public constructions within their social processes. I explore the ways in which monuments can be emergent from tribal cultural processes and effective in securing and furthering them.

The "T" Word: The Tribe Concept in Anthropology

The modern anthropological notion of the tribe has its roots in Lewis Henry Morgan's 1851 study of the Iroquois. Morgan (1996 [1851]: 77–103) characterized "tribes" as emerging from a given region and segmenting into distinct territorial and linguistic groups to counteract an inherent tendency toward disintegration. Morgan was part of the crystallization of anthropology as a discipline in the nineteenth century, when it came to fill the "Savage slot" (Trouillot 2003: 19). He and others who focused on sociocultural evolution during this period (Spencer 1851, 1857, 1897; Tylor 1870, 1871), working with limited and anecdotal ethnographic data from disparate parts of the world, further defined this slot. Their models of sociocultural evolution embraced the concept of "savage" as an appropriate descriptor for the "simplest" stage of human societal development, which included the tribe as one type of "savage" society (Marcus 2008: 252).

While shedding such racist conceptions and terminology, social evolution continued to inform anthropology, which was influenced in the mid-twentieth century by a "second wave" of evolutionists (Marcus 2008: 252). This included scholars such as Julian H. Steward, Morton H. Fried, Marshall D. Sahlins, Elman R. Service, and Leslie A. White. They crafted controlled comparisons and based their work on richer and more systematically collected ethnographic data (Marcus 2008: 252). The now infamous Band-Tribe-Chiefdom-State framework (Service 1962) emerged from this social evolutionary focus in anthropology. The conceptualization of the tribe within this taxonomic framework was influenced in part by Morgan's early formulation, in which the tribe was viewed as a discrete type of society, a segmental organization that constituted one "stage" in social evolution (see Sahlins 1961, 1968; Sahlins and Service [eds.] 1960; Service 1962; Steward 1955). The term "tribe" was carved out as the transitional stage of cultural evolution between simple hunter-gatherer societies and more complex chiefdoms and states (Fowles 2002: 13).

Almost as soon as these models emerging from the second wave were established, anthropologists, including several evolutionists themselves, began to question them (see, for instance, Fried 1966, 1975). Anthropologists and archaeologists have engaged in an intense "unpacking of the evolutionary portmanteau" as applied to social organization (McIntosh 1999: 4), calling into question traditional typologies that rely on a suite of "bipolar traits" (tribes do *X* but not *Y*) to categorize what a society *is* (Feinman and Neitzel 1984; O'Shea and Barker 1996). This unpacking has revealed several problems in trying to "group together societies based upon a plethora of characteristics which are understood to be intimately intertwined" (Parkinson 2002b: 3; see Arnold [ed.] 1996; Barth 1967; Chapman 2003; Feinman and Neitzel 1984; Feinman et al. 2000; Gregg [ed.] 1991; Mills 2000; O'Shea and Barker 1996; Paynter 1989; Upham [ed.] 1990). Scholars have consistently demonstrated that employing a cultural taxonomy that assigns traits as diagnostic of societal types ignores variation and change, which are critical aspects of human communities (Barth 1967: 669). Different organizational variables manifest in societies in varying degrees; for example, societies labeled tribes within a cultural evolutionary model may have traits more often associated with chiefdoms and vice versa (O'Shea and Barker 1996).

As a result of this unpacking, some scholars have suggested a total "excision" of the cultural-form concept from our work (Yoffee 2005: 6). The concepts of chiefdom and state, while still debated (see Pauketat 2007), have largely been reformulated and retained. In contrast, "tribe" was an immediate target of critique and a particularly acceptable candidate for excision. Just a few years after Service (1962) created his framework, Fried (1966, 1967) suggested abolishing the term. Central to the discrediting of the concept of the tribe was the view that tribes only emerged as a response to European contact and therefore could not be considered a universal stage in sociopolitical development (Carneiro 2002: 35). Service himself was willing to eliminate the term "tribe," changing his evolutionary sequence to Egalitarian Society–Hierarchical Society–Archaic Civilization (Carneiro 2002: 35; Service 1968: 167).

Discarding the term, however, did not make those egalitarian societies that had been called "tribes" disappear. Scholars searched (and continue to search) for a way to describe egalitarian societies organized into lineages, clans, and (sometimes) moieties with socioeconomic links transcending the local community (Marcus 2008: 255–56). Several terms carrying less theoretical (social evolutionary) baggage have been offered: Service's egalitarian society, small-scale society, politically autonomous village society, transegalitarian, middle-range, and corporate (cf. Bender 1990; Blanton et al. 1996; Carneiro 1987; Feinman and Neitzel 1984; Feinman et al. 2000; Mills 2000; Owens and Hayden 1997; Peregrine 2001; Schachner 2001; Spielmann 2002).

The use of these terms encourages archaeology to avoid the flaws of a strict social evolutionary paradigm and focus on explaining the tremendous diversity in noncomplex societies (Mills 2002: 77). But the proliferation and use of multiple terms, several of which are conceptually vague, complicates cross-cultural comparisons and discussions and has not resolved the problems identified with the term "tribe." Each new term is as much an arbitrary descriptor as "tribe" (Parkinson 2002b: 2) and still conceptualizes these societies as nebulous, somewhere betwixt and between—not too big, not too small, not a chiefdom, not strictly mobile hunter-gatherers (Fowles 2002: 18). This furthers the view that these societies are ephemeral, emergent from contact with something more "complex" and not complicated in their own right. A latent sense remains that these noncomplex societies are by-products of organizational simplicity rather than emerging from complicated institutions and ideologies that conferred advantages on participating communities (Wiessner 2002: 235).

In his seminal work *Europe and the People without History*, Eric Wolf (1997 [1982]: 19) calls on anthropologists to develop a new theory of cultural forms that focuses on connections and processes rather than trait lists and bounded entities. Wolf urges the discipline to concentrate on understanding "more precisely how cultural forms work to mediate social relationships among particular populations." The archaeological record offers the only information on cultural forms and the mediation of social relationships in a noncolonial, precapitalist setting. Archaeology has an unparalleled perspective on theories of human societies; it can illuminate "ways of being" in the world that have been ethnographically unavailable since capitalism and other globalizing forces began homogenizing communities throughout the world. Rather than excising the culture-form concept from our work, I suggest that we use process-based understandings of cultural forms: study what actors in societies *do,* with awareness that they do it within a cultural form that mediates their social worlds. We should undertake deep contextual studies of particular communities to understand their historical and emergent contingencies (Watanabe 2007: 321) and use our studies to build better theoretical appreciations of human societies.

An overreliance on the ethnographic present has contributed to the woes of the "tribe" concept; from the snapshot provided by ethnographic observation in postcontact or postapocalyptic (Larson 2007) situations, tribes appear to be transitory and tending toward disintegration. Incorporating the long-term historical perspective of archaeology provides a look at tribal systems in contexts outside of contact with colonial powers. We can see how people chose to participate in tribal societies for the advantages they offered and how participation was not some inelegant reaction to an outside force. An archaeological approach offers a diachronic perspective on the diverse trajectories of tribal systems and the powerful and elaborate behavioral patterns that maintain equality in small-scale societies (Trigger 1990a: 145).

Thus, following the lead of several scholars, I suggest that the tribal concept is salvageable if we take these important considerations into account (see, for example, Arnold [ed.] 1996; Barker 1999; Fowles 2002; Gregg [ed.] 1991; O'Shea and Milner 2002; Parkinson 1999, 2002b; Parkinson [ed.] 2002; Upham [ed.] 1990). We need words to talk about the past in ways that make sense to people beyond ourselves. As Pauketat (2007: 17) said of the term "civilization" (although I am not suggesting that he would agree with the following statement), "tribe" is awaiting reclamation from the ethnocentrism and racism of nineteenth-century anthropology and its role in filling the "Savage slot" (Trouillot 2003). By showing how complicated and dynamic the histories of societies viewed as "savage" or "tribal" in this early era can be we can leave behind the theoretical baggage of the term "tribe" and help it again become a constructive tool in facilitating cross-cultural comparisons in ethnography and archaeology (Fowles 2002: 14; Parkinson 2002b: 10). I retain the concept "tribe" not as a type of society stuck in between stages of social evolution but as a processual, historically emergent, and embedded cultural form that provides a productive anthropological framework for investigating the social, economic, and ideological organization of egalitarian societies.

"Tribe" in Native North America

In North America the term "tribe" proper carries several embedded legal and historic meanings related to American Indian communities (see Wilkins 1997). From first contact through the founding of the United States, Europeans and Euro-Americans had difficulty understanding what were often diffuse and flexible identities among the indigenous communities they encountered (DuVal 2006; Ethridge 2003; Shepherd 2008; White 1991; Witgen 2007). The foreigners were confronted by people living "relationships" in ways that ran counter to their own understanding of the world. They were interacting with people who had a way of relating to everything else in the cosmos (Miller 2009: 27). The indigenous world was full of structured and intertwined interrelationships involving humans, animals, plants, societies, the spirit world, and the land (Holm et al. 2003: 18). These interrelationships conferred on people rights and responsibilities for ensuring the health and well-being of everything in the cosmos, including their families and communities (Miller 2009: 28).

Europeans and Euro-Americans had to deal with these indigenous views that challenged their frames of reference. They struggled to understand how people could take on different identities in different spaces or shape-shift (possibly even into nonhuman form) as context necessitated (Witgen 2007: 641). They also struggled to understand the people themselves, who held deep ties to a living landscape offering wisdom, sustaining identity, and demanding mutual interaction (see Basso 1996). Europeans and later Americans came with "visions and conceptualizations of identity that drew upon Western philosophy, political theory, and social organization" (Shepherd 2008: 21). Sequential colonial empires in North America worked to create categories out of complex indigenous social formations that defied easy categorization (Witgen 2007: 642).

The constructed categories were "tribes," seen as linguistically and ethnically homogeneous, discretely bounded, and easily identifiable distinct groups. These constructed and bounded historic tribes were imposed on communities, named with words that were not their own, and viewed in a way that did not align with actual indigenous relationships. For instance, in the Great Lakes the indigenous peoples considered themselves Anishinaabeg (Spontaneous People, meaning indigenous, natural, always people) (Warren 1984 [1885]: 56). During early contact the French Empire worked to carve out discrete tribes, such as the Saulteurs or Chippewas, from these fluid, mobile, and multiethnic Algonquian groups (Witgen 2007: 642). Throughout America discrete "tribes" solidified over time: they were the social formations that made sense and held weight with imperial powers in the postcontact setting. These reified homogeneous identities helped further the colonial aim of erasing the distinct histories and cultural relationships of indigenous communities (Shepherd 2008: 21).

It may seem unusual that in a study of precontact American Indian social organization I use a term with this problematic history. But the fluidity observed in historic Indian communities, their shape-shifting, and their deep ties to place—the senses of identity that colonial powers could not understand—are tribal cultural processes. Organizational flexibility, the ability to strike different structural poses as conditions require, is a tribal cultural process, as are fluidity in ethnicity and relatedness (Snow 2002) and territorial ties in identity formation.

By using a process-based framework of tribal society, we can better understand historical contingencies in specific communities and compare cases from other times and places. We are able to build better ideas about the distinctiveness and dynamism in nonhierarchical societies. By considering tribal cultural processes in detailed contexts, we can more effectively highlight the limits and problems of the colonial invention of bounded "tribes" than by completely abandoning the concept.

Tribal Social Organization

Tribal social organization is a means of predictably organizing individuals in a defined territory without permanent hierarchical structures of social and political control (O'Shea and Milner 2002: 200). A defined territory ties groups to a localized, bounded set of resources (Adler 2002). Tribal communities exert (or attempt to exert) control over access to resources within the confines of the defined territory (see Ackerman and Ackerman 1973; Adler 2002; Cashdan 1983; Chapman 1995; Dyson-Hudson and Smith 1978; Peterson 1975).

Although territory offers a means of controlling resources, the restriction to a territory results in stresses for tribal systems that "are always in existence but not always expressed" (Barker 1999: 3). These stresses include the risk and uncertainty inherent in a set resource base and the social pressures that emerge when autonomous communities live within a circumscribed space (Binford 1980; Bird-David 1992; Cashdan 1983; Dyson-Hudson and Smith 1978; Halstead and O'Shea 1989; Harpending and Davis 1977; Ladefoged and Graves 2000; Smith and Winterhalder [eds.] 1992; Wiessner 1982). Resource availability and production vary spatially and temporally in predictable and unpredictable ways across all subsistence systems, from predominantly agricultural-subsistence systems to foraging systems to mixed-strategy systems (see Cashdan [ed.] 1990; Halstead and O'Shea 1989; Rowley-Conwy 2001).

All tribal societies have to develop strategies to deal with the constant social and economic stresses within defined territories. Organizational flexibility, deep claims to territory, and panresidential social integration are effective cultural trajectories in addressing emergent stresses internally. People in tribal social systems also have to develop strategies for interacting with and potentially gaining access to the resources of distant external groups. Regional interaction offers a diversity of resources that can amplify each group's resource base as well as provide people with the opportunity to build reciprocal social relations that can be activated in times of need. I suggest that internal cultural processes involving flexibility, ties to the landscape, and suprahousehold integration and external cultural processes involving regional intertribal interaction together form the operational repertoire of tribal social systems.

Internal Cultural Processes

Organizational flexibility is an inherent feature of tribal systems because it offers an effective internal tool for dealing with the risk, uncertainty, and social pressures of restricted spatial settings. Tribal fluidity is expressed when individuals within a larger tribal system rearrange their spatial and social associations to deal with predictable, new, or intermittent socioeconomic stresses (Gearing 1958: 1148). This ability to reorganize has been recognized as central to tribal social systems. The earliest definition of tribe by Morgan (1996 [1851]: 77–103) recognized a process of "segmenting." As noted, this idea of segmental organization remained important in second wave conceptions of tribal communities. William A. Parkinson (2002b: 8) argues that segmentation is perhaps the only characterization of tribal cultural processes worth retaining from type-based approaches.

Frederick O. Gearing (1958: 1150) offers the term "structural poses" to explain the "rhythmic changes" in social and spatial roles within a tribal community. Sociospatial rearrangements in a tribal population occur at different temporal scales, ranging from the annual cycle to the longer term (Fowles 2002; Parkinson 1999, 2002a).

Developing a seasonal cycle of resource procurement and population movement reduces the uncertainty inherent within any resource base in ecological zones characterized by seasonal variation (Blakeslee 2002). Within the annual round, tribal organizational flexibility is often most notable in the spatial shifts along seasonal lines (O'Shea and Milner 2002). Within a pattern of regular seasonal moves, tribal populations also shift in response to sporadic (rather than regularized) events, such as sudden and intense environmental changes, unexpected deaths, or unarranged encroachments from outside communities.

The work on the structural poses of eighteenth-century Cherokee villages by Gearing (1958) provides an ethnographic account of tribal flexibility within an annual round. Gearing documented Cherokee villagers moving in and out of social relations to accomplish both resource procurement and the tasks of regulating social relations. The village as an aggregate of independent households was one structural pose (incorporating the lowest amount of active social relations). The intrahousehold social relationships (such as child rearing) were addressed in the village, and the resource task of hunting was regulated. At the opposite end of the spectrum, each village operated as an organized entity, making major social decisions about matters as critical as war as well as minor decisions, such as those about village maintenance. Villages also operated in this manner to accomplish the major resource tasks of agriculture.

Over the long term, tribal organization flexibility results in major spatial shifts and reorganization of populations in response to dramatic internal and external changes, such as the development of new procurement strategies (e.g., farming), prolonged episodes of economic crisis (e.g., drought), or the rise of chiefdom/state societies in the vicinity (or contact, as in the historical case of the Great Lakes). The resulting shifts can be cyclical, containing episodes of tribal aggregation and dispersal (Parkinson 2002a), or directional and resulting in permanent changes in tribal systems (Minc and Smith 1989). The flexibility critical to tribal organization is useful only if it is tempered with integration. Tribal social systems must maintain a suprahousehold level of coherence to be effective.

The defined territory of tribal systems is one feature that facilitates internal tribal integration at a level beyond the residential unit. A territory provides a limit to the extent of the spatial shifts and areal distribution of a tribal population. Defining (and frequently physically marking) a territory creates a social boundary that serves to teach and remind members of their place within a larger tribal system. For instance, in an ethnographic study of West Kimberly Australian Aborigines, Valda Blundell (1980: 115) found that territorial organization "served as a blueprint for behavior," which included dictating readjustments in the affiliations of individuals. This exemplifies the power that territory can have in forging a sense of identity among individuals and underscores just how critical ties to specific landscapes become in securing social well-being (see Basso 1996). Even Morgan, who always asserted the primacy of biology in defining human relationships (see Morgan 1997 [1871]), became aware of the deep and direct relationship between the land and individuals as his involvement with the Iroquois increased over his lifetime (Feeley-Harnick 2001).

Because most of the interaction and daily practices of tribal communities occur among local residential groups, it is necessary to have "ideological and social mechanisms that will promote the tribal identity beyond the range of normal, face to face or familial connections" (O'Shea and Milner 2002: 201). In the absence of political hierarchies, a variety of "lateral" integrative mechanisms or panresidential social institutions, including kinship (both biological and fictive), ideology, religious orders, cosmology, and language, fulfill this end (O'Shea and Milner 2002: 201; Snow 2002: 97). Shared styles in material-culture media can also be used to express and mark group identity (see Stark [ed.] 1998; Wiessner 1983, 1984; Wobst 1977). Together these panresidential, lateral mechanisms build fundamental and durable connections between autonomous groups, thereby creating and maintaining shared identities and integration essential to coherence of the larger tribal social system.

Intratribal aggregation events at defined places within territories present opportunities for face-to-face interactions, which are necessary for the pronouncement and perpetuation of lateral mechanisms within a tribal system. Periodic intratribal aggregations become the "means by which a sense of community, a cultural oneness, is maintained" (Meyer and Thistle 1995: 406). The periodic congregation of otherwise dispersed residential groups that compose a tribal society provides regular opportunities for individuals to express suprahousehold social identities, renegotiating and affirming their larger tribal identity (Bernardini 2004: 331). The cross-cultural importance of suprahousehold interaction for the economic and social welfare of egalitarian societies has been widely documented (Buikstra and Charles 1999; Carlson 1994; Conkey 1980; Hayden 1993; Johnson 1982; Marcus and Flannery 2004; McCarthy 1939; Meyer and Thistle 1995; Minc and Smith 1989; Snow 2002; Spielmann 2002; Wallace 1970).

The gatherings are routinely located in places that have critical resource potential and are scheduled for times when resources are abundant (see Meyer and Thistle 1995). Intratribal gatherings serve essential economic functions as well as integrative ones: they resolve the inequality of resource production, providing all community members with access to the gathering site's seasonally abundant resources. Furthermore, trade has been documented as an important aspect of intratribal gatherings (Carlson 1994; McCarthy 1939; Meyer and Thistle 1995). Trade at these events allows household/residential groups that have experienced productive stress to be aided by their counterparts who have not.

External Cultural Processes

Intertribal interaction and trade are vital processes in sustaining egalitarian communities; extensive regional exchange networks are well-documented aspects of tribal social systems (see Bourque 1994; Braun and Plog 1982; Ewers 1988; Ford 1972; Fortier

2001; Hegmon et al. 2000; Morrison and Junker [eds.] 2002; Spielmann and Eder 1994; Trigger 1990a; Vehik 2002; Wiessner 2002). Regional exchange provides tribal societies with an external means of dealing with the resource uncertainty inherent within circumscribed territories. These networks can occur at multiple scales. Most commonly, exchange occurs between groups producing different resources, which results in complementary exchange relations (Halstead and O'Shea 1989). Exchange can also occur between groups producing similar resources, in which case the exchange is supplementary (Halstead and O'Shea 1989). In both situations, the exchange reduces resource uncertainty by providing "more efficient access to subsistence resources" (Spielmann and Eder 1994: 317).

Economically, these interaction networks provide access to the resources of other groups that diversifies local resource bases and reduces the annual and interannual variations in resource productivity within single territories. The economic benefit is immediate as well as long-term: individuals gain access to what a trade partner has to offer currently as well as in the future. Communities in intersocietal exchange networks also gain an array of social benefits, including alliances and expanded information sharing, reducing potential competition for territory, opening the mating pool (which ensures genetic viability), sharing in bonds of friendship, and gaining access to raw materials and technologies not found at home (see Jackson 1991; Mahoney 2000; Spielmann 2002; Wiessner 2002).

Complementary intertribal exchange relations between farming and foraging communities were widespread among historic Native American groups throughout North America. These specific ethnohistoric cases illustrate the advantages that intersocietal trade can confer. In the Upper Missouri region, for example, a long-established exchange network existed between horticultural tribal communities such as the Mandans and mobile groups from the west (Ewers 1988). Foodstuffs were the main products traded. Mobile hunter-gatherers "enjoyed the benefits of a vegetable diet without the necessity of raising crops themselves," and horticultural groups did not have to rely on the buffalo hunt for protein and "freed themselves of dressing large numbers of skins and of making dress clothing" (Ewers 1988: 22). Such exchanges conferred advantages on the economies of both groups in a system that lasted for centuries. Sixteenth-century Spanish explorers in the American Southwest recorded a similar complementary intertribal exchange system between Southern Plains nomadic tribes and eastern Pueblo tribes. The nomadic groups brought hunted items to trade events at the Pueblos, where they traded for agricultural products, most notably corn (Ford 1972; Spielmann [ed.] 1991). This system evolved into an interdependence between these tribal societies (Spielmann 1983). A similar pattern of complementary intertribal trade occurred in the Great Lakes between historic horticultural Huron and Northern Algonquian foraging communities (Smith 1996; Trigger 1987).

Regional intertribal exchange networks are actualized through and sustained by periodic aggregations of separate tribal communities at defined locations. Intertribal interaction events, most commonly referred to in the anthropological literature as trade rendezvous or trade fairs (Jackson 1991: 271; Smith 2001: 217), have been documented around the world. In the historic American Indian cases, nomadic groups traveled to the more sedentary agricultural groups for trading events and interaction. When one group hosts events at defined locations within its own territory, these can be conceptualized as *attached* intertribal interaction places. While this is common, cross-cultural variations exist. Defined locations of intertribal interaction can also be located in medial positions near the juncture of several territories or in vacant, neutral locales to attract strangers (Jackson 1991: 276). For instance, Australian Aboriginal communities hold intercommunity events at totemic centers "situated along mythical ancestral tracks that crossed numerous tribal territories" (Jackson 1991: 274). Defined places in areas that are not exclusively the property of one tribal community, in vacant places or boundaries between cultural groups (DeBoer and Blitz 1991; Smith 2001: 217), can be conceptualized as *detached* intertribal centers. Communities will develop either attached centers, detached centers, or some variation that best suits their particular economic and ecological parameters (Junker 2002).

Negotiating Intratribal and Intertribal Interaction

Intra- and intertribal interaction and integration are needs that must be filled in *all* tribal social systems and yet pose problems within tribal organization. Each need relies on the fulfillment of multiple commitments by individuals across social distances, a risky endeavor. The production of intratribal integration contradicts (and counteracts) the flexibility and fluidity within tribal social systems; having individuals participate in building a suprahousehold sense of identity can be a tenuous proposition. Developing systems of intertribal interaction and exchange causes problems, because it involves creating reliable interaction and durable bonds between what may be socially distant entities not linked by any political hegemony (and with strong internal senses of identity if intratribal integration is successful). While offering many advantages, intersocietal networks of marriage and exchange can be fraught with tension and misunderstandings (Wiessner 2002: 238). As Richard I. Ford (1972) characterizes intertribal interaction, it can result in "barter, gift, or violence."

The Liturgical Order. The process of both intra- and intertribal interaction and exchange offers ample opportunity for any participant to deceive others, to manipulate the exchange and interaction, to negate relationships, and to aggrandize rather than forge social connection. This creates the potential to transform the nonhierarchical social order (Watanabe 2007: 317; see also Mauss 1990 [1922]). What keeps individuals from taking these opportunities and *binds* actors to honor commitments that go beyond their immediate households? My use of the term "binds" in this question is intentional. Religion (from the Latin *religare*) means to bind, and it is (always?) through public and communal ritual that these cultural processes are enacted and ensured in nonhierarchical communities. Through liturgy, participants become formally bound to and reify (and thus perpetuate) the moral, social, and political order of their society. Ritual both requires and allows individuals to understand their ways of being in the world: their communities and their multiple cultural roles and obligations in these communities. Liturgy (the public performance of rituals) becomes the means of conformance (Keane 2007; Kelleher 1985; Rappaport 1979, 1999).

The importance of communal ritual to small-scale societies cannot be emphasized enough. As Katherine A. Spielmann (2002: 196) observes, in a synthetic analysis of ritual production in nonhierarchical societies "it is not, then, irrelevant that political action takes place in the public context of communal ritual in small-scale societies. While the political fortunes of individuals and corporate groups wax and wane, the ritual realm endures as a context for display, distribution, interaction, and consumption." Taking control of the ritual realm has been shown to be a means that aspiring leaders in foraging societies target to create hierarchical order (see Aldenderfer 1993). Given the ritual realm's central and potentially transformative role, it is imperative that we consider the ways in which individuals living in egalitarian societies use liturgy to extend and maintain their moral, social, and political order.

Following Roy A. Rappaport (1979: 175–76), ritual can be defined as "the performance of more or less invariant sequences of formal acts and utterances not encoded by the performers," and liturgy is "more or less invariant sequences of formal acts and utterances repeated in specified contexts." These specified contexts are and must be public. The public, the shared, is the essence of liturgy, which comes from the Greek *leitourgia,* meaning "public work." Liturgy is the prescribed form or set of forms for *public* religious worship (Kelleher 1985).

Above all else, liturgy is a phenomenon of communities; it is a public act dependent upon and undertaken, created, mediated, and sustained by community members. A community, of course, is made of individuals, but individuals are constituted by their relationship to their communities: liturgy is *circular.* Liturgy not only depends on individuals who participate but also establishes individual identity by binding individuals to the social (and moral) order of their community. Christianity offers an example of this circularity: "liturgy is an act of ecclesial performative meaning in which the church symbolically mediates itself" (Kelleher 1985: 482). The church, the Body of Christ, is dependent on a circle of believers, but it is only through liturgy that believers can come to see themselves as Christians (Irwin 2004: 20).

The social contract finds its commemoration *and* its enactment in liturgy, which contains the acceptance and consummation of a social contract by its participants. When individuals participate in liturgical orders, they offer their public acceptance of the social order, regardless of their private belief (Rappaport 1979: 194). Liturgical ritual is *the* basic social act, because it protects the public social order against the private and obligates (or binds) individuals to their commitment against what may be the vagaries of individual private feelings (Rappaport 1979: 197). The inherent risk of failure, given the omnipresence of interpersonal competition in these ritual obligation enactments, makes them vulnerable but ultimately that much more powerful (Keane 2007).

Morality is thus intrinsic to liturgical performance. By obligating individuals to the social contract, liturgy subsumes the moral within the social; the breaking of social obligation becomes an immoral act. Liturgical orders draw participants into a web of moral, not just utilitarian, obligations (Watanabe 2007: 319). Liturgy impacts individual conscience and points to and embeds the immaterial ideas of moral order that it expresses (Keane 2007: 109). As such a fundamental social and moral-forming act, liturgy is essential in regulating the internal and external levels of socioeconomic reciprocity and interdependence. The morality of liturgy sanctifies, standardizes, and ultimately vouchsafes intra- and intergroup interaction and exchange; public ritual binds participants to the commitments of tribal social organization.

Tribal Ceremonial Monuments

Monumentalism, the use of monuments to anchor a "symbolically interactive, topographically bounded, aesthetically effective, and meaningfully holistic landscape" (Dillehay 2007: 318), can directly further tribal social organization. Because ceremonial monuments give material form to the immaterial ideas of social and moral order that liturgy expresses (Keane 2007: 109), they offer a highly effective means of obligating the enactment of both intratribal and intertribal interaction. Providing materialized sacred loci for the participation in and performance of shared ritual, monuments come to form permanent and enduring symbolic centers in the landscape for groups whose settlements are widely dispersed (Bradley 1998: 17; DeMarrais et al. 1996).

As noted above, monuments are more than passive memorials. Once monuments exist and are engaged in public ritual, they become a shaping force in the lives of the people who built them, organizing their responses and patterns of interaction (Bradley 2002; Dillehay 2007: 5). By creating networks of permanent symbolic centers that demand people act a certain way, monumentalism provides a powerful way to regulate the internal and external levels of socioeconomic reciprocity and interdependence essential to tribal societies.

Researchers investigating specific regions have found that different, multiple, and overlapping arrays of ceremonial monument use can exist within single regions. These include one group employing multiple ceremonial monuments, a single monument employed by multiple communities, groups reusing older monuments, or all of these happening at once (e.g., Barrett et al. [eds.] 1991; Bradley 1998; Chapman 1995; Clay 2009; Edmonds 1999; Goldstein 1995; Holtorf 1998). When examining variation in the constructed landscapes of "simple" societies, it is important to consider the processes of intra- and intertribal integration as sufficiently distinct operations that necessitated the production of monuments with contrasting scales, positions, and roles. More simply put, monuments intended for use by members of a single community are materialized differently than monuments intended for use by a broader population. Understanding this can help us analyze how monumentalism was used to order social worlds by people in the past.

In their cross-cultural study of twenty-eight ethnographic noncentralized hierarchical societies, Michael A. Adler and Richard H. Wilshusen (1990) found groups constructing different "high-level" (multiple community) and "low-level" (single community) social integrative monuments. In his detailed study of the Araucanian polity in modern-day Chile, Dillehay (2007) demonstrates how mound centers were central in ordering social worlds and navigating the changes after Spanish contact. He illustrates that communities used two different types of mound centers to achieve different purposes and that together these constituted a living monumental landscape. *Kuel* (single-mound centers) were constructed and maintained to reflect lineages (Dillehay 2007: 17). They were familial: they served families and had to be treated as family, showing hundreds of years of stability in the region. This is salient in an era based on egalitarian kin-based rulership as well as after the rise of political hierarchy and political power postcontact (Dillehay 2007: 17). In contrast, *rehuekeul* (multimound centers that each formed a spatially planned and socially integrated single site complex) were used for communal feasting, such as the *nguillatun* fertility ceremony (Dillehay 2007: 17). *Rehuekeul* mound complexes were sites of inclusivity and feasting by all social levels and facilitated a complex set of interlineage relations (Dillehay 2007: 381).

As even this brief review shows, in looking at the ways in which tribal communities developed and maintained monumental landscapes to accommodate varied socioeconomic demands, it is reasonable to expect that they will "build and use multiple monuments with different functions" (Bernardini 2004: 336). In the following discussion I consider how intra- and intertribal monuments may develop and function across a landscape and offer preliminary expectations for these constructed places. It is my hope that these generalized findings may become one more tool in the growing arsenal that archaeologists working across North America and beyond use for investigating the multilayered monumental landscapes crafted by egalitarian societies.

Intratribal Monuments and Archaeological Expectations for Egalitarian Monumental Landscapes

Embedding intratribal events in public ritual and establishing monuments for these events confer many advantages. Intratribal events provide members of tribal communities with opportunities to assert (and understand) claims on what and who is part of their larger community. The construction of a ceremonial monument provides a physical, permanent marker of these claims; it serves as a materialization of group membership. The addition of sacred monuments to panresidential interaction sites transforms them into permanently marked symbolic centers that attract individuals for participation in liturgical (shared ritual) events. These sites are often located in critical resource zones, so the addition of permanent ceremonial monuments also adds an important legitimization to claims on these key resources.

Cross-cultural ethnographic and archaeological studies have widely documented how corporate groups legitimize claims to restricted resources through lineal descent, which is frequently ritualized through the maintenance of a permanent, specialized, bounded area exclusively for disposal of the dead. This is known as the Goldstein–Saxe Hypothesis (Goldstein 1981; Saxe 1970). Mortuary monuments have been shown to be one technique that corporate groups use to create these formal specialized spaces.

Constructing mortuary monuments at intratribal centers legitimizes corporate claims to control over these important resource-dense sites. By erecting permanent constructions, groups assert these use rights even when they are not physically present. In addition, placing their ancestors at these sites promotes a sense of shared ancestry during events and embeds the activities in tradition and ritual renewal. In a study of ceremonial constructions in the Illinois River Valley from the Middle Archaic (4000 B.C.) through the Late Woodland periods, Douglas K. Charles and Jane E. Buikstra (2002) documented intratribal mortuary monuments serving these roles over a long period. The association of intratribal centers with mortuary remains provided a reference to ancestors and created a physical link between the ancestors and the land. By recalling ancestors, these sites provided explicit and direct claims to territory and resources for a single tribal community or descent group (Buikstra and Charles 1999; Charles and Buikstra 2002). Furthermore, associating ancestors with these sites facilitated social negotiations between dispersed communities in the Illinois River Valley by providing a physical reminder of common descent (Charles and Buikstra 2002).

Dillehay (2007) states that the lineage mounds of the Auragnacian are not simply connected to family but become family, demanding attention as humans do. Marking monuments at intratribal centers with an additional layer of interrelationship gives people rights and responsibilities for ensuring the health and well-being of these monuments, just as they have to care for their families and communities (Miller 2009: 28). Thus connecting to ancestry and to family is a way of mandating moral obligation; combined, they ensure the continuation of panresidential interaction. Through overt monumentality, mortuary ceremonial constructions at intratribal gathering sites "reinforce local group identity, honor ancestors, and claim important local resources" (Adler 2002: 214).

In a multilayered monumental landscape, monuments built to fill internal tribal processes can be expected to be located within defined tribal territories at critical resource zones. The zones claimed with these monuments can be expected to have offered seasonally dense, predictable resources that could support the periodic dense aggregations of dispersed community members. The utilization of the resources should appear archaeologically as a major component of site activities, as access to seasonally rich resources provided an important internal buffer against resource uncertainty.

Events at intratribal ceremonial centers, critical to easing the uncertainty of resource production, would have been scheduled on a regular basis (at least once each year during the peak season of the resource) so that the resource could be harvested by dispersed residential units. Given that the bulk of the material remains at intratribal gathering sites would have been used to procure and process seasonally abundant resources, the material assemblages can be expected to form tight suites indicative of the seasonal economic-extraction activities conducted (for example, fishing gear, including net weights, hooks, and so forth, if the resource had been a fish-spawning run).

Monuments used in securing internal tribal cultural processes can be expected to be specialized structures to dispose of the dead. As noted, mortuary association would benefit intratribal monument centers by using claims of ancestry for further legitimization of claims to the resource zones in which intratribal gatherings were held. The material remains at intratribal monumental centers should show an overarching stylistic homogeneity typical of the local tribal community using the site. Material variability can be expected but should be subtle, because members of the larger social unit would have learned and practiced manufacturing traditions while living and interacting in seasonally dispersed residential social groups.

Intertribal Monuments and Archaeological Expectations for Egalitarian Monumental Landscapes

As noted in my discussion above, regional intertribal exchange typically occurs in defined locations. The links of these locations with cultural group boundaries and territories (attached vs. detached) can vary. In both scenarios, using ceremonial monuments to mark the locales of regional multicommunity exchange events offers benefits for facilitating these events, which fill critical social, economic, and ideological needs.

Intertribal exchange and interaction events are socially complicated, because they draw together entities not linked by political hegemony. Some social integration is necessary for the events to be successful and for larger interaction networks to function. These events can be fraught with social tension. Obtaining cross-cultural integration will undoubtedly be complicated even in a best-case cooperative scenario. In this regional, intertribal context, monuments provide a spatially predictable place for temporally predictable, periodic large gatherings of culturally disparate communities. Developing a standardized context for this interaction reduces the potential for overt hostilities during the promotion of intersocietal integration.

Monuments hold specific advantages where territorialism is strongly expressed or contested. In such settings, regional monument centers are more likely to be (1) located according to a detached model and (2) embedded in the sacred. While not necessarily completely vacant ceremonial centers, regional exchange centers benefit by being in positions that reduce the potential for turf battles between cultural groups. (They may also be completely vacant, however: see the study of the Chachis, 3,000 individuals inhabiting the Cayapas Basin in Ecuador, by Warren DeBoer and John H. Blitz [1991].) Embedding these centers in the sacred allows members of communities from separate territories (potentially hostile and distrusting) to meet and exchange goods where the liturgical order ensures moral behavior. Public ritual restrains individual competition and any proclivities to deceive or corrupt, thereby binding participants to the social order. While the unity may be temporary, public ritual still ensures it for these events, which draw together individuals whose daily lives rarely include such interaction. Ritual order is political order. Ceremony unites separate entities and extends these connections through time (Adler and Wilshusen 1990: 136). Ritual participation then becomes a major impetus for intertribal gatherings.

Intersocietal ceremonial centers are interpreted across disparate communities. They must develop in ways that are symbolically salient regionally, with forms or associations that are powerful across disparate peoples. The case of Chaco Canyon is an example of how this is materialized.

Chaco Canyon, of course, is a widely studied (and contested) archaeological phenomenon, and I do not pretend to present a thorough review of it here. Archaeologists disagree about the communities responsible for Chaco, with ideas ranging from egalitarian communities to states. Today most archaeologists working on Chaco have stopped trying to pinpoint the social form and instead focus on the ways in which leadership was organized (Mills 2002). Despite unresolved debates, it is well accepted that Chaco was communally oriented, involving consensual politics and feasting (Mills 2002: 94), that it was ritually ordered (Renfrew 2001; Yoffee 2001), and that it had a major regional (and extraregional: see Crown and Hurst 2009 for definitive evidence of cacao from Mesoamerica in vessels at Chaco Canyon) draw. Moreover, the strong contrast in population between Chaco Canyon proper and the surrounding San Juan Basin provides demographic support for Chaco being some kind of mostly empty ceremonial center (Mills 2002: 78; see Judge 1989; Malville and Malville 2001). Chaco Canyon was based on a regional ceremonial system organized around elaborate central ceremonial precincts (Bernardini 2004: 352; some scholars have suggested that its precincts were formal pilgrimage centers: see Malville and Malville 2001 and Renfrew 2001). Thus I draw on Chaco here as a well-documented study of a regional, detached ceremonial center to develop a kind of "hypermodel."

Between A.D. 900 and 1150 almost twelve great houses were built in the center of the rugged San Juan Basin. They were carefully crafted, multistoried buildings with hundreds of oversized rectangular rooms, round kivas, and one or more sub-terranean "great kivas," all requiring roof beams from distant forests (Cameron and Toll 2001; Lekson 2000; Mahoney 2001). Architecture was the "principal fact" of the Chaco Phenomenon (Lekson 1999a: 21) and was found in geometric forms in great houses and kivas throughout the Chaco region. Architecture was taken to an extreme in the canyon, reaching its pinnacle in the 800-room Pueblo Bonito, argu-ably the center of the Chaco World (see Neitzel [ed.] 2003). The distribution of great houses throughout the region and the grand investment in architecture imply that in Chaco this regional collective ideal was enshrined or incarnated in the twelve great houses (Van Dyke 2004, 2008). Furthermore, this architecture, particularly Pueblo Bonito, was set into spectacular canyon bluffs and appears to be coming out from them, associating the buildings with the sacred power of geography.

In a multilayered monumental landscape, the forms of monuments built to fill external tribal cultural processes can be expected to be repeated across the land-scape in nonmonument structures or other monument sites. They can be expected to enshrine regional ideals and values that make them salient to multiple communi-ties. An association with distinctive or sacred geography is also possible. All fac-tors being equal, ceremonial monuments built for intertribal interaction can also be expected to be more substantial and elaborate than those built for intratribal gatherings.

Located in positions accessible to different societies in geographically separate ter-ritories, intersocietal monuments will have a culturally heterogeneous social catch-ment. Again, Chaco Canyon offers us a hyperexample.

During the years of the Chaco Phenomenon, Chaco Canyon was a magnet for imported and unusual goods. A widespread network of roads provided links to bring people and goods to the canyon (Windes 1991). The presence of ceramic ves-sels produced in distant locations (southeast Utah, northeast and eastern Arizona, central western New Mexico, the Mogollon region in southern New Mexico, and all over the San Juan Basin) demonstrates that Chaco drew individuals from a wide area and had a high level of interactions (Toll 2001). Lithic raw materials also came from multiple long-distance regions: Narbona Pass chert from the Chuska Mountains, 75 kilometers west of the site, is the most common nonlocal lithic material found dur-ing the Chacoan era in Chaco Canyon (Cameron 2001: 85). Furthermore, turquoise (the nearest source of which was 200 kilometers to the east) came to Chaco in nota-ble amounts (Cameron and Toll 2001: 10). Extraregional materials also entered the site: copper bells and macaw feathers from Mesoamerica and shells from the Pacific coast (Nelson 2006).

Special ritual items were deposited in the structures at Chaco Canyon. Pueblo Bonito and Pueblo Alto, both great houses, had caches of Narbona Pass chert in the form of projectile points (Cameron 2001). These points, as well as special-use pot-tery forms, were ritual objects produced explicitly as offerings to the great houses in Chaco. Cylinder jars, one of the rarest vessel forms at Chaco Canyon, were ritual paraphernalia brought to the site. Many of these special jars were from the Chuska

Mountains, but close to one-third of the assemblage of this vessel form came from the Mogollon region in southern New Mexico, showing that other groups also brought special ritual-associated items to Chaco (Toll 2001: 63). In addition, as noted above, Patricia Crown and Jeffery Hurst (2009) proved definitively that some of these cylinder vessels have cacao residue inside them, an item imported from Mesoamerica.

Archaeologically, monuments built to fill external tribal cultural processes can be expected to have material culture remains that reflect a notable geographic diversity for individuals participating in the gatherings held there. As illustrated by the Chaco Canyon case, materials from considerable distances would have been brought to and deposited at the site (see Pollard 2008 for a case from a monument center in Neolithic Britain). In addition to diverse material remains, intertribal ceremonial monuments should have materials related specifically to the ceremonial activities occurring at these centers. Special-purpose materials may be detectable as more elaborate or as completely distinct from the materials typically manufactured and used by the individuals attending the ceremonies. If ritual-material production occurs on site, it will leave a detectable archaeological signature (Spielmann 2002). When individuals bring paraphernalia, however, the archaeological evidence may be more complicated. As with the Narbona chert projectiles in Chaco Canyon, the paraphernalia may be deposited as ceremonial offerings, in which case they will be archaeologically visible. But special ritual materials brought from long distances might not be left behind.

The scheduling of events at intertribal monuments had to accommodate a large number of individuals in atypical circumstances. These pressures are particularly notable at events in detached centers, which had to support a residential population (albeit temporary) that otherwise never occurred. Large regional gatherings entailing such preparation as well as travel time should occur less frequently than local intratribal events.

The evidence at Chaco Canyon shows that very few people lived in Chaco's great houses. Most rooms in the great houses were never occupied; instead they served as places for nondomestic storage, transient visiting quarters, massing, and other purposes, but not as homes (Lekson 1999a: 21). The few residents in Chaco Canyon proper contrasted strongly with the surrounding San Juan Basin, with much larger populations (Mills 2002: 78; see Lekson 1999a: 21, who estimates the basin population in the several tens of thousands and the population in Chaco Canyon proper in the range of 2,000 to 3,000 people).

These data indicate that the major constructions of Chaco Canyon were specifically built to accommodate periodic influxes of individuals in big numbers (Judge 1989). Feasting was a method of provisioning these influxes of people, forming an important component of the ritual practices at the canyon's ceremonial centers (Mahoney 2000; Potter 2000).

We can expect the stress of periodic influxes of people to produce a unique archaeological signature consisting of the remains of provisioning activities by and for the participating individuals in the ritual events. The provisioning activities can be expected to have included temporary visiting living quarters of some kind, large areas of storage for foodstuffs, and large-scale subsistence activities. These activities are likely to have included feasting, which is well documented as a primary component of large ritual gatherings (see Dietler and Hayden [eds.] 2001).

Summary Thoughts

Ceremonial monuments are not exclusively the products of complex societies; nor are they unique, rare features when constructed by nonhierarchical social systems. Rather, they can be understood as emerging from standard tribal cultural processes. By creating permanent, meaningful, easily interpreted, consistent, and predictable contexts for the enactment of liturgical orders, monuments confer distinct advantages for facilitating both intra- and intertribal interaction, which fills imperative social, economic, and ideological needs in tribal systems. Archaeologically, we know that not all tribal societies chose to construct monuments; but constructing them offered a productive solution to the often conflicting claims that subsistence and political demands pose in tribal populations (DeBoer and Blitz 1991: 62).

The processes of intra- and intertribal integration are sufficiently distinct to necessitate the production of monuments with contrasting scales, positions, and roles that may produce archaeologically detectable patterns. This generalized framework of how monuments develop and of archaeological expectations for these monuments offers a means of approaching and modeling the regional dynamics of the specific context of the late Late Woodland/Late Prehistoric period (ca. A.D. 1200–1600) in northern Michigan. The next chapter offers background on this time and place, with particular emphasis on the long-standing model used to study this period.

CHAPTER 2

Modeling Late Prehistory in the Northern Great Lakes

CURRENT APPROACHES AND LIMITATIONS

The indigenous communities living in the northern Great Lakes developed their social and economic strategies within the context of their beautiful yet often harsh and unpredictable environment. The region is distinguished by its complex glaciated landscape sculpted by the last continental ice sheet, the Wisconsinan Glaciation. This last advance of the Pleistocene Epoch began in Canada 85,000 years ago and reached as far south as the Ohio River. Around 20,000 years ago the glacier began to retreat, and this ice age ended around 10,000 years ago with the beginning of the Holocene. The ice retreated in stages, leaving a variety of glacial landforms in its wake, including terminal moraines, recessional moraines, drumlins, eskers, kames, and glacial outwash plains. Michigan might be almost flat without these hilly landforms.

Initial Populations

The first humans to inhabit the Great Lakes area arrived at the end of the Pleistocene Epoch between 12,000 and 10,000 years ago. During this time, known as the Paleo-Indian period, early inhabitants lived in small hunting and gathering "bands" that moved frequently, following large game mammals such as caribou and mastodons.

As the Holocene began, some large game, such as mastodons, went extinct; and other large mammals, such as caribou, elk, and moose, retreated north of Michigan. The modern landscape emerged as the five Great Lakes were formed by meltwater pooling at the rim of receding glaciers.

The Great Lakes have been at their current levels for about 4,000 years. Three of the lakes surround the Lower Peninsula of Michigan: Lake Erie, Lake Huron, and Lake Michigan. Lake Michigan, Lake Huron, and Lake Superior form the Upper Peninsula of Michigan. Surrounded by Great Lakes, the state of Michigan has 3,200 miles of coastline, more than any other state in the United States except Alaska (Keen 1993: 7). The Mackinac Straits separate the Upper and Lower Peninsulas (fig. 2.1).

In addition to the major lakes, numerous inland lakes also formed in the glacial landscape. Today 11,037 inland lakes are spread throughout Michigan. As the glacier retreated, swamps and marshes emerged as vegetation colonized shallow depressions. Over time, rivers began to cross-cut the landscape, depositing fluvial sediments in some places and eroding glacial deposits in others.

The environmental changes at the end of the glacial period and the emergence of the modern environment meant that the inhabitants of the Great Lakes region were no longer able to rely on large game and had to adopt subsistence practices that took advantage of new opportunities. Early communities adopted a hunting and gathering economy, which involved diverse strategies to procure resources and maximize returns from seasonally available foods. This broad-spectrum foraging system involved the exploitation of a wider variety of foods, including wild game, fish, nuts, berries, aquatic tubers, and other resources (Lovis 1985, 1989, 1999; Lovis and Robertson 1989; Lovis et al. 2005; Robertson et al. 1999). Archaeologists call this period the Archaic (ca. 8000–800 B.C.), which is traditionally divided into Early (ca. 8000–6000 B.C.), Middle (ca. 6000–3000 B.C.), and Late (ca. 3000–800 B.C.) phases.

The Saginaw River system, the largest in the entire state of Michigan, was a particular focus for Archaic peoples. The Saginaw River is only 20 miles long; together with its tributaries (which include the Flint River, the Cass River, the Shiawassee River, and the Tittabawassee River), however, the system drains over 6,000 square miles and flows into the Saginaw Bay of Lake Huron (fig. 2.1). This system is bound by the Saginaw Valley terraces (Eagan 1990: 11). The valley's rivers and wetlands made it a veritable hunter-gatherer smorgasbord with intensive occupation (Brashler and Holman 1985; Fitting [ed.] 1972; Lovis 1985; Lovis et al. 2005; O'Shea and Shott [eds.] 1990).

The new social and economic system was fully developed throughout Michigan by the Late Archaic. Its success depended on groups (1) freely moving between resource zones, (2) having widespread kin networks, (3) developing extensive trade connections, (4) conducting visits over great distances, and (5) engaging in a high level of cooperation and intergroup tolerance. This system was so successful that people maintained it in the northern Great Lakes for millennia until about A.D. 1000/1100.

Woodland Traditions

The first use of ceramics in the Great Lakes region marks the beginning of the Early Woodland period (ca. 800 B.C. to A.D. 1). The use of ceramics created small but significant changes in subsistence practices (Garland and Beld 1999). Nuts and starchy seeds were used in greater quantity as people found ways to process them and to extract oil by simmering them in pots over fires (Ozker 1982: 77). In general, however, the only changes during the Early Woodland period were additional subsistence strategies augmenting the repertoire of Archaic strategies.

During the Middle Woodland (ca. A.D. 1–500/600) significant cultural developments occurred throughout the Midwest. Known as the Hopewellian Complex, these developments influenced communities in southern Michigan. A sudden, abrupt, and seemingly complete adoption of Hopewellian mortuary, ceremonial, and technological traits occurred in southwestern Michigan (ca. 10 B.C.). This development has been called the Norton Tradition after the Norton Mounds site located near modern-day Grand Rapids (Griffin et al. 1970: 189). Groups seem to have participated fully in the Hopewell Interaction Sphere (Struever 1964), engaging in extraregional trade, building large burial mounds, and adopting elaborate Hopewellian mortuary practices, ceramic styles, and lithic technology (for detailed discussions of Hopewell, see Brose and Greber [eds.] 1979; Carr and Case [eds.] 2005; Dancey and Pacheco [eds.] 1997). Meanwhile, communities in the Saginaw Valley adopted several, but not all, Hopewellian traits (Kingsley 1999).

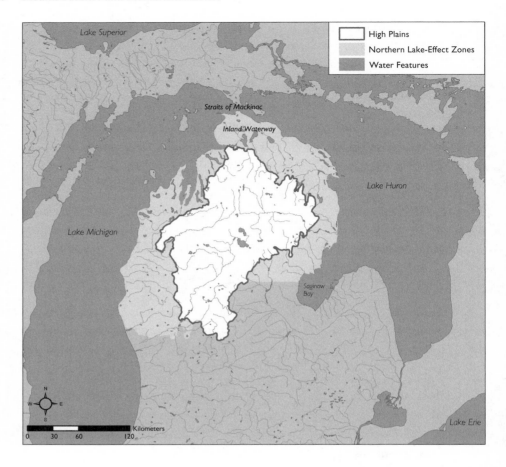

Figure 2.1. Map of
Michigan (focused on
the northern section),
showing the Great
Lakes, array of inland
lakes, rivers, and major
ecosystems of the modern
landscape.

In contrast, Hopewellian traditions were never practiced in northern Michigan (Brose and Hambacher 1999). Groups continued to follow the socioeconomic strategies that they had followed since the Late Archaic (O'Shea 2003). These developments during the Middle Woodland are referred to as the Lake Forest Middle Woodland, a term incorporating a continuum of non-Hopewell Middle Woodland ceramic styles produced by hunting-gathering communities dispersed throughout the northern Great Lakes area (Brose and Hambacher 1999: 173; Fitting 1975: 98–99).

The transition from the Middle Woodland to the Late Woodland period is not well understood by archaeologists, but we do know that early Late Woodland systems (ca. A.D. 600–1000) developed locally in both southern and northern Michigan (Holman and Brashler 1999). Analysis of ceramic styles has demonstrated that during the early Late Woodland social boundaries were permeable, group membership was flexible, and territories were weakly defined (Brashler 1981). While the cultivation of maize began around A.D. 500–600, it did not become a significant crop until around A.D. 1000/1100. The diffuse socioeconomic strategy so effective since the Late Archaic, which included reliance on an array of wild foods from many resource zones, remained effective in the early Late Woodland.

Changes after A.D. 1000/1100

Communities throughout northern Michigan had been practicing a broad spectrum strategy of foraging in which groups could move easily between different resource zones on the shorelines of the Great Lakes and on inland lakes and rivers for millennia. After A.D. 1000/1100 more efficient production and consumption of food resources (both cultivated and wild) brought the first notable changes to this system. Limited cultivation of maize had begun in the Great Lakes around A.D. 500–600, but it became a significant crop around A.D. 1000–1200 (Crawford et al. 1997; Katzenberg et al. 1995; Martin 2008). In the Upper Great Lakes, "one of the effective limits of prehistoric Indian agriculture was the line marking the limits of the 120-day average frost-free period" (Yarnell 1964: 128). Michigan has a differential distribution of areas with this minimally sufficient growing season. The southern Lower Peninsula and northern Great Lakes lake-effect coastal zones are the main areas open for cultivation, and the interior of the Lower Peninsula (designated by the High Plains ecosystem) falls short of this growing season (fig. 2.1; I discuss the lake-effect later in this chapter). In terms of wild resources, the introduction of the bow and arrow with associated small triangular and notched points led to more efficient hunting (Cleland 1992: 25). More notably, fishing practices intensified and specialized on seasonal spawns in the northern Great Lakes, and these activities assumed new importance (Cleland 1982).

These more specialized subsistence economies led to the "restructuring of patterns of settlement, territoriality, subsistence scheduling, and social alliance" (O'Shea 2003: 6) and brought an end to the long-established socioeconomic system that featured high mobility, fluid social boundaries, and ready procurement of items across resource zones. Associated with the end of this long-established system across Michigan was an increase in community size, the emergence of strong territorial systems with less permeable boundaries, the formalization of decision making, and the development of stronger group identity (Cleland 1982, 1992; Holman and Lovis 2008; O'Shea and Milner 2002). These changes mark the start of the "late Late Woodland/Late Prehistoric period" (A.D. 1200–1600; referred to herein as the Late Prehistoric period).[1]

The Traditional Model of Late Prehistory (ca. A.D. 1200–1600) in Northern Michigan

Expectations and explanations of the subsistence practices and cultural patterns of Late Prehistory have been, and remain, largely derived from one model: the Biotic/Historic Model. This model was developed and explicated most clearly forty years ago by James Fitting and Charles Cleland (1969). It has inspired, framed, and guided much subsequent research on the northern Great Lakes and continues to influence archaeological research today (see Holman and Lovis 2008).

Based on the temporal adjacency of Late Prehistory (ca. A.D. 1200–1600) to the post–European contact period, the Biotic/Historic Model assigns a pattern from one of three early American Indian tribal groupings to three main biotic provinces identified for Michigan. The model uses these historically "known cultural adaptations to specific ecological settings" to project "back onto the prehistoric period" in order to "elucidate late prehistoric cultural patterns in the Upper Great Lakes Region" (Fitting and Cleland 1969: 289). In developing this model, Fitting and Cleland acknowledge that historic communities observed postcontact would have been somewhat different precontact, but they consider the differences to be primarily technological.[2] As such, Fitting and Cleland (1969: 292) conclude that overall historic cultural adaptations, including subsistence strategies and settlement systems, would still be applicable to the past. Their model does not use the direct historical approach—it focuses on tracking the patterns of adaptation of historic tribal groups back into prehistory, not the groups themselves (Holman and Lovis 2008: 286; see Brose 1971 for details on problems with the application of the direct historic approach [ethnic continuity] in Michigan).

The three biotic provinces are summarized as the Carolinian, the Canadian, and the transition zone between the two (fig. 2.2). Fitting and Cleland assigned the "Miami and Potawatomi Pattern" to the Carolinian (Fitting and Cleland 1969: 297); the "Chippewa Pattern" to the Canadian (Fitting and Cleland 1969: 293); and the "Ottawa Pattern" to the transition zone (Fitting and Cleland 1969: 295).

The Carolinian and the "Miami and Potawatomi Pattern"

The Carolinian biotic province is characterized by Lower Michigan's rolling hills, flat lake plain, warm climate, long growing season, and deciduous forest communities (Fitting and Cleland 1969: 289; fig. 2.2). Abundant animals and plants prosper in deciduous forest communities, including deer, nuts, and berries, and the area has both soils and a climate amenable to agriculture. Based on this climate suitable for agriculture, Fitting and Cleland assigned the Miami and Potawatomi pattern, a cultural adaptation relying on agriculture supplemented by hunting. Large permanent agricultural villages are occupied during the summer when hunting occurs in the surrounding zones. Men and women move together into large temporary hunting camps in the winter (Fitting and Cleland 1969: 297).

Projecting the Miami and Potawatomi pattern back to Late Prehistory, this southern region settlement pattern is based on large summer villages with evidence of agriculture as well as some hunting activities and winter hunting villages with no permanent structures and a dominance of hunting activities (Fitting and Cleland 1969: 299). Both summer and winter sites were large and show balanced male-female activities. The Moccasin Bluff site (20BE8) in Berrien County in the southwest corner of Michigan is one example of a Late Woodland/Late Prehistoric summer village conforming to the Miami and Potawatomi pattern (Fitting and Cleland 1969: 297).

The Canadian and the "Chippewa Pattern"

In almost complete contrast to the warm and moderate Carolinian biotic zone, the Upper Peninsula of Michigan as well as part of the interior and northeastern portion of the Lower Peninsula fall into the Canadian biotic province (Cleland 1966: 9; Fitting and Cleland 1969: 290; fig. 2.2). In this cool area, with a short annual growing season, resources are highly variable (Holman and Lovis 2008). The dominant floral association of this province is the Lake Forest, containing sugar maple, beech, elm, aspen,

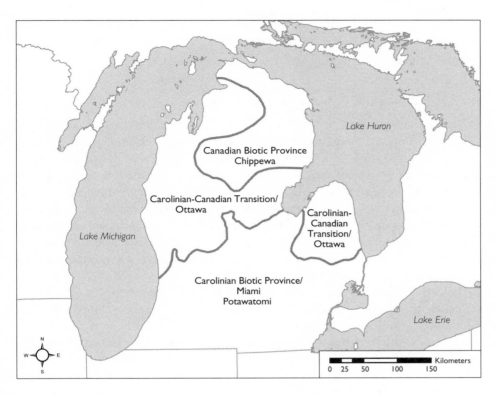

Figure 2.2. The biotic zones and their associated historic American Indian adaptations as designated by the Biotic/Historic Model of Late Prehistory for the Lower Peninsula (adapted from Fitting and Cleland 1969).

basswood, hemlock, black spruce, tamarack, cedar, fir, white pine, Norway pine, and jack pine (Cleland 1966: 9).

Fitting and Cleland (1969: 291), drawing heavily on the work of George I. Quimby (1962) detailing the year (1763–64) that Alexander Henry spent with a Chippewa family in Michigan, suggest the Chippewas as the early historic period example of a tribal community in the Canadian biotic province. Farming was not a component of the Chippewa economic repertoire. Fishing on the coasts and off islands of the northern Great Lakes was the main economic activity (Cleland 1992: 19–27). People aggregated in large villages during the late summer and fall and engaged in large-scale fishing operations of spawning fish, constituting what Cleland (1982) would later distinguish as the Inland Shore Fishery. This fishing strategy was based on the use of the gill net in deep water to capture fall-spawning anadromous fish, particularly whitefish and lake trout (Cleland 1982).

Other plant and mammal economic resources were so dispersed throughout the province that the fall fishing industry provided the primary context in which people could congregate in high density in the Canadian zone (Fitting and Cleland 1969: 294). During the winter, when resources were scarce, family groups dispersed, moving inland from the Great Lakes coasts to engage in small-scale hunting and other economic activities.

Projecting the Chippewa pattern back to Late Prehistory, settlement in this zone includes intensively and repeatedly occupied sites on the coasts of the Great Lakes with evidence of large-scale fall-focused fishing, such as the Juntunen site (20MK1) on Bois Blanc Island (Fitting and Cleland 1969: 299; McPherron 1967). All sites show no agricultural activity. Small, nonintensive winter occupation sites may be found inland from the Great Lakes, but these were used only by family groups (Fitting and Cleland 1969: 299).

The Transition Zone and the "Ottawa Pattern"

The transition zone between the Carolinian and Canadian provinces is designated as the third biotic province in Michigan (Fitting and Cleland 1969: 291; fig. 2.2). This area is also called the "Edge Area" (Fitting 1966). As a transition zone, it holds an unusually diverse array of plant and animal foods, making it abundant in wild resources (Holman and Lovis 2008: 288). It has a growing season sufficient to support prehistoric agriculture as well. The size and shape of this zone vary from east to west. In the eastern half of the state the transition zone encompasses the Saginaw Valley with its large expanses of wetlands; near the center of the state the Carolinian-Canadian transition zone widens and extends up the west coast; the Traverse Corridor forms the northern end of the transition zone (Hambacher 1992: 26).

The early historic Ottawas are seen as "specifically adapted to this Carolinian-Canadian transition area" (Fitting and Cleland 1969: 295). Developed from the ethnohistoric work of W. Vernon Kinietz (1940), the "Ottawa Pattern" was characterized by a commitment to a semisedentary way of life supported by crops and fishing in a variable environment (Holman and Lovis 2008: 299). Large mixed-economy fisher-horticultural villages were located in the coastal areas. Male hunting parties left these camps on winter hunts "directed toward the interior areas" (Fitting and Cleland 1969: 295). Hunting parties would select a defined territory and establish a winter camp in its center. Game was processed and transported back to the main coastal villages.

Projecting Ottawa patterns back, Late Prehistory settlement patterns developed as communities engaged in a seasonal round where late spring through late fall was spent on the coasts of the Great Lakes, the interior hosted winter hunting parties, and early spring was spent in locales between winter and late spring occupations (Holman 1984). Logistical residential mobility characterized this pattern (see Binford 1980). Larger villages located along the coasts show mixed fisher-horticultural economies. These were substantial and multiseasonal villages where hunted game came to the site already processed from the big winter hunts (Fitting and Cleland 1969: 295). A specialized use of the interior resulted in small Late Prehistoric sites reflecting male winter hunting camps (Holman and Lovis 2008). Other seasonal resource extraction activities also occurred in the interior, including maple sugaring in early spring as people traveled back to their coastal villages; but otherwise it was a place of sparse habitation, a kind of "vacantscape" (Holman 1984; Lovis 1973; Wright 1966).

The Colonial Encounter and Late Prehistory: Limitations of the Biotic/Historic Model

The Biotic/Historic Model provides a set of historically derived predictions for Late Prehistoric cultural developments (summarized in table 2.1). While this model does not use the direct historical approach, it is nevertheless based on some static assumptions: (1) that historic tribes are distinct, homogeneous entities for which discrete

TABLE 2.1. SUMMARY OF THE BIOTIC/HISTORIC MODEL'S EXPECTATIONS FOR LATE PREHISTORIC SUBSISTENCE PRACTICES AND SETTLEMENT PATTERNS

	Site types	Location	Seasonality	Subsistence (occurring at site)	Permanency
Carolinian/ Potawatomi	Large villages	Productive farming locales	Spring/summer/ fall	Agriculture and Hunting	Permanent
	Large camps	Protected areas	Winter	Hunting	Temporary
Canadian/ Chippewa	Large villages	Coasts of northern Great Lakes	Summer/fall	Specialized Fall Spawner Fishing	Reused year to year
	Small camps	Interior of Lower Peninsula	Winter	Hunting	Temporary
Transitional area/Ottawa	Large villages	Coasts of northern Great Lakes	Spring/summer/ fall	Mixed fishing-horticulture	Semipermanent
	Small camps	Interior of Lower Peninsula	Winter/early spring	Hunting/maple-sugaring	Temporary, low-intensity, small resource-extraction groups

cultural adaptations can be determined (such as "The Ottawas are a unit and they did *X*," "The Potawatomis are a unit and they did *Y*") and (2) that patterns observed during the postcontact period can be projected backward in time to understand the precontact cultural patterns in the Great Lakes. Entire adaptations are for the most part "uncritically projected backwards" (Trigger 1987: 14).

Even a brief review of colonial encounters in the Great Lakes (see below) raises obvious but also deeper intrinsic problems involved in relying on the historic activities of discrete tribes to predict past social, economic, and ideological activity.[3] I suggest that the reliance on postcontact developments as templates for the past places an inaccurate limit on the range of possible cultural developments in Michigan during Late Prehistory.

It is noteworthy that archaeologies of other times and places in North America have moved past the use of such static paradigms for interpreting the archaeological record. These archaeologies readily prioritize writing the deep histories of pre-Columbian life on the continent by using the great dynamism evident in the material record (see Alt [ed.] 2010 for examples of these contemporary archaeologies). An evaluation of this static paradigm in the Great Lakes may seem outdated to those familiar with these archaeologies, but I contend that it is vital because this framework is still the driving interpretive force behind archaeology in the region. Reviewing the limitations of this model is necessary if we want to see a new kind of archaeology emerge in the Great Lakes that is in line with contemporary work in North America.

The Colonial Encounter in the Great Lakes

The Northeast and the Great Lakes formed one extensive indigenous space where Algonquian and Haudenosaunee (Iroquoian) communities had forged interdependent and long-term connections over millennia by linking people and goods in networks of waterways and pathways (see Brooks 2008: map 1).[4] These connections ensured resource sharing vital to social stability and physical health (Brooks 2008: 5). Given these intimate connections, colonial encounters on the Atlantic seaboard were not and could not have remained disconnected from the Great Lakes. Thus the colonial encounter in the Great Lakes began with first contact on the seaboard.

Early Encounters: The Fur Trade and Competing Interests While some intermittent European presence was documented in the late fifteenth century (e.g., John Cabot), the sixteenth century saw the first notable European presence on the Atlantic seaboard, with both the Basques and French. Almost immediately, Europeans started the fur trade. This came to be a dominating conduit for cultural contact between American Indians and Euro-Americans. It is impossible to talk about interaction between indigenous and European peoples without considering the central place of the North American fur trade (Wagner 1998: 430). Evidence indicates that the initial phases of the fur trade provided numerous openings for participation by Indian men as well as women, offering more opportunities for indigenous communities to direct and even expand their socioeconomic systems than would exist later (White 1999).

Informal trading for furs had begun as early as the 1520s on the coast of Maine (Salisbury 1996: 452). Formalized trading accelerated along the seaboard to the Gulf and Estuary of St. Lawrence after the mid-1500s, however, when European demand for fancy furs increased (Fitzgerald et al. 1993: 44). The first formalized trade networks emerged with the Basques, an ethnic population in northern Spanish territory renowned as accomplished sailors, shipwrights, fishers, and whalers (Ross 1985). Basque mariners became involved in whaling and fishing along the Atlantic seaboard in the early 1500s (Ross 1985). They started formal trading in the Gulf and Estuary of St. Lawrence around 1580 (Fitzgerald et al. 1993: 44).

The French arrived in the region shortly after the Basques. The first formal French explorations of the Atlantic seaboard and the land inward toward the Great Lakes began in 1534 with French explorer Jacques Cartier's journey on the Gulf of the St. Lawrence and the St. Lawrence River system. Cartier met a number of Algonquian- and Iroquoian-speaking groups throughout his explorations (Trigger 1987: 177).

Iroquoian speakers, which included the Iroquois nations, the Huron confederacy, the Neutral confederacy, the Eries, the Petuns, the Wenros, and the Susquehannocks, were spread across modern-day New York, southern Ontario, and adjacent portions of Pennsylvania, Ohio, and Quebec (Snow 1994: 1). Algonquian speakers occupied the land north and west of the Iroquoian range, living on lands that the French came to call the *pays d'en haut* (fig. 2.3). These lands included areas around Lake Erie but not near southern Lake Ontario (which fell within Iroquoia), took in the rest of the Great Lakes, and stretched to the Mississippi River (White 1991: x).

The Algonquian speakers of the northern *pays d'en haut* understood themselves collectively as An-ish-in-aub-ag (Anishinaabeg). While this is often translated to mean "Common People," William Whipple Warren, an Ojibwa scholar and native speaker who wrote a history of his community in the nineteenth century, argued that this is a misinterpretation. The term actually translates as "Spontaneous People" (Warren 1984 [1885]: 56). This translation connects directly to the cosmological story of origins shared across Anishinaabeg communities based on a cycle of creation, destruction, and re-creation (Johnston 1990: 15). In this cycle, Kitche Manitou

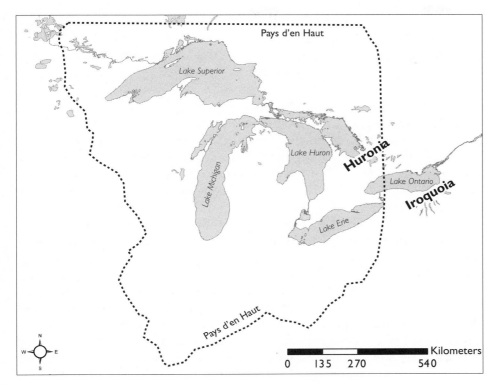

Figure 2.3. The *pays d'en haut* (adapted from White 1991).

creates plants, animals, the elements, and humans; floods (the seas) destroy the earth; and Sky-Woman re-creates the earth by placing soil brought up from the seas by muskrat on turtle's back and then re-creates humans by giving birth to a man and woman. The newly re-created men and women were called Anishinaabeg, "beings made of nothing because their substances were not rock, or fire, or water, or wind" (Johnston 1990: 15). Made of soul-spirit substance, they were "spontaneous beings": indigenous, natural, arising from Sky-Woman and intimately connected to her other creation, re-created earth, their homeland (see Johnston 1990: 13–16).

By the 1540s specialized French fur traders had traveled as far south as the Chesapeake Bay (Salisbury 1996: 452). By the mid-1500s or soon thereafter the French were holding regular trade rendezvous with tribes along the shores of New England and the Maritimes and inland on the St. Lawrence (Salisbury 1996: 452). French explorer Samuel de Champlain followed Cartier, pushing up the St. Lawrence River and establishing Quebec in 1608. From there the French launched even more formalized fur trading (Cleland 1992: 79). While the French originally favored alliances with the Algonquian groups along the northeastern Atlantic seaboard, who lived closer to the heart of New France, their relationships with the Iroquoian-speaking Huron confederacy in the interior grew as they formalized their control of the fur trade in the early 1600s. The Huron confederacy consisted of four tribes clustered together in Huron country, which the French called Huronia (Trigger 1987: 50; fig. 2.3).

The early French explorations of the Northeast and St. Lawrence region, while penetrating the range of Iroquoian-speaking groups, did not enter Iroquoia itself (the territory of the Iroquois confederacy [or Haudenosaunee] in upstate New York), because the Adirondack mountains stood in the way. The first major interaction between Europeans and the Iroquois confederacy came during Dutch explorations in the early 1600s in what is now New York (Bradley 2007; Fenton 1998; Trelease 1960, 1962).

The Dutch had commissioned Englishman Henry Hudson to find a passage to the Pacific. In 1609 Hudson traveled down the river that now bears his name to modern Albany. He met the Algonquian-speaking Mahicans who lived along the river. Hudson had not found a passage to the Pacific, so he opted to establish trading posts along the river (Bradley 2007). The Dutch followed his explorations by constructing Fort Nassau on an island on the southern side of Albany in 1614 (Snow 1994: 80).

The Mohawk tribe of the Iroquois confederacy lived just west of Albany and began competing with their already established rivals, the Mahicans, for participation in the Dutch fur trade. In 1624 the Dutch built a new fort in Albany, Fort Orange, which rekindled Mohawk interest and involvement in the fur trade (Trelease 1962: 138). While the Mahicans disliked the Mohawks' involvement, which led to a four-year Mohawk-Mahican war, the four other tribes of the Iroquois confederacy joined the Mohawks in trade with the Dutch. As Dean Snow (1994: 89) describes, "the years between 1614 and 1634 were exhilarating ones for the Iroquois. The Dutch trade enriched their lives and drew them together as a League as never before."

In 1634 an epidemic swept through the St. Lawrence Valley (Trigger 1987: 500), beginning six years of illness among all American Indian communities in the broader northeastern region of the United States and Canada, including the Iroquois and Huron confederacies. Between 1634 and 1640 the epidemics ravaged communities, reducing populations by as much as 50% (Snow 1994: 100; Trigger 1987: 499). The diseases "penetrated along the trade routes into areas no European had yet visited" (Trigger 1987: 499), including areas in the *pays d'en haut*. While the number of those who died is not known, it is certain that the epidemics devastated indigenous populations in the *pays d'en haut* (Brose 2001; Cleland 1992; White 1991).

In Iroquoia the immense loss of family and community members was coupled with a rapidly declining supply of fur-bearing animals. This combination led the Iroquois, who were well equipped by the Dutch, to seek both revenge and new hunting grounds (Fox 2009; Snow 1994). They first vented their anger on the Hurons. As Snow (1994: 114–15) describes, "driven mainly by the desire for revenge, prestige, and power, along with a desire for captives to replace lost family members, the Iroquois battered the Huron mercilessly from 1641 on." The Huron confederacy disintegrated in 1649 after enduring years of Iroquois attacks. Members of the confederacy dispersed from Huronia; some moved with French Jesuits and traders to Montreal; some were adopted by the Iroquois; and others became refugees among Algonquian-speaking groups to the west in the *pays d'en haut* (for details, see Trigger 1987: 789–840).

These adoptions failed to make up for Iroquois losses (Fenton 1998: 6), so, after displacing the Hurons from their territory, the Iroquois turned their aggressions toward other Iroquoian-speaking tribes living around southern Lake Ontario and Lake Erie (Keener 1999; Kinietz 1940). They had displaced the Neutrals, who lived around Lake Ontario, by 1653 and the Eries, who resided along the south side of

Lake Erie, by 1656. When the refugees from these Iroquois attacks (like the Hurons) fled west, the Iroquois followed. They extended their attacks into the upper Great Lakes and even struck as far as the Mississippi River, displacing indigenous communities from these areas as well.

Refugees and the Pays d'en Haut The French were the first Europeans to enter the Upper Great Lakes region, arriving sporadically in the early to mid-1600s and developing a solid presence after 1650. The Anishinaabeg peoples living in these lands were hardly living in some kind of "virgin" world when these French explorers arrived. Years of contact and trade on the seaboard had facilitated the rapid movement of trade goods deep into this country before European peoples themselves came in large numbers (Turgeon 1997). European goods moved along and inland from the Atlantic seaboard by two means: (1) along the extant intertribal trade routes that had been forged between communities over millennia (Branstner 1992: 179); and (2) via Indian brokers like the Micmacs, who controlled the movement and introduction of European trade goods into the Gulf of Maine for twenty to thirty years before Europeans made significant contacts with tribal populations there around 1610 (Bourque and Whitehead 1985).

Moreover, European disease epidemics had come early along these routes as well. The western Great Lakes region (modern-day Michigan and west) had sustained major demographic losses already by the mid-1500s due to trends in place before contact, which were magnified by waves of disease during early contact (Milner and Chaplin 2010: 721). When the destructive reality of intertribal competition over the fur trade sent violent ripples through the region, the Lower Peninsula of Michigan was left almost completely empty by the mid-1600s (see Brose 1971: 54; Cleland 1992: 93; Pilling 1968; Quimby 1960: 128).

As refugees "moved west to avoid the Iroquois hammer, they encountered an anvil formed by the Sioux, a people whom the Jesuits called the Iroquois of the West" (White 1991: 11). Surrounded by two strong and aggressive powers, the Indian refugees "recoiled and concentrated themselves within an inverted triangle whose point rested on Starved Rock in the Illinois country and whose base ran between Sault Sainte Marie and Michilimackinac in the east and Chequamegon in the west. Green Bay was approximately at its center" (White 1991: 11; fig. 2.4). This refugee triangle was a multiethnic community of Algonquian-speaking groups including Ottawas (or Odawas), Potawatomis, Chippewas (or Ojibwas), Fox, Sauks, Kickapoos, Miamis, Illinois, Mascoutens, and many others (Brose 1971; White 1991: 11).

By the mid-1600s the *pays d'en haut* was dissected into two distinct sections: refugee lands and emptied lands (fig. 2.4). This amalgamation of previously separate communities had several important social consequences. These refugees, displaced from their ancestral lands, were unable to maintain geographic boundaries; this led to reenvisionings of previous notions of territoriality that had been important prior to displacement. The social practices of communities living in new landscapes were altered by these spaces, which became their new, if temporary, homes. Kinship, another key organizing principle of Algonquian life, remained important, but people operationalized it in new ways. Algonquian kinship was based on a formal system of clan membership, largely determined through patrilineal descent (see Clifton

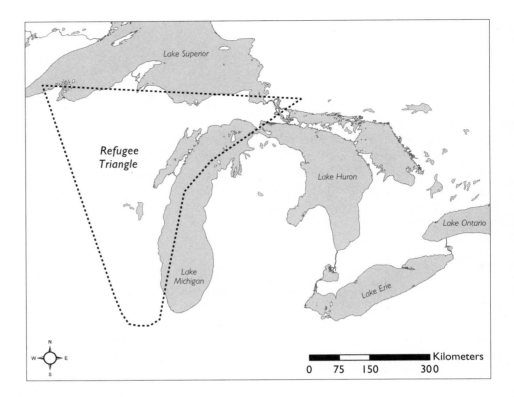

Figure 2.4. The refugee triangle (adapted from White 1991).

et al. 1986: 6–7; Warren 1984 [1885]: chapter 2). Previously distinct groups had to live side by side on a daily basis, however, so new identities were created as neighbors crafted multiple ties of real and symbolic kinship; "kinship moved far away from actual descent" (White 1991: 18). In this refugee world, identity and kinship became contingent rather than fixed by actual descent, activated and maintained in ways that let individuals best deal with rapidly changing social and economic conditions.

In some cases, these "denser connections between refugee groups" led to "the dissolution of old groups and the creation of new ones" (White 1991: 18). For example, the coalescence of various patrilineal bands laid the foundation for the two large divisions of Ojibwas recorded historically, the Chippewas and the Mississaugas (see Hickerson 1966). Furthermore, the Iroquoian-speaking Hurons and Petuns, minorities in the *pays d'en haut*, merged to form the Huron-Petuns (see Kinietz 1940).

Within this complex array of kinship and identity formation, pantribal organizations that transcended kinship became important. The Catholic Church filled this role to some degree. It also played a role in divisions within tribal groups, however, creating breaks between those Indians who became Christians and those who did not. The most important pantribal organization was an Indian-constructed religious organization, the Midewiwin Society (Densmore 1929; Hickerson 1962, 1963; Hoffman 1891). This organization is relevant to one of the monument sites discussed here (see the more detailed discussion in chapter 5).

While the refugee world was a place where "fragments" of previous worlds were melded into new and interesting notions of social structure, this world still needed something other than common loss and a common enemy to hold it together (White 1991: 1). The political glue came in the form of a French-Algonquian alliance crafted in the last two decades of the seventeenth century. This alliance principally concerned the fur trade but entailed much more, as the French and the Algonquian refugees of the *pays d'en haut* created an "elaborate network of economic, political, cultural, and social ties to meet the demands of a particular historical situation" (White 1991: 33). Mediation of conflicts between the French and Algonquians as well as among various Algonquian groups was at the heart of the alliance. Richard White (1991) has eloquently termed the world that emerged from this alliance the "Middle Ground." It was a form of "odd imperialism where mediation succeeded and force failed, where colonizers gave gifts to the colonized and patriarchal metaphors were the heart of politics" (White 1991: 145).

While significant, this alliance could not curb the economic and environmental instability the refugees faced in the late seventeenth century. With such large groups of people (many of them sick) concentrated together, epidemics swept through village centers. These large concentrations of people depleted the local natural resources. These stresses were paramount in the last two decades of the seventeenth century, finally easing when the French-Algonquian alliance for the first time was able to fight back the Iroquois and reach the Grand Settlement of 1701, a peace accord with the Iroquois (see Brandão and Starna [1996] for a different perspective on this settlement as positive for the Iroquois). The refugee centers in the triangle quickly dissolved as groups repopulated the emptied portion of the *pays d'en haut* to secure lands with more abundant subsistence bases.

Regional Blocs Repopulating the Pays d'en Haut The early eighteenth century saw six regional blocs develop in the *pays d'en haut*. One was on lower Lake Michigan, including southwestern Michigan and running through present-day Milwaukee and Green Bay. This bloc included Sauks, Fox, Kickapoos, and Mascoutens, who maintained very close ties, as well as Winnebagos and Menominees in the bloc's northern end and the Potawatomis in southwestern Michigan (Clifton 1977; Edmunds 1978; White 1991: 146). The second bloc was Illinois country (Blasingham 1956; Ehrhardt 2005). The third centered on modern Detroit; this was the most volatile bloc, including Ottawas, Huron-Petuns, Potawatomis, and Miamis, who became the Mississaugas east of Detroit (Tanner 1987: 58–59).

The fourth bloc centered on Michilimackinac and included the Chippewa village at Sault Ste Marie and the Ottawa village on Manitoulin Island (White 1991: 147). These northern Chippewas were the second division of the Ojibwas that emerged during the coalescence of patrilineal bands in the refugee centers. A growing difference existed between the western Chippewas in the Lake Superior region and those at Sault Ste Marie (the Saulteurs proper), who were closely linked with the Ottawa groups at Michilimackinac. Together, the Chippewas of Sault Ste Marie and the Ottawas colonized the Saginaw Bay in Michigan (Tanner 1987: 41). The Ottawas gradually shifted their settlements from Michilimackinac west to the shores and islands of northern Lake Michigan; by the 1740s their settlement centered on Arbor Croche on Little Traverse Bay (Blackbird 1897; McClurken 1991). The western Chippewas of Lake Superior formed the fifth regional subunit or bloc in the eighteenth century expansion in the *pays d'en haut* (Hickerson 1970; Kinietz 1947).

The sixth regional bloc emerged in the Ohio Valley. A variety of refugee groups moved into the valley, including Miamis, Kickapoos, and Mascoutens as well as the Huron-Petun group, who proclaimed themselves to be the Wyandots after resettling in Ohio (Dowd 2002: 41). Groups from outside the *pays d'en haut* also moved in throughout the eighteenth century. Shawnees, who had once lived in the Ohio Valley but had been expelled by war and were living in Pennsylvania, returned to their homelands (Dowd 2002: 41; Mann 2003; Tanner 1987: 43). Delawares from Pennsylvania and remnants of the Iroquois nation also moved their villages into Ohio country (Dowd 2002: 41). The Ohio Valley had a complicated and often conflict-ridden history in the eighteenth century (cf. Griffin 2005; Hinderaker 1997).

During this time Algonquian groups located their villages in locales that optimized their access to the French fur trade. Groups also moved to locations where corn agriculture was easy or fisheries were abundant. Having spent the previous decades in the desperate conditions of refugee centers, communities considered both subsistence and trade when deciding where to locate their villages.

As groups expanded into reopened homelands, they developed new senses of territory, mobility, and identity. By the late seventeenth century the postrefugee bands of Algonquians increasingly assumed "national" or tribal identities, such as Ottawas and Saulteurs, when in the *pays d'en haut* (Witgen 2007: 641). Even as these "national" identities took shape, however, they remained flexible and interchangeable (Witgen 2007: 641). As Michael Witgen (2007: 641) explains, the same people took on different identities in different spaces. Fulfilling roles of discrete tribal identities held weight with the French and allowed postrefugee communities to further their trading power. Using these situational, flexible identities, communities were able to capitalize on other opportunities as well, such as trade systems farther west and outside the French alliance (Witgen 2007: 641). But over time discrete tribal groupings frequently developed into the historically named and located American Indian tribes or nations of the Great Lakes and Midwest that the American government would make treaties with, remove, and place on reservations during the first half of the nineteenth century. These are also the groups that ethnographers studied during the nineteenth and early twentieth centuries, as anthropology crystallized as a discipline.

The communities that moved into Michigan during the eighteenth-century expansion out of the triangle of refugee centers developed into the recognized tribes of Michigan (Brose 1971). These include the Potawatomis in southwestern Michigan, the Chippewas in the Upper Peninsula, the Ottawas along the shores of northern Lake Michigan, the combined group of Chippewas and Ottawas in the Saginaw Valley, and the Mississauga Ojibwas in eastern Lower Michigan.

The twelve federally recognized and two state recognized tribes in Michigan today reflect the history of life after European contact and stand as examples of survivance.[5] These groups are the Bay Mills Chippewa Indian Community, Burt Lake Band of Ottawa and Chippewa Indians, Gun Lake Band of Potawatomi Match-e-be-nash-she-wish, Grand Traverse Bay Band of Ottawa and Chippewa Indians, Hannahville Potawatomi Indian Community, Keweenaw Bay Indian Community, Lac Vieux Desert Band of Lake Superior Chippewa Indians, Little River Band of Odawa Indians, Little Traverse Bay Band of Odawa Indians, Match-e-be-nash-she-wish Band of Potawatomi Indians of Michigan, Nottawasppi Huron Band of Potawatomi,

Pokagon Band of Potawatomi Indians, Saginaw Chippewa Indian Tribe of Michigan, and Sault Ste. Marie Tribe of Chippewa Indians (MACPRA 2009).

Implications for the Archaeology of Late Prehistory

Ethnohistorians working in other parts of eastern North America have mapped similar patterns of disruption, dispersion, reconfiguration, and repopulation during the early stages of European contact (see Axtell 1997; Brose et al. [eds.] 2001; Ethridge and Hudson [eds.] 2002; Galloway 1995, 2002; Merrell 1989; O'Brien 1997). Robbie Ethridge (2009: 21) coined the term "Shatter Zone" to explain the deep, integrated, and widespread instability that followed European contact and the inauguration of the capitalist modern world system in eastern North America. Postapocalyptic histories (Larson 2007) suggest that relying on cultural adaptations from this time as prototypes for Late Prehistory works only if we ignore many realities.

Those working within the Biotic/Historic Model are aware that contact impacted historically observed American Indian communities. But they argue that the impacts were primarily technological; thus cultural adaptations, such as settlement patterns, mobility, and subsistence choices, are appropriate and useful templates for Late Prehistory. People were displaced, occupied a refugee world, and developed social realignments to navigate and actively manipulate the postapocalyptic imperial world, however, so we have absolutely no reason to think that socioeconomic strategies, choices, and systems in place during Late Prehistory were not different, perhaps radically so, from those observed historically. Others have also argued that the cultural changes between precontact and postcontact Michigan involved more than simple shifts in technology and that continuity in subsistence activities and settlement choices between pre- and postcontact times may have shifted significantly (O'Gorman 2007: 375). In the following discussion I consider some of the practical as well as deeper intrinsic issues of economy, identity, and landscape raised by the review of the colonial encounter that support this latter proposition.

Economy: Subprime Subsistence Choices? The postcontact economic setting is a poor match for Late Prehistory. Prior to European contact, the Anishinaabeg communities in Michigan did not live in a capitalist world system that demanded prioritizing the fur trade into their location and subsistence decisions. While fluctuations in resource productivity during the year were common, Late Prehistoric communities had not experienced years of massive subsistence stress as historically observed communities did.

Late Prehistoric Anishinaabeg communities occupied the beautiful, sometimes harsh, landscape of northern Michigan in ways that responded to their specific economic milieu. This meant that they could choose living locations without considering the need to participate in the fur trade. Tribal groups living prior to contact could also make subsistence choices that were not necessarily the most productive but were sufficient and reliable; unlike historic communities, they had mechanisms other than the fur trade to buffer resource risk. The range of subsistence activities and settlement locations among historic American Indian communities may predict some Late Prehistoric patterns but cannot account for all possible economic choices made prior to contact. The archaeological record bears this out, showing significant

divergences between archaeological finds and the Biotic/Historic Model's historically derived subsistence predictions (see table 2.1 for a summary of these).

Archaeological research conducted along the northern coast of Lake Huron, in
what the Biotic/Historic Model designated as the Canadian/Chippewa Pattern (fig.
2.2; table 2.1), has concluded that people engaged in maize cultivation even in this
somewhat marginal environment. During the Late Prehistoric period maize was
adopted by the established forager communities on the northern coasts of Lake
Huron and became a significant subsistence resource (Brandt 1996; Katzenberg et
al 1995; O'Shea 2003; O'Shea and Milner 2002). In fact, maize is relatively abundant
in the botanical remains recovered at the Juntunen site (McPherron 1967: 188), the
very site that the Biotic/Historic Model offered as an exemplar of a fall fishing village
in the Canadian/Chippewa Pattern, predicting no maize agriculture. The variability
of the region presented challenges to growing maize, making it perhaps not a prime
resource choice but clearly one that communities made anyway.

In the Upper Great Lakes "one of the effective limits of prehistoric Indian agriculture was the line marking the limits of the 120-day average frost-free period"
(Yarnell 1964: 128). "Lake-effect" is a term used in the Great Lakes area to describe
the environmental influence that the lakes have on growing season and duration
(Burnett et al. 2003; Leighly 1941; Liu and Moore 2004; Schaetzl et al. 2005). As the
growing season begins, the lakes' cooling effect protects plants until the spring frost
season is over. The lakes store daytime heat as the growing season continues; the
warm water lessens the variation between day and night temperatures, lengthening
the growing season by as much as four weeks along the shorelines. As summer draws
to an end, the stored warmth of the waters delays frost that might damage fall crops.
In summary, the lake-effect produces a growing season that is longer in areas adjacent to the Great Lakes than in inland areas (see fig. 2.1). Along the northern coasts
of both Lake Huron and Lake Michigan, the lake-effect produces a growing season
ranging from 130 to 150 days, which is sufficient for prehistoric horticulture (Albert
1995; Lovis 1973; Yarnell 1964).

Looking at the Lake Huron area, sufficient frost-free days do not mean that the climate was never harsh or unpredictable. While maize could be grown in this coastal
area, its cultivation still entailed substantial risk. An analysis of maize yields in four
counties (Iosco, Alcona, Alpena, and Arenac) along Lake Huron's northern zone
from the first half of the twentieth century (before farmers used high-productiv-
ity hybrid crops) reveals a pattern of dramatic interannual fluctuation. Prehistoric
communities would have faced an unpredictable pattern of productive years inter-
spersed with years of severe crop failure (O'Shea 2003: 7–8; O'Shea and Milner 2002:
203). Maize agriculture in these marginal environments would have offered "a substantial potential increase in caloric capture," but this "potential was tempered by
the inherent year-to-year variation in maize productivity" (O'Shea 2003: 7). With
the Biotic/Historic Model predicting backward from historic economic adaptations
made with prime productivity in mind, this dynamic subsistence development of
Late Prehistory had gone overlooked.

In addition to expecting this northeastern region not to have horticulture as
part of the economy, the Biotic/Historic Model also expected fall fishing or Inland
Shore Fishery to have supremacy (table 2.1). An intensive research program along

northern Lake Huron, however, found that the major Late Prehistoric fishing site, the Hampsher site (20AL44), was a spring site (Milner 1998). Looking again at the subsistence evidence from the Juntunen site, which the Biotic/Historic Model held as an exemplar of a fall fishing village in the Canadian/Chippewa Pattern, we see further divergences from this expectation. The data show that both spring and fall spawning runs of fish (not just fall) had crucial importance there (McPherron 1967: 198).

This evidence aligns with work by Susan Martin (1989). Through an analysis of settlement and faunal data from fifty-one Middle and Late Woodland sites on the coasts and islands of the northern Great Lakes, Martin (1989: 596) demonstrates that the fishing of fall spawners and the use of gill nets predated the Late Woodland. She concludes that the key feature of Late Woodland subsistence practices was opportunism, which resulted in a diversified fishing industry, not one that specialized in fall spawning, with sites positioned to maximize fish resources abundant in many seasons (including fall- and spring-spawning species).

While work on Lake Huron has uncovered these notable economic divergences, archaeological research in coastal areas of the transition zone has found the large mixed-economy, more permanent villages during Late Prehistory predicted by the Biotic/Historic Model, such as the Skegemog site (20GT8) in the Traverse Corridor (fig. 2.2; table 2.1). Work on the Inland Waterway (marked in fig. 2.1) has suggested that this locale was complementary to these coastal villages—the place for specialized seasonal resource extraction, strong in winter resource catchments as well as spring maple sugaring (Holman 1978, 1984; Holman and Krist 2001; Lovis 1978, 2001).

It is important to note that the large interior of the Lower Peninsula formed by what is called the High Plains ecosystem (designated in fig. 2.1) has remained largely uninvestigated because it is predicted to have been an even more marginal locale of empty winter hunting grounds (a "vacantscape") by the Biotic/Historic Model. This underinvestigated area is addressed in more detail in chapter 3. The emerging archaeological patterns, like the evidence just reviewed from Lake Huron, suggest further divergence from the predictions based on the traditional model.

Identity: Fluidity and Discrete Historic Tribes? Metalevel concerns include identity and the landscape. The realignments and fluidity that we know occurred in tribal community identity during the early historic period problematize one of the assumptions central to the Biotic/Historic Model: that a tribal entity was a static, observable unit that did *X*. Such national identities were important, but they were often assigned by the French and occupied by indigenous peoples in ways that filled French ideals. These identities remained flexible and could even be dismissed as people moved in and out of socioeconomic settings. The very idea of distinct, essential "Ottawa/Chippewa/Potawatomi Patterns" that can be observed historically is open to doubt.

We could argue that this is an issue of ethnicity and that the Biotic/Historic Model does not expect to trace ethnicity over time. But can identity be completely separated from "cultural adaptation"? The events of early colonial encounters show that the complicated process of identity formation was fundamentally tied to economics. Identity was essential to all that falls under the broad umbrella of "cultural adaptation," as people used identity (as well as nonidentity) to ensure social persistence, economic vitality, and their basic survival.

Landscape: How to Explain Monumentalism? Landscape is an intimate part of any tribal community's identity, social order, and practice. As noted in chapter 1, relationships to distinct territories can inform, even control, behavior. Historic communities occupied and were occupied by (see Basso 1996) different landscapes than precontact communities, which undoubtedly produced different behaviors. Dwelling in varying natural landscapes can be expected to produce differences in cultural patterns (see Ingold 2000).

In dealing with the Potawatomis, Jodie A. O'Gorman (2007) suggests that we have good reasons to expect discontinuities in cultural patterns between precontact and postcontact times due to landscape differences. Historic Potawatomi life as observed in northeastern Wisconsin was not the same as in southwestern Michigan. It could not be the same, because the physical and social differences between the landscapes are all part of the Potawatomi culture's dynamics and would have affected the remains of behavior studied by archaeologists (O'Gorman 2007: 394).

Indeed, in *Ethnohistory*, the same journal that published Fitting and Cleland's 1969 outline of the Biotic/Historic Model, O'Gorman (2007) systematically debunks what she calls the "Myth of Moccasin Bluff." O'Gorman (2007: 375) demonstrates that Moccasin Bluff, the key archaeological site thought to be an agricultural village of the Potawatomi Pattern, offers little evidence of intensive corn agriculture. Even after intensive surveys in southwestern Michigan conducted in the almost forty years since Fitting and Cleland's article, "no other sites that might be comparable to the kind of village represented by the mythical large agricultural village of Moccasin Bluff have been located" (O'Gorman 2007: 390). Their imported historic pattern simply does not match the archaeological evidence (table 2.1; this lack of fit between the Potowatomi Pattern and Late Prehistoric archaeology is becoming well accepted: see Holman and Lovis 2008; O'Gorman and Lovis 2006).

We might expect even more drastic differences in cultural patterns when one community constructs and occupies a monumental landscape and another does not. A most obvious divergence between Late Prehistoric and historic occupations is the construction of earthworks and mounds. Numerous mounds and earthworks were built preceding contact; several, in fact, were spread throughout the interior of the Lower Peninsula, presumed to be an empty hunting ground (see chapter 3).

These mounds and earthworks suggest that monumentalism (see Dillehay 2007) was important during Late Prehistory in northern Michigan. Monuments are not superfluous to subsistence, settlement, and social developments; they are intimately intertwined with every aspect of community organization. Once built, all monuments became hubs in networks of social interaction; monumental investment in and engagement with the landscape must have had correlated impacts on social, economic, and ideological behaviors of Late Prehistoric communities. Monumentalism was part of the process of "cultural adaptation" during Late Prehistory that has no historic counterpart yet demands an explanation. The monuments' presence highlights again that the changes after contact were more than simple shifts in technology and should give us pause in considering how we draw on historic adaptations to interpret the past.

Summary: Where Do We Go from Here? The utility (at a practical level) and the validity (at a metalevel) of using historically "known cultural adaptations to specific ecological settings" to project "back onto the prehistoric period" in order to "elucidate late prehistoric cultural patterns in the Upper Great Lakes Region" are questionable (Fitting and Cleland 1969: 289). Late Prehistory had a dynamism that was significant in its own right and left a material record that can be investigated and understood (Howey and O'Shea 2009). It is true that in Late Prehistory people made some choices similar to those made historically. But people also made choices that we should expect to differ from historical observations.

Native peoples were far from passive bystanders in the postcontact geopolitical landscape, and specific developments played out in a dialectical fashion between Native American and European views (Ethridge 2009: 18). But colonialism was a destructive experience in which Europeans ultimately gained and wielded (often ruthlessly) the structural power (Wolf 1999: 275).

We should expect different, perhaps even radically different, cultural patterns before contact because people were living in a *structurally different world* that was not based on capitalist economies, territorial dispossession, and militaristic colonialism. Limiting the possibilities for Late Prehistory to the choices and patterns that people followed in the remade world of postcontact obscures our ability to understand the actual dynamism present in the northern Great Lakes during Late Prehistory. Understanding these dynamics is essential for unfolding the complicated story of Late Prehistoric to Early Historic population dynamics, social interaction, and cultural change in the Great Lakes. We cannot understand the "Shatter Zone" by assuming that we know what came before contact; we must reconstruct the lives of the people who were indigenous to the landscape on their terms on the basis of the material remains that they left behind.

As noted in the introduction, we need to build archaeologies showing that American Indian history did not begin with Columbus. If we continue to rely heavily on importing cultural patterns from post-Columbian observations to explain pre-Columbian pasts, we risk reifying the view that nothing dynamic or novel or notable occurred before "true history." We should not keep using the precontact world to fill that "Savage slot."

In criticizing the Biotic/Historic Model's overtendency toward continuity, it is important to avoid falling prey to the opposite tendency, where an overly skeptical approach to ethnohistory assigns an acculturative origin to everything in historic American Indian communities (Trigger 1987: 14). All known historic American Indian economic patterns and social systems in the Great Lakes clearly did not develop from an entirely new cloth. Historic Indian groups attempted to deal with "forces that threatened their existence" (Angel 2002: 74). These new forces were of a scale and severity that they had never faced in prehistory, yet Indian groups used cultural systems and understandings in place prior to contact to deal with them.

The challenge before us is to consider organizing principles (including territory, kinship, social roles, religious practices, and economic structures) that retained meaning and efficacy even as they were repurposed for new and emergent milieus, from the precontact to postcontact worlds (Norder 2003: 84). Such "traces" in historic and modern Anishinaabeg communities offer a vital perspective for archaeological investigations of the Late Prehistoric period in northern Michigan.

So where do we go from here? The Biotic/Historic Model's command to consider both environment and ethnohistory in order to move away from studying only cultural history must still be heeded. But we also need to approach the Late Prehistoric period with a framework that allows us to remain open to finding different dynamics. I contend that a focus on tribal cultural processes, and how monuments can emerge within them, offers one such framework.

CHAPTER 3

Monuments and Tribal Ritual Organization

NORTHERN MICHIGAN, A.D. 1200–1600

The patterns and trends marking Late Prehistory (ca. A.D. 1200–1600) emerged from regional processes of tribalization among Anishinaabeg communities in the northern Great Lakes. Communities throughout northern Michigan had practiced a broad spectrum strategy of foraging in which groups could move easily between resource zones on the shorelines of the Great Lakes, inland lakes, and rivers for millennia. Anthropologists agree that a dramatic shift occurred after A.D. 1000/1100 and brought an end to the long-established socioeconomic system. Associated with the end of this system was an increase in community size, the emergence of strong territorial systems with less permeable boundaries, the formalization of decision making, and the development of stronger group identity (Cleland 1982, 1992; Holman and Lovis 2008; O'Shea and Milner 2002).

These changes were related to notable resource transformations. Communities living along Lake Michigan and Lake Huron developed specialized subsistence economies that involved an intensified exploitation of fall- as well as spring-spawning fish species (Cleland 1982; Holman and Lovis 2008: Martin 1989; O'Shea and Milner 2002; Smith 2004). Indeed, along both lakes, several Late Woodland sites are located near historically documented fisheries (Milner 1998: 58).

More dramatically, Late Prehistory saw an increase in maize horticulture along the coasts of the northern Great Lakes. Sufficient climactic amelioration was caused by the lake-effect along both Lake Michigan and Lake Huron to permit successful maize horticulture on these coasts (see chapter 2). Maize (*Zea mays*) was first cultivated in a limited manner around A.D. 500–600 in the Great Lakes (Crawford et al. 1997: 116), but after A.D. 1000/1100 maize horticulture increased among established forager communities along the shorelines and coasts. It quickly filled a dominant role in the communities' diet, and evidence suggests that by about A.D. 1350 some communities consumed fewer wild animals, relying more and more on maize (Katzenberg et al. 1995: 335).

Both of these specialized economic activities—maize cultivation and intensified fishing—benefited from a growing focus on shoreline and coastal settlements. Increasing sedentism improved prospects for successful maize horticulture in the region's highly variable climate (O'Shea 2003) and allowed groups to secure access to key fall- and spring-spawning fishing locations (Holman and Lovis 2008). These shifts, which involved intensive local interactions and restricted ranges of movement, precipitated major social transformations, including the "restructuring of patterns of settlement, territoriality, subsistence scheduling, and social alliance"

(O'Shea 2003: 6). Communities living in northern Michigan during Late Prehistory (ca. A.D. 1200–1600) came to participate in tribal systems based on defined, stable, and eventually exclusive territories and social boundaries.

Ceramic Wares and Tribal Social Boundaries

One of the most notable material culture developments in Late Prehistory was the emergence and persistence of distinct, strong, homogeneous ceramic stylistic traditions with discrete spatial extents (see fig. 3.1). Traverse wares have been defined from northwestern Michigan in the Traverse Corridor, dating to the Late Prehistoric (ca. A.D. 1200–1600) (Hambacher 1992: 7). Juntunen ware (dating to A.D. 1200–1650) has been defined from Lake Huron (Milner 1998) and the Straits of Mackinac region (McPherron 1967). Younge tradition wares developed in southeastern Michigan (Stothers 1999); Oneota ceramics in southwestern Michigan, Indiana, and westward (McAllister 1999); Wisconsin Lake Phase pottery northwest of Lake Michigan (Milner 1998); and Iroquois styles east of Lake Huron (Milner 1998: 105–106).[1]

These Late Prehistoric ceramic wares show an almost rigid uniformity in the degree to which decorative attributes occur together (McPherron 1967: 297). This "contrasts sharply with the stylistic profile of earlier phases during which ceramic variation is minimal and occurs in a pattern that largely reflects declines in interaction among relatively mobile pot producers with distance" (O'Shea and Milner 2002: 213). During the early Late Woodland (ca. A.D. 600–1000) the few distinct wares across northern and southern Michigan shared a high level of stylistic overlap, reflecting the presence of some, but still fluid, social boundaries (Brashler 1981; Lovis 1973; McPherron 1967). These ceramic patterns suggest the presence of an intermediate social system between a highly diffuse and exclusive system (Brashler 1981: 383).[2]

The emergence of spatially restrained uniform styles maps the process of tribalization, providing an index of the shift from a more open social pattern to the increasingly exclusive sphere of Late Prehistory. The restricted production and distribution zones of these ceramic wares illustrate the rigid social boundaries developing throughout the northern Great Lakes during the Late Prehistoric period (Krakker 1999: 233; fig. 3.1).

Perspectives on the Process of Tribalization from the Juntunen Region

Research conducted in the Juntunen region, along northeastern Lake Huron (fig. 3.1), provides an example of the nature of the process of tribalization as established foragers along the coasts specialized their resource activities during Late Prehistory, including incorporating maize horticulture into their activities.

Research shows that an increase in maize cultivation occurred in the lake-effect areas along northern Lake Huron (see chapter 2). Maize cultivation still entailed substantial risk, including both interannual temporal variability and spatial variability. A strong spatial correlation does not exist between good and bad crop years: a bad year in some cultivators' area would not necessarily have been a bad year in

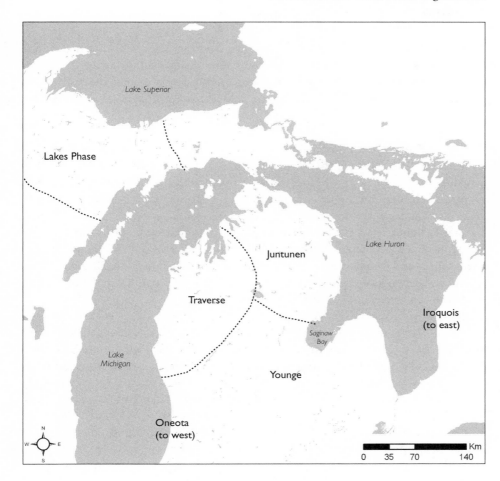

Figure 3.1. Late Prehistoric ceramic stylistic zones (adapted from Milner 1998: 106).

their neighbors' area. This situation made social connections between neighboring communities particularly important. In order to deal with the variability, the Juntunen communities "were tied both to the lake effect zone of the major lakes and to a spatially extensive network of relatives and trade partners" (O'Shea and Milner 2002: 203).

The Juntunen tribal system developed linearly along the coast of Lake Huron and contained a "nested series of progressively larger interaction zones" (O'Shea and Milner 2002: 203). Day-to-day interaction occurred among local residential units, the most spatially proximate of which formed bands. A loose affiliation (which researchers termed a confederacy) of these bands formed the larger Juntunen tribal system, expressing their connection with that homogenous ceramic style (fig. 3.1). The system was composed of "a series of small social units that during normal years shifted from subsistence focus to subsistence focus within the limits of a defined home territory" (O'Shea and Milner 2002: 206). Tribal-level affiliation, while not necessarily active and on people's minds daily, was an essential structural pose of the confederacy (see Gearing 1958). Interaction among bands provided opportunities to level out subsistence shortfalls and ease social tensions from both inside and outside the system.

Associated Material Culture Changes: Lithics

Increased territoriality and tribal identity formation in Late Prehistory had associated material culture changes in Juntunen territory. In addition to the distinctive Juntunen ceramic style increased tribal territorialism also restricted the distribution of primary lithic raw material sources across Juntunen territory (O'Shea and Milner 2002: 220).

Michigan's Lithic Raw Material Profile The profile of lithic raw material sources in Michigan is well established (Luedtke 1976; see also Clark 1982; Fitting 1968; Krakker 1997; O'Shea and Milner 2002). Four main lithic raw material resources were used throughout Michigan prehistory: (1) high-quality localized in-state primary chert sources; (2) distant localized chert sources of very high quality; (3) nonlocalized (nonquarry) glacial till chert of varying quality ubiquitous in the state but typically of lower quality than localized chert sources; and (4) the low-quality metamorphosed rocks quartzite and argillite. Chert, which includes all sedimentary microcrystalline silicates, is "by far the most common type of lithic material used for stone tools in Michigan" (Luedtke 1976: 7).

Michigan is covered in deep glacial deposits, so bedrock is exposed in very few areas. This creates a pattern of localized primary chert sources. Chert exposures in Michigan fall along the coasts of the Great Lakes, where more weathering has occurred (see fig. 3.2). These sources include Bayport chert, which outcrops "in an arc across Saginaw Bay" (Luedtke 1976: 197); Bois Blanc or Northern Gray chert, which outcrops in northeastern Michigan in the Lake Huron area (Luedtke 1976: 212); Norwood chert, which outcrops in northwestern Michigan along Lake Michigan near modern-day Charlevoix (Luedtke 1976: 257); and Lambrix chert, which outcrops in southwestern Michigan along the shore of Lake Michigan (Luedtke 1976: 248). Norwood, Northern Gray, and Bayport cherts are visually distinct, but Lambrix has a less distinguishable visual appearance.

In addition to these lithic raw material sources, a number of readily identifiable chert sources from outside of Michigan are found on archaeological sites within the state. These include Upper Mercer chert from southern Ohio (the most common extraregional chert on Late Woodland sites in Michigan); Flint Ridge chert from southern Ohio; Kettle Point chert from Ontario; Onondaga chert, which outcrops in eastern New York; and Indiana hornstone, which outcrops in southern Indiana (Luedtke 1976: 187–88; fig. 3.2). These high-quality materials from afar are exotic, and typically low in abundance, on archaeological sites in Michigan.

Along with the distinct and localized primary chert sources described above, chert is also available in glacial gravel almost everywhere in the state (Luedtke 1976: 90). With this suitable lithic material available everywhere locally, the distribution of nonlocal primary cherts on sites throughout Michigan carries important social information about groups' level of access to and interest in nonlocal materials and how they were able to procure them, either directly or indirectly (Luedtke 1976).

Patterns of Direct versus Indirect Access to Lithic Raw Materials in Small-Scale Societies
Lithic raw material procurement is shaped by the abundance and quality of materials in a region, but lithic procurement in small-scale societies is often socially

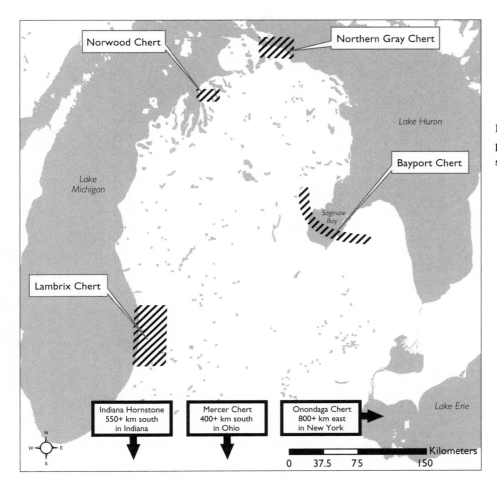

Figure 3.2. Location of primary lithic raw material sources in Lower Michigan.

embedded as well. The specific social and economic setting of a time/place constrains access to materials; groups with quarries in their home territory who live in an exclusive social sphere may regulate access to this source (overtly or passively), whereas a quarry in a more diffuse social sphere may not be regulated. Furthermore, as social, economic, and ideological settings vary, demands for specific materials can develop, cease, or transform. A commonly documented situation in small-scale societies is that distant rock sources are still preferred even when adequate raw materials abound locally (Bradley 2000: 88). Groups travel extensive distances to procure preferred lithic resources; when access to such materials is limited, either physically or socially, societies rely on trade networks to obtain these preferred or exotic lithic raw materials (Andrefsky 1994; Spielmann 2002; Yerkes 2002).[3]

In addition to amounts of material, the form in which lithic raw material reaches a site offers another proxy for access to the material source itself. Raw material can be "transported to a site in the form of unworked nodules, partially reduced cores, or already worked preforms" (Dibble et al. 2005: 546). If raw materials reach sites in early stages of reduction, groups probably had direct access to the sources themselves. If raw materials enter sites in more reduced stages, groups using the site probably had indirect access to the sources, trading for the material in an already worked form with groups living near the source. The amount of cortex from raw materials is a useful initial indicator of core reduction (and thus the form in which materials reached sites). Generally speaking, the reduction of unworked nodules produces more cortical flakes than reduction of already partially worked cores or preforms, although raw material geometry can influence this to some degree (Dibble et al. 2005).

The amount of formal versus informal tool production from raw materials in an assemblage can also suggest the level of access to the material sources themselves. Informal or expedient tool production involves a low expenditure of energy and results in easily made but short-lasting tools. Informal tool production produces large waste flakes, waste cores, and simple situational tools (Binford 1979). Informal tools are commonly made from lower-quality lithic materials in both high and low abundance and from high-quality material when it is abundant (Andrefsky 1994: 30). Formal tool production involves a higher level of energy expenditure and results in longer-lasting tools (Andrefsky 1994: 22). Formal tools tend to be made from only high-quality material in both high and low abundance (Andrefsky 1994: 30). Formal tool production results in carefully prepared cores, bifaces, and retouched tools (Andrefsky 1994: 22). Formal production suggests limited, indirect access to materials, and informal production suggests ready, direct access (because waste was not a concern).

Another aspect of lithic production worth noting is bipolar reduction. This is a form of lithic reduction that is typically a last attempt to produce a sharp flake from a chert source. It is common on smaller raw material nodules. This process produces a lot of shatter (Binford and Quimby 1963), and bipolar cores are the exhausted remnants (Shott 1990). Bipolar reduction indicates that a tool producer tried to maximize a core of material, suggesting (as a rough proxy) that the material was valuable and perhaps in short supply and offering another measure of a group's access to sources and production strategies (Andrefsky 1998: 226).

Lithic Procurement and Production in the Juntunen Tribal System These general observations extend appreciations of the specific case of interest. Barbara E. Luedtke (1976) conducted an extensive study of the major lithic raw material sources found on sites in Michigan and their distribution over the entire Late Woodland period (ca. A.D. 600–1600) and reported that the major factor influencing the distribution of raw materials throughout this period was distance from the source. Luedtke (1976: 408) determined that the decline of percentages of raw materials with distance from the source was exponential and created a series of expectations for the proportion of major chert sources that archaeologists should find in the lithic assemblages.

Luedtke argued that the farther a Late Woodland site was from a primary chert source, the fewer lithic remains from production (debitage) on these materials should be found and that these nonlocal materials should predominantly be found, if at all, as finished products (artifacts) that were procured indirectly through exchange networks (Luedtke 1976: 361). Distance from a primary chert source was *the* limiting factor in a group's procurement of a material.

The distribution of Bayport (one of Michigan's primary coastal cherts) on Late Prehistoric sites in the Juntunen region, however, does not follow Luedtke's predicted pattern of smooth, exponential distance decay. Rather, the fall-off north of the Saginaw area, where Bayport outcrops, is stepped; "these steps broadly correspond to the marked territories of Juntunen bands" (O'Shea and Milner 2002: 220). This pattern reveals that the increased territoriality of the Late Prehistoric period precipitated increased fall-off in the percentage of Bayport chert in Juntunen territory.

The habitual patterns of movement and resource activities of coastal tribal groups conditioned their habitual interaction throughout the region, thereby changing the distribution of raw materials (O'Shea and Milner 2002: 220). The emergence of bounded tribal systems during Late Prehistory altered previously smooth distance-decay patterns of lithic raw material procurement, access, and distribution.

Concurrent Developments in the Interior of the Lower Peninsula

Research has provided a nice picture of the ways in which coastal horticulturalist-fisher communities developed coherent tribal social systems during Late Prehistory, with specialized resource activities, defined territories, and strong group identities signaled by ceramic styles. Taking a quick glance at the distribution zones of Late Prehistoric ceramic wares, we see that they converge in some undefined location in the center of the northern Lower Peninsula (Milner 1998: 106; fig. 3.1). This observation illustrates a common view that a decided lack of significant concurrent cultural developments took place in the interior of the Lower Peninsula, which was designated as a kind of "vacantscape" more than forty years ago by the Biotic/Historic Model. This idea remains salient. Even though various aspects of the model have been challenged (see chapter 2), the view of the interior as a land of intersections (a vacantscape) on the periphery of larger developments without any of its own has gone largely unchallenged.

Looking at figure 3.3, it is clear that the spatial extent of the Great Lakes' ameliorating effect depends on the distance between the coast and the rise of the High Plains, a prominent inland plateau formed by glacial outwash and end moraines (Albert 1995). The High Plains ecosystem forms a distinct interior in the northern Lower Peninsula (Albert 1995; Albert et al. 1986; Kashian et al. 2003; Pearsall et al. [eds.] 1995; Walker et al. 2003). The northern latitude and high elevations of the High Plains create the most severe climate in Lower Michigan. Growing seasons range from only 70 to 120 days. Extreme minimum temperatures have been recorded as low as minus 50 degrees F. The climactic profile of this region indicates that prehistoric agriculture would have been unfeasible. This, combined with the obvious lack of Great Lakes spawning fish, sets up a clear resource contrast with the coasts.[4] These aspects of the zone's environmental setting support the archaeological view of the interior as an empty zone, a place with "sparse occupation" (Lovis 1973: 4).

The general perception is that this interior area was a vacant winter hunting ground for Late Prehistoric coastal communities busy growing corn, intensifying fishing, and becoming "tribal." This ignores the possibility that foraging communities occupied the interior of the Lower Peninsula and that they were impacted by coastal developments and engaged in contemporary social developments. This perception both causes and is furthered by infrequent archaeological work in the interior.

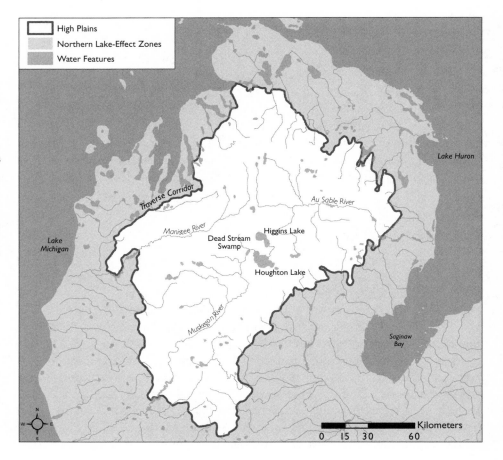

Figure 3.3. The High Plains ecosystem and its major waterscapes. Note the fall-off of the Great Lakes coastal lake-effect with the rise of the High Plains.

As work has slowly increased in the interior, however, we are starting to see (1) late sites that are not just small winter hunting camps and (2) people residing in the interior who were expressing weaker material and social ties to the Great Lakes coasts than would be expected if they were coastal mobile hunting parties passing through. Lithic patterns show that communities residing in the interior during Late Prehistory lacked direct access to the coasts; likewise, Late Prehistoric vessels found in these interior sites do not always fit with the formal defined wares from the coasts or southern Michigan (Beld, personal communication, 2004; Howey 2006). Preliminary observations suggest that certain decorative characteristics are more common on late vessels from the interior than on coastal wares. Distinctive features include (1) a channel running along the entire lip; (2) a high frequency of protruding rolled lips; (3) a high frequency of decoration (both lip and exterior) applied with fingers (Beld, personal communication, 2004); and (4) cord-marked exteriors, which are typical of early Late Woodland ceramic vessels throughout Michigan (Brashler 1981), persisting on vessels in the interior into the Late Prehistoric period (note, in contrast, that the well-defined coastal wares of this later period have smoothed exteriors).

Many things about Late Prehistoric interior occupation have not been fully explained. Is the lack of Great Lakes fisheries and potential for maize agriculture sufficient cause to write off the possibility of Late Prehistoric occupation and cultural investment in the interior? A closer look shows that the High Plains would have offered communities more resource diversity and potential than a coarse assessment of its climate suggests.

Waterscapes and Resource Potential in the Interior

The major forest type of the High Plains before European land clearing was northern hardwoods, which were dominated by beech and sugar maple. They also included red oak, hemlock, and white pine, although these species were not common along the northwestern portion of the end moraines (Barnes and Wagner 2004; Comer et al. 1995; Daniel and Sullivan 1981). Sandy ridges in the northern section of the plains and outwash in the southern portion supported oak-pine forests of red and white pine and oak, red maple, and aspen; forests of white and red pine were also common in broad undissected regions of outwash (Albert 1995). The interior floral profile contains the same edible resources as the northern Great Lakes' lake-effect zone forests, including oak trees and berry plants. Although interior forests perhaps included a lower abundance of nut-bearing trees, oak trees grew in stands of not inconsequential size (Comer et al. 1995). The interior also offered many of the same fauna as the coastal zones, including a wide array of mammal and bird resources and migratory waterfowl.

More notable are the distinctive waterscapes found in the High Plains, features that diversify and enhance the wild-resource profile on which American Indian communities could have capitalized. As figure 3.3 shows, the headwaters of three major rivers (the Manistee, Au Sable, and Muskegon) are in the Grayling Outwash Plain, in the center of the High Plains (Albert 1995; Kashian et al. 2003; Walker et al. 2003). The convergence of the headwaters of three of Michigan's major rivers (the Muskegon, Michigan's fifth largest river, which flows into Lake Michigan; the Manistee, the eighth largest river, which also flows into Lake Michigan; and the Au Sable, which flows into Lake Huron) allows both major Great Lakes of the Lower Peninsula to be accessible by water travel. This situation is unique in the Great Lakes.

Michigan's largest inland lakes, Houghton and Higgins, are also located in the Grayling Outwash Plain and are connected by the Cut River (fig. 3.3). Houghton Lake, the larger, more southern, and shallower of the two, has an area of 20,075.1 acres (8,124 hectares), a volume of 165,072 acre-feet (53,288 million gallons [Mgal]), and a mean depth of 8.4 feet (2.6 m); its deepest point is 21 feet (6.4 m) (Breck 2004). Of Michigan's 11,037 inland lakes, Houghton Lake is the largest, but its shallow waters make it warm. Higgins Lake, the smaller, more northern, and deeper of the two, has an area of 10,185.6 acres (4,122 hectares), a volume of 51,9751 acre-feet (169,360 Mgal), and a mean depth of 52.2 feet (15.9 m); its deepest point is 135 feet (41.1 m) (Breck 2004), which makes its waters cool and crisp.

The Muskegon River's source is the small streams from Houghton and Higgins (fig. 3.3). Wetlands are located at the margins of Houghton Lake and Higgins Lake and in the headwaters of the Muskegon River. Although the Muskegon River has a humble start in small feeder streams, it emerges as a major river some 219 miles (352.4 km) long and drains 2,723 square miles (705,253.8 hectares) of land before flowing into Lake Michigan. As the Muskegon twists and turns and emerges as a real river from feeder streams, it runs through the Dead Stream Swamp, one of the largest northern white-cedar swamps in the United States and a national natural landmark (MDNR 2009).

Although this interior zone does not contain the dense autumn- and spring-spawning anadromous fish runs found along the Great Lakes's northern coasts (Cleland 1982), these inland lakes and the rivers host an array of native, economically productive fish, including walleye, yellow bullhead catfish, brown bullhead catfish, channel catfish, northern pike, rock bass, bluegill, smallmouth bass, largemouth bass, black crappie, yellow perch, northern logperch, longnose gar, bowfin, white sucker, and shorthead redhorse sucker (Bailey et al. 2004). These fish would have been available all year, so ice fishing would have been a productive winter activity. Both Houghton and Higgins are consistently rated as two of Michigan's best lakes for ice fishing, an impressive distinction given the state's large number of inland lakes (Gnatkowski 2010). Fish would have been a particularly dense resource during the spring-spawning runs, as they swim up riverine tributaries of lakes (Cleland 1982; Jones et al. 2003). River headwaters also offer freshwater shellfish, such as mussels.

The large Dead Stream Swamp, which supports a high diversity and density of flora and wildlife, adds another layer to the resource profile. The swamp hosts a variety of undergrowth, including edible blueberry, raspberry, and huckleberry plants. Northern cedar swamps have been documented as supporting a major portion of the region's deer (Habeck 1960: 327) as well as other terrestrial mammals, such as black bear and porcupine. In fact, Michigan's first state-organized bear hunt took place in the Dead Stream Swamp in 1946. Water-based mammals, such as muskrat and beaver, abound in swamps, which are the ideal habitat for a variety of reptiles, particularly snapping, wood, Blanding's, and painted turtles (Harding and Holman 1997). This swamp also attracts a variety of migratory waterfowl, including ducks and geese, providing seasonally abundant resources in the fall and spring (Cleland 1982; Tacha et al. 1991).

Domestic Life in the Interior

Recent findings from domestic sites along the prominent waterscapes of the High Plains provide a glimpse into local community dynamics in the interior. They show that groups capitalized on the interior's resource offerings for millennia and that this use increased (or the orientation of this use shifted) during Late Prehistory in response to broader socioeconomic transformations along the coasts. Two sites are discussed below: (1) the Meade's Bridge site (20RO5) along the Muskegon River and Dead Stream Swamp and (2) the Chief White Bird site (20RO50) on the southern "High Banks" region of Houghton Lake.

The Meade's Bridge Site: Setting and Evaluation The Meade's Bridge site (20RO5) is located in Lake Township, Roscommon County, Michigan (23N04W) (fig. 3.4). The site is positioned on high ground between two meanders potentially shaped to form oxbow lakes in the Muskegon River. The meanders are just under three kilometers from the beginning of the Muskegon at Houghton Lake. As the Muskegon River flows westward from the site, the horizon opens immediately onto the Dead Stream Swamp.

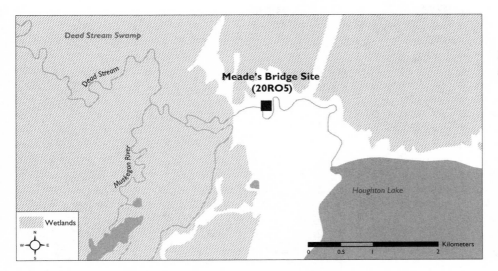

Figure 3.4. Meade's Bridge site location.

This site's location on the bank of the Muskegon River and the edge of the large Dead Stream Swamp renders it rich in economically productive wild resources. Inhabitants would have had access to large mammals such as bears and deer wintering in the swamp as well as water-focused mammals such as muskrats and beavers. Migratory waterfowl, notably the great blue heron, which breeds in the summer in swamps such as the Dead Stream Swamp, would also have been an available resource. Furthermore, the Dead Stream Swamp is an ideal habitat for a variety of reptiles, particularly turtles, and the Muskegon River would have added additional important aquatic resources, such as fish and freshwater shellfish, especially mussels.

Today the Michigan Department of Natural Resources (DNR) owns the land, which is used for fishing and as a boat launch on the Muskegon River. Its current ground cover is a combination of open field and thick forest. No formal work had ever been conducted at the site prior to this research program. Archaeological investigation of the site entailed topographic mapping with a total-station shovel test survey to determine the spatial layout of the site and test excavations in spatially discrete occupation areas discerned during the shovel test survey.

The shovel tests and subsequent excavations identified two spatially discrete zones of distinct temporal occupation: one along an old marsh set back from the river's edge and another along the bank of the Muskegon River (fig. 3.5). Unfortunately, the subsurface work also revealed that the site stratigraphy had been badly disturbed by modern activities, particularly plowing and camping. No intact cultural features were found. Despite these limitations, some conclusions about the nature of socioeconomic activity at this interior domestic site can be drawn from the material assemblages recovered in the discrete occupation zones.

Meade's Bridge Marsh Zone: A Late Archaic Occupation One of the site's occupation zones was located next to an old marshy area several meters from the Muskegon River bank. The shovel test survey revealed a topographic depression reflecting the now mostly dry marshy area with a dense occupation band alongside (see fig. 3.5).

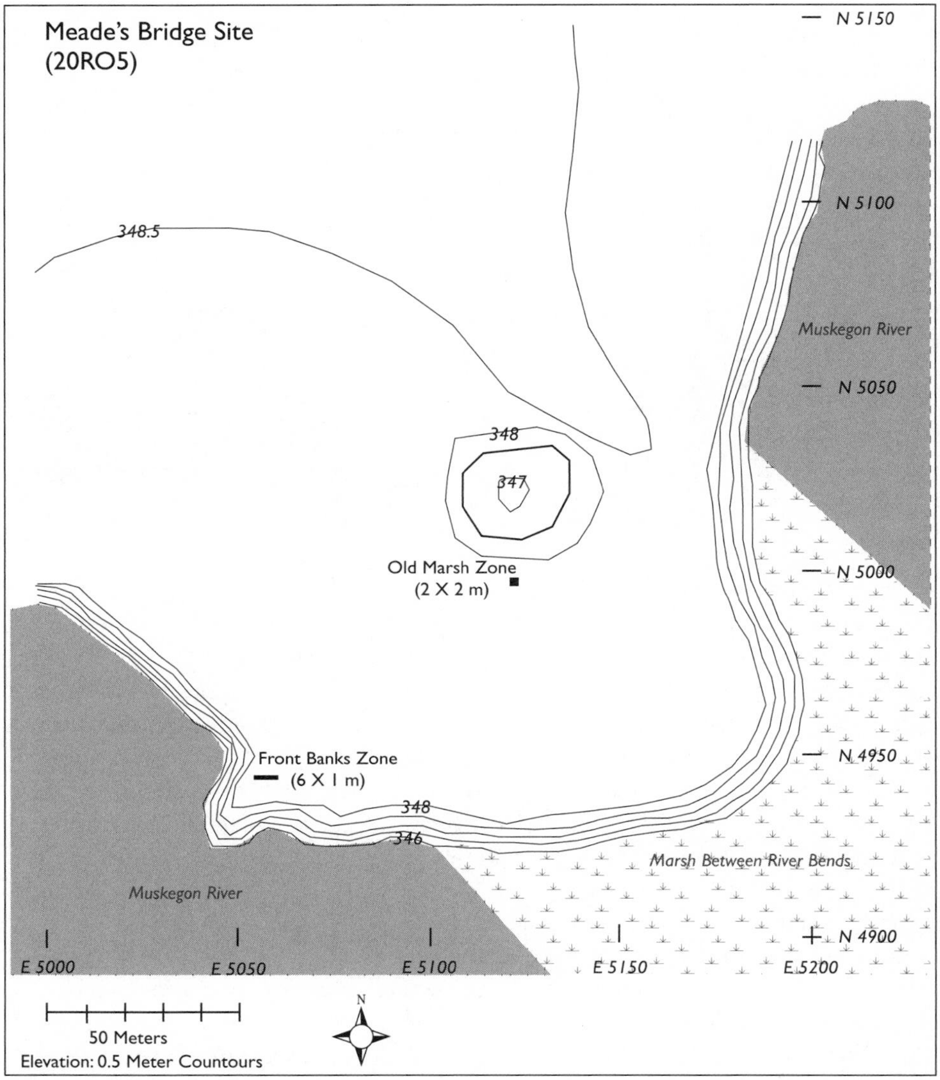

Figure 3.5. Topographic map of Meade's Bridge site (20RO5) with excavation units in two occupation zones identified in shovel testing.

Excavations were limited to four units, forming a 2 by 2 meter square, because of the extensive modern damage and absence of ceramic remains.

Lithic density in this excavation unit was twice as high as in the excavations conducted in this site's other occupation zone, a 6 by 1 meter trench along the front banks of the Muskegon River discussed below (0.33 grams/liter soil vs. 0.16 grams/liter soil). The lithic assemblage recovered in this marsh zone evidences a Late Archaic occupation. Bayport chert from the Saginaw Bay region constituted over 50% of the lithic raw material (table 3.1). Local glacial cherts formed the assemblage's second most prevalent raw material, at 20%. Norwood chert from the Traverse Corridor in northwestern Michigan was the third most frequent lithic material source, composing almost 16% of the assemblage. Even more exotic lithic raw materials were also present, including dark-banded chert from the Upper Peninsula, Flint Ridge chert from over 650 kilometers south in Ohio, and Onondaga chert, which outcrops 500

TABLE 3.1. PERCENTAGES OF RAW MATERIALS IN THE
MARSH OCCUPATION ZONE LITHIC ASSEMBLAGE

Lithic raw material	Count	Percentage of assemblage
Bayport	402	53.0
Northern Gray	64	8.4
Norwood	120	15.8
Glacial	152	20.0
Quartzite	7	0.9
Dark-Banded Upper Peninsula	2	0.2
Flint Ridge	1	0.1
Onondaga	12	1.6
TOTAL	**760**	**100.0**

kilometers west in Ontario. The majority of lithic items consisted of flakes and shatter. Twenty-five tools, composing 3.3% of the assemblage, were recovered. These include one very small side-notched projectile point made on Bayport chert and four parts of finely worked drills, a tool type common in Late Archaic tool assemblages (Robertson et al. 1999). Seven cores, including one of Flint Ridge and one of dark-banded chert from the Upper Peninsula, were recovered as well as one core rejuvenation flake from a Bayport nodule.

The lack of ceramics and the high density of lithic material, including patterned tools and exotic material, support this area's designation as a Late Archaic occupation. The presence of nonbipolar cores of raw materials from regional locations in Michigan (Bayport from the Saginaw Bay, Northern Gray from northern Lake Huron, and Norwood from northwestern Lake Michigan) suggests that the groups using this site ranged throughout wide territories, a pattern expected for dispersed Archaic groups. The large core rejuvenation flake with the cortex from a Bayport nodule supports the interpretation that the cores were derived from unworked nodules that the groups brought with them to the site. This suggests that they moved within the area of these outcrops, rather than receiving these materials through trade. These Late Archaic groups had the embedded lithic procurement strategy predicted for this period, incorporating direct visits to Michigan's primary chert sources into their seasonal rounds. The well-curated core of highly exotic material (Flint Ridge) and the presence of Onondaga chert suggest that these groups were also involved in even wider regional interaction spheres. This behavior was characteristic of Late Archaic times (see chapter 2; Robertson et al. 1999: 113).

The lack of floral and faunal remains, the low density of fire-cracked rock (used for cooking and heat), and the lack of cultural features suggest that this occupation zone reflects a temporary use of the site. Summer Late Archaic sites tend to contain "fishing, gathering, and wood working tools such as concave scrapers, drills, and unifacial tools" as opposed to hunting tools such as bifaces, which typify winter hunting sites (Houghten 1990: 5). Drills and unifaces are well represented in this tool assemblage. These six tools form 24% of the tool assemblage, greatly outrepresenting the single projectile point. While evidence and excavations were limited, the

Marsh Zone occupation at the Meade's Bridge site seems to reflect a locale visited by Late Archaic groups during their summer foraging rounds.

Meade's Bridge Front Bank Zone: Late Woodland and Historic Occupation The other occupation zone located through the shovel test survey at the Meade's Bridge site is on the high ground along the Muskegon River, on the western side of the second U-loop (fig. 3.4). The shovel test survey showed dense cultural materials that followed this entire portion of the riverbank. Materials fell off rapidly from this zone of occupation, both east as the river curves away and the marsh emerges and north as the distance from the river increases.

A 6 by 1 meter trench was excavated along this front bank occupation (in 1 by 1 m units). These units showed clear evidence of plowing, which resulted in a mixed cultural material assemblage and no in situ remains. Historic and prehistoric materials were recovered together in the plow zone. Despite these limitations, this area produced a late Late Woodland/Late Prehistoric radiocarbon date and a material assemblage clearly indicative of a historic (ca. A.D. 1610–1800) utilization, most likely related to fur trapping.

The trench contained an abundance of well-preserved faunal remains and shell. In total, almost 23 kilograms of bone and 8 kilograms of freshwater mussel shells were recovered from the plow zone in these six units. The faunal assemblage is dominated by muskrat and beaver remains but also includes migratory waterfowl, including duck and great blue heron; terrestrial mammals, including porcupine, deer, and bear; and a variety of fish. Although the assemblage was not analyzed beyond the level of simple identification, it indicates that groups using the site capitalized on the freshwater mussels found nearby as well as the other food resources abounding in the Muskegon River and the Dead Stream Swamp.

The faunal assemblage is dominated by muskrat and beaver remains, two mammals used for fur, which points toward a historic fur trapping use for this portion of the site. Three items recovered with these faunal remains support this: two gun flints and one gun spawl. One flint is French and the other is British, and the spawl is made from Michigan native Bayport chert. The Bayport gun spawl is significant, strongly suggesting that this was not only a historic fur-trapping site but an American Indian fur-trapping site. At the very least, the historic fur trapper occupants had an Indian member in their group. European fur trappers would not have regarded Michigan cherts as appropriate for making gun flints; this suggests that it was an American Indian product.

While a large part of the faunal assemblage was produced during the historic fur-trapping use of the site, some remains also were produced during Late Woodland activities. Radiocarbon dating on a freshwater mussel shell produced a date of 810 ± 40 B.P., calibrated to A.D. 1170–1280. This indicates that late Late Woodland/Late Prehistoric use of the site (ca. A.D. 1200–1600) involved the exploitation of its rich aquatic resources. Other late Late Woodland materials were limited: no diagnostic lithics and only one very small rim (1.06 g) were recovered. The lack of diagnostics hinders insights into the use of the area during this period.

Obviously, inferences that can be made about seasonality are limited, particularly because the late Late Woodland and historic faunal remains cannot be securely disentangled. The historic fur-trapping use of the site was likely a winter occupation, and the deer and bear remains support this inference. The presence of great blue heron remains suggests that the site was occupied at a different season: this migratory bird is only available in Michigan between March and October and is most vulnerable to capture while breeding in the summer. The extant faunal data indicate that the use of this inland resource zone in one or both of these later periods was not exclusively in the winter.[5]

The Chief White Bird Site: Setting and Evaluation Recent findings from the Chief White Bird site (20RO50) provide more insight into how communities capitalized on the resource offerings of the interior region during Late Prehistory. The site is located in a prime position on Houghton Lake, on the highest elevation area along the lakeshore known colloquially as the "High Banks" (fig. 3.6). This area, being the most secure dry land along the lake, is prime real-estate today. Heavy development means that the excavations at this site probably provide the only chance for a site along the High Banks to be documented. This site—on a small sliver of land protected by its owner, Mrs. Hiroko Cook (wife of the now deceased Chief White Bird)—is undoubtedly representative of the larger pattern of the Late Prehistoric period (ca. A.D. 1200–1600) throughout this interior resource area.

The site's location is well suited for the extraction of a variety of economic resources. Inhabitants would have had access to generalized water-based resources such as open-water fish and marshy aquatic vegetation. The combination of deciduous and coniferous forests on the higher ground would have offered access to a variety of terrestrial mammals and birds. Moreover, the site is also located close to what would have been one of the largest acorn-producing areas around all of Houghton Lake before modern land clearing (Comer et al. 1995).

Research at the Chief White Bird site entailed topographic mapping, test excavations across the High Bank, and expanded excavations around productive tests. Twenty-two square meters were excavated on Cook's property, with contiguous

Figure 3.6. Location of the Chief White Bird site on a Digital Elevation Model.

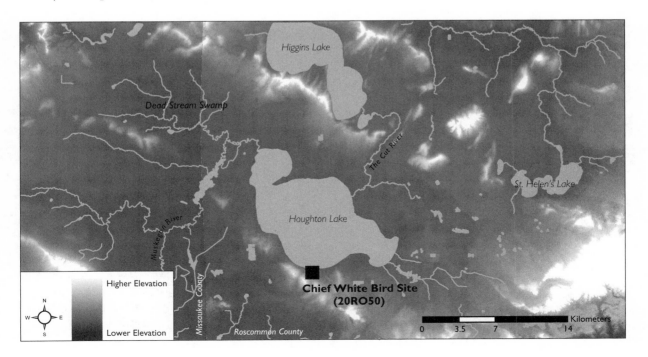

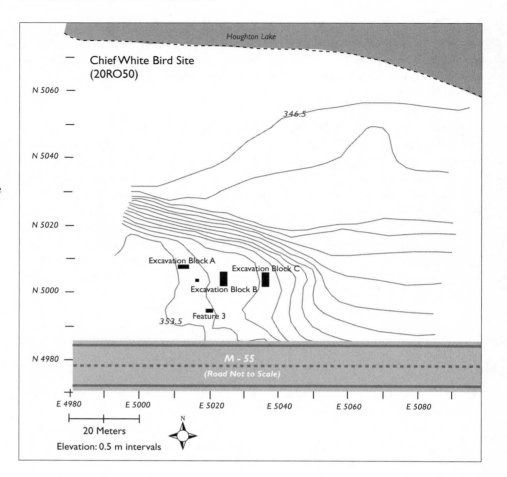

Figure 3.7. Distribution of test excavations conducted at the Chief White Bird Site (20RO50).

excavations in three areas (fig. 3.7). All areas produced cultural materials. The site stratigraphy, diagnostic lithics and ceramic remains recovered at the site, and three radiometric dates (table 3.2) demonstrate conclusively that 20RO50 is a single-component Late Prehistoric period site dating circa A.D. 1300–1660. No evidence exists to suggest that the Chief White Bird site was occupied prior to the Late Prehistoric period or that it was occupied beyond this time.

The combination of evidence offering a picture of life at this site indicates that at around A.D. 1300 regional communities incorporated the Chief White Bird site, with its variety of resources, into their seasonal rounds. Faunal remains show that groups took advantage of the resources in the site's vicinity: the deer and small mammals in the forest, migratory waterfowl stopping over on the lake (geese remains), the aquatic mammals and reptiles in the marshy land along Houghton Lake's shore, and of course the abundant fish in the lake itself. The ubiquity of acorns at the site indicates that groups also took advantage of the oaks in the nearby pine-oak forest. These resource remains are particularly suggestive of a fall occupation (geese and acorns), showing that this site was not occupied exclusively in the winter by a small hunting party (this is likely reflective of the larger occupation pattern, as this site is one of the only slices of undeveloped property along the entire southern shore of Houghton Lake).

TABLE 3.2. RADIOMETRIC DATES FROM THE CHIEF WHITE BIRD SITE (20RO50)

Dated item	Conventional radio-carbon date	Calibrated date
Charred Acorn, Level 1, Feature 3	310 ± 40 B.P.	A.D. 1470–1660
Bulk Charcoal, Level 4, Feature 3	310 ± 40 B.P.	A.D. 1470–1660
Charred Residue, Vessel 14, Feature 6	580 ± 40 B.P.	A.D. 1300–1420

While six feature numbers were assigned during field operations at the site, only features 3 and 6 proved to be cultural constructions: a hearth and a small storage pit, respectively. No evidence of a substantial structure of any kind (such as post holes) was recovered. This was a seasonal economic extraction site, a place where daily life played out.

The Chief White Bird Ceramic Assemblage A vessel count based on diagnostics and provenience identified a minimum of 13 Late Prehistoric period vessels (all jars) in the ceramic assemblage. Of these, only 4 were from clearly defined Late Prehistoric coastal ceramic wares: 3 Traverse wares and 1 from the Juntunen stylistic tradition (see fig. 3.1 for the locations of these coastal styles). The other 9 Late Prehistoric jars, making up almost 70% of the assemblage, did not have characteristics that directly fit within well-known Late Prehistoric coastal ceramic styles.

Residue from one interesting vessel that has both a collar (a typical late ceramic feature) and a rough cord-marked exterior (a typical earlier ceramic feature) produced an AMS (accelerator mass spectrometry) date of 580 ± 40 B.P., calibrated to A.D. 1300–1420 (table 3.2; fig. 3.8). This date adds an important layer to the discussion of the presence of distinctive trends in ceramics found in the interior of the Lower Peninsula during Late Prehistory. One noted trend was that people continue to apply rough cord-marked exteriors, typical on early Late Woodland vessels, on vessels in the interior during Late Prehistory (while people along the coasts largely switched to smoothed exteriors). This date confirms that this happened.

Enough data are not currently available to support the definition of a formal ceramic style produced by a late interior tribal system. But the assemblage from this exclusively Late Prehistoric site, where the majority of vessels fail to fit nicely into coastal styles, adds to the growing sense of distinct ceramic trends in the interior during Late Prehistory. This must be recognized and appreciated; Late Prehistoric interior ceramic producers clearly were not exclusively tied to the homogenized canon of contemporary coastal ceramic styles, so here I refer to late ceramic vessels showing distinctive interior stylistic tendencies as "White Bird ware" (in quotation marks because the data for a formal definition of this ware are lacking). As new work produces larger assemblages and as researchers look back at extant late collections where these interior traits have gone un(der)appreciated, I expect that evidence will emerge that will allow this ware to become formally (typologically) defined.

Figure 3.8. Chief White Bird site vessel for which an AMS date of A.D. 1300–1420 was produced from residue (see table 3.2). Note that this vessel has a collar, a typical Late Prehistoric ceramic feature, as well as a heavily cord-marked exterior. Cord-marked exteriors are typical of early Late Woodland vessels, but emerging trends suggest that they persisted in the inland on later ceramics. This date adds support to the observation of unique inland stylistic choices during Late Prehistory.

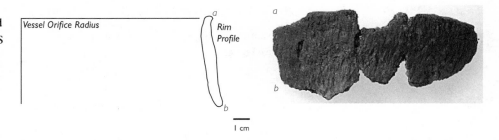

Chief White Bird Lithic Assemblage The lithic assemblage from the Chief White Bird site includes 417 lithics, primarily composed of debitage, with only 7 patterned tools, including 5 bifaces and 2 bipolar cores. Of the small triangular points, 2 were made on Norwood chert, 2 more on local glacial till, and the fifth (an unfinished biface) was on Bayport chert. One bipolar core was local glacial till and the other quartzite. The dominant raw material type in the lithic assemblage recovered at the Chief White Bird site is Bayport chert (64.7%). Local glacial chert is the second most common at 25%, and Norwood chert is third at 10.1%; one piece of quartzite is present (table 3.3).

Norwood chert, which outcrops in coastal northwestern Michigan (fig. 3.2), occurs in slightly lower quantities than predicted by a distance-decay model (Luedtke 1976: 352). Two formal tools made of Norwood chert were found. As discussed earlier, formal tool production tends to occur on high-quality material (Andrefsky 1994: 30). No Norwood cores or Norwood cortex were recovered at this site, which indicates that this material was not brought there in raw primary form and tool production did not occur on site. The low abundance of the material, the lack of cores or cortex, and the fact that tools arrived in processed form all indicate that the communities had only limited, indirect access to this lithic material outcropping in the northwestern coastal Lake Michigan area. While the distance decay model predicts the very low presence of Northern Gray, which outcrops along northern Lake Huron, the complete absence of this chert indicates that the groups using this site had no access to it.

The dominance of one coastal primary chert source, Bayport chert from the Saginaw Bay region, is interesting (see fig. 3.2 for its location). Only 29 pieces of Bayport chert cortex were found (10.7% of the Bayport from the site), and no cores were recovered. This low abundance of cortex combined with a lack of cores suggests that Bayport chert entered the site in an already reduced stage.

Work in the Juntunen tribal region suggested that the habitual patterns of movement and resource activities of tribal coastal groups with chert outcrops in their territories restricted the distribution of raw materials, altering smooth distance-decay patterns of procurement, access, and distribution (O'Shea and Milner 2002). At the Chief White Bird site, however, more (not less) Bayport is present than a smooth-decay pattern predicts (Luedtke 1976: 340). Even though the groups using this site during Late Prehistory had only indirect access to this chert, they favored it. Substantial indirect access to Bayport suggests that something more active than simply changes in habitual movements was occurring to produce this pattern. Groups were probably getting Bayport in an already worked stage through active exchange

TABLE 3.3. LITHIC RAW MATERIAL PROPORTIONS FROM THE CHIEF WHITE BIRD SITE (20RO50)

Lithic raw material	Count	Percentage of assemblage
Bayport	270	64.7
Norwood	42	10.1
Glacial	104	25.0
Quartzite	1	0.2
TOTAL	**417**	**100.0**

Note: See figure 3.2 for a map locating the Bayport and Norwood primary chert sources.

with those living in the vicinity of the source. In contrast, the trends that we saw for the primary chert sources on the northern coasts of Lake Michigan and Huron (Norwood and Northern Gray) suggest that an opposite process was operating: communities using this inland site faced boundaries actively maintained by coastal tribal communities that they could not (or chose not to?) develop bridges across.

What is clear from these lithic patterns is that the people using this site during Late Prehistory had developed what seems to be a socially based means of acquiring Bayport chert but lacked direct access to coastal areas where primary cherts outcrop. The ceramic assemblage corresponds with these lithic trends, showing people in the interior expressing weaker material ties to the coast than would be expected if the people making the pots were actually mobile hunting parties who lived primarily on the coasts moving through the area.

Evidencing Circumscription to the Interior: A Comparison of the Chief White Bird Late Prehistoric and Meade's Bridge Late Archaic Lithic Assemblages

A comparison of the lithic assemblages from the Late Archaic component of the Meade's Bridge site (20RO5) and the Late Prehistoric Chief White Bird site (20RO50) allows an assessment of how interior materials look in an open social setting (which typified the Late Archaic) and subsequent evaluation of developments in the interior after about A.D. 1100/1200 when the regional setting became more closed. The results show a reduction in direct access to coastal sources with the emergence of tribal systems along the Great Lakes coasts during Late Prehistory, indicating an increasing circumscription of groups to the interior. Furthermore, this comparison indicates that inland communities' raw material procurement strategies in Late Prehistory cannot be understood as the result of passive effects such as distance decay or passive marking of tribal coastal territories (Luedtke 1976; O'Shea and Milner 2002). Rather, the lithic trends point toward active interaction between separate coastal and inland (tribal) entities during Late Prehistory.

Raw Material Transport The lithic assemblage from the Chief White Bird site has significantly more local glacial material than the Late Archaic component of the Meade's Bridge site (table 3.4). The Chief White Bird assemblage has no true exotic cherts. In contrast, the assemblage from the Late Archaic component of Meade's

Bridge has Onondaga from 500 kilometers west and Flint Ridge from 650 kilometers south in Ohio (table 3.1).

Bayport outcrops 70–100 kilometers from both of these interior sites and is the dominant chert at both (fig. 3.2). Forming 64.7% of the assemblage recovered at the Chief White Bird site, Bayport, admittedly unexpectedly, composes significantly more of this late site assemblage than of the Late Archaic assemblage recovered at Meade's Bridge (table 3.4). Norwood chert, which outcrops over 130 kilometers northwest of these sites in the Traverse Corridor along northern Lake Michigan, occurs in a significantly higher proportion at the Late Archaic Meade's Bridge site than at the Chief White Bird site. Northern Gray, which outcrops over 140 kilometers northeast of these sites in the Lake Huron area, composes 8.4% of the Late Archaic assemblage from Meade's Bridge. This chert is completely absent at the Chief White Bird site, a statistically and, I believe, socially significant difference.

The disparities in raw material proportions indicate major differences in raw material transport and use between Late Archaic and Late Prehistoric routine domestic interior sites. These differences reflect the contrasting social settings of the two periods: an earlier open, fluid setting and a later closed, exclusive one. Groups using the interior in the Late Archaic exploited a diversity of coastal primary cherts as well as exotic materials, relying significantly less on glacial materials because they had ready access to the array of higher-quality coastal cherts. In contrast, the inland communities using the Chief White Bird site (20RO50) in the Late Prehistoric period used more local glacial material because they had extremely limited access to coastal cherts and an absence of highly exotic materials. Most of these raw material patterns thus fit the expectations for these two periods. The Late Prehistoric Chief White Bird site has an abundance of one primary coastal chert source, Bayport, from the Saginaw Bay area. This diverges from the expected pattern.

An evaluation of how raw materials arrived at these two interior sites adds detail to the temporal shifts in the interior groups' access to primary coastal chert and helps clarify the unusual pattern seen in Bayport at the Late Prehistoric Chief White Bird site.

To reiterate, raw material can be "transported to a site in the form of unworked nodules, partially reduced cores, or already worked preforms" (Dibble et al. 2005: 546). In this case, the form in which coastal cherts reached these inland sites offers another proxy for changes in access to these raw material sources over time. If coastal cherts reached the sites in early stages of reduction, it is likely that groups had direct access to the sources themselves, traveling to outcroppings and bringing back complete unworked nodules. If coastal cherts entered these sites in more reduced stages, however, it is more likely that groups had indirect access to the sources, trading for the material in an already worked form with the coastal groups living near the source.

The amount of cortex from raw materials present in an assemblage is a useful initial indicator of core reduction (Dibble et al. 2005). Generally speaking, the reduction of unworked nodules produces more cortical flakes than reduction of already partially worked cores or preforms, although raw material geometry can influence this to some degree (Dibble et al. 2005; this is not a problem here because the material is held constant).

TABLE 3.4. COMPARISON OF RAW LITHIC MATERIALS BETWEEN
CHIEF WHITE BIRD (LATE PREHISTORIC) AND MEADE'S
BRIDGE (LATE ARCHAIC) COMPONENT ASSEMBLAGES

	Local glacial material (%)	Other material (%)
Chief White Bird (20RO50)	104 (24.9)	313 (75.1)
Meade's Bridge (20RO5)	152 (20)	608 (80)
	Fisher's Exact Test p-value < .05	
	Bayport chert	**Other material**
Chief White Bird (20RO50)	270 (64.7)	147 (35.3)
Meade's Bridge (20RO5)	402 (52.9)	358 (47.1)
	Fisher's Exact Test p-value < .0001	
	Norwood chert	**Other material**
Chief White Bird (20RO50)	42 (10.1)	375 (89.9)
Meade's Bridge (20RO5)	120 (15.8)	640 (84.2)
	Fisher's Exact Test p-value < .006	
	Northern Gray	**Other material**
Chief White Bird (20RO50)	0 (0)	417 (100)
Meade's Bridge (20RO5)	64 (8.4)	696 (91.6)
	Fisher's Exact Test p-value < .006	

Three raw material types co-occur at both the Late Archaic component of Meade's Bridge and the Chief White Bird site: Bayport, Norwood, and local glacial material. But the amount of cortex by raw material type differs significantly at these two sites. The Late Archaic site at Meade's Bridge has significantly more Norwood and Bayport cortex and significantly less glacial cortex than in the Late Prehistoric Chief White Bird site assemblage (table 3.5). This emphasizes the increasing direct use of local materials in Late Prehistory seen in the raw material comparison above.

The patterns of cortex from Norwood chert highlight the difference in terms of access to coastal cherts already evident in the raw material proportions from the sites discussed above (table 3.4). The abundance of Norwood chert combined with the presence of three Norwood cores indicates that the groups using Meade's Bridge during the Late Archaic brought Norwood chert to the site in some form that still had significant amounts of cortex and reduced cores on site, suggesting again that they had access to the chert source itself. This was not the case at the Chief White Bird Late Prehistoric site, which had only 1 Norwood cortex flake out of all 417 lithics recovered and no cores (indeed only 42 Norwood lithics in all).

Bayport chert in general occurs in a significantly higher percentage at the Chief White Bird site than at the Late Archaic Meade's Bridge occupation (table 3.4). This does not seem to fit with the modeled patterns of lithic material access for the Late Prehistoric period, when the strong tribal systems along the coasts should have limited inland groups' access to Bayport and other coastal sources.

**TABLE 3.5. COMPARISON OF CORTEX BY RAW MATERIAL BETWEEN
CHIEF WHITE BIRD (LATE PREHISTORIC) AND MEADE'S
BRIDGE (LATE ARCHAIC) COMPONENT ASSEMBLAGES**

	Glacial cortex	Glacial not cortex
Chief White Bird (20RO50)	25 (24.0%)	79 (76.0%)
Meade's Bridge (20RO5)	8 (5.3%)	144 (94.7%)
	Fisher's Exact Test p-value < .001	

	Bayport cortex	Bayport not cortex
Chief White Bird (20RO50)	29 (10.7%)	241 (89.3%)
Meade's Bridge (20RO5)	68 (16.9%)	334 (83.1%)
	Fisher's Exact Test p-value < .05	

	Norwood cortex	Norwood not cortex
Chief White Bird (20RO50)	1 (2.4%)	41 (97.6%)
Meade's Bridge (20RO5)	16 (13.3%)	104 (86.7%)
	Fisher's Exact Test p-value < .05	

The cortex comparison helps clarify this situation. Significantly more Bayport cortex is found at the Late Archaic Meade's Bridge site than at the Late Prehistoric Chief White Bird site (table 3.5), which indicates several things. First, the abundance of Bayport cortex combined with the presence of a nonbipolar Bayport core and a large core rejuvenation flake with the cortex from a Bayport nodule suggests that Late Archaic groups using the Meade's Bridge site moved within the area of Bayport's outcrops, like Norwood chert, and brought unworked nodules with them on their seasonal rounds.

The scarcity of Bayport cortex combined with a lack of Bayport cores indicates that although Late Prehistoric groups at the Chief White Bird site had access to Bayport chert in much higher quantities than expected, they received it in some already worked form. This illustrates that the access to Bayport chert by inland communities in the Late Prehistoric period was indeed significantly different than during the Late Archaic. Late Prehistoric communities were able to acquire Bayport chert but did not have direct access to the source itself, unlike the situation in the open social setting of the Late Archaic.

This coarse comparison of cortex by raw material, like the sheer abundance of raw material, suggests that Late Prehistoric tribal communities in the interior had a restricted territory that did not include direct access to coastal chert sources. This highlights a circumscription of the interior territory during the Late Prehistoric period that was not present in the Late Archaic. Also, these trends may indicate that a preferred axis of exchange to the southeast was actively established as a response to the circumscription to the interior (see below).

Lithic Production A comparison of lithic production at the two sites adds support to the conclusions above: groups using the Meade's Bridge site in the Late Archaic

TABLE 3.6. COMPARISON OF LITHIC DEBRIS SIZE BETWEEN CHIEF WHITE BIRD (LATE PREHISTORIC) AND MEADE'S BRIDGE (LATE ARCHAIC) COMPONENT ASSEMBLAGES

Lithic debris measurement	Chief White Bird (20RO50)	Meade's Bridge (20RO5)	Compare means (t-test)	Significantly different (at .05 alpha level)?
Mean weight (g)	.47	.57	.039	Yes
Mean length (mm)	15.09	16.29	.003	Yes
Mean thickness (mm)	2.35	2.85	.000	Yes

Note: Flakes and shatter only.

had direct access to primary coastal chert sources, but by the Late Prehistoric inland groups had limited, indirect access to those sources.

Thus the amount of formal versus informal tool production in an assemblage suggests the access that groups had to the raw material sources themselves (indirect versus direct). Formal production indicates limited, indirect access, and informal production suggests ready, direct access, because waste was not a concern. Informal tool production produces large waste flakes, waste cores, and simple situational tools (Andrefsky 1994; Binford 1979). Formal tool production results in carefully prepared cores, bifaces, and retouched tools (Andrefsky 1994: 22).

The average weight, length, and thickness of the lithic debris (flakes and shatter) at the Chief White Bird site are significantly lower than those of the Late Archaic material from Meade's Bridge (table 3.6). The greater debris at Meade's Bridge and the smaller amount of lithic waste at the Chief White Bird site suggest that informal tool production was occurring at the Late Archaic site and not at the Late Prehistoric site. These patterns again support the notion that Late Archaic groups had ready and direct access to coastal cherts, so waste was not an issue; but by Late Prehistory inland communities did not have direct access to any coastal cherts and were more conservative with raw material (Shott 1990).

A comparison of only Bayport lithic debris (flakes and shatter) between these two sites further indicates that sheer abundance does not portray actual Bayport procurement patterns in Late Prehistory. The average weight, length, and thickness of Bayport lithic debris at the Chief White Bird site are significantly lower than those for the debris from the Late Archaic material from Meade's Bridge (table 3.7). This suggests that Late Archaic groups practiced informal tool production on Bayport while Bayport was conserved at Chief White Bird through less waste-producing, more formal tool production.

The lithic distribution pattern found for the Bayport was not predicted by either distance from the source (Luedtke 1976) or passive marking of tribal coastal systems (O'Shea and Milner 2002). Instead, it indicates a different strategy of lithic procurement by Late Prehistoric inland groups. When communities were circumscribed to the interior by the changes along the coasts and lost direct access to coastal territories, they established a preferred exchange axis with coastal communities to the southeast, in the Saginaw Bay area, where Bayport outcrops. This trade ensured, among other things, the availability of at least one high-quality primary chert material for inland groups.

TABLE 3.7. COMPARISON OF BAYPORT CHERT LITHIC DEBRIS SIZE BETWEEN CHIEF WHITE BIRD (LATE PREHISTORIC) AND MEADE'S BRIDGE (LATE ARCHAIC) COMPONENT ASSEMBLAGES

Lithic debris measurement	Chief White Bird (20RO50)	Meade's Bridge (20RO5)	Compare means (t-test)	Significantly different (at .05 alpha level)?
Mean weight (g)	.415	.725	.000	Yes
Mean length (mm)	14.74	17.22	.001	Yes
Mean thickness (mm)	2.17	2.9	.001	Yes

Note: Bayport flakes and shatter only.

Earthen Constructions and Local Interior Developments

Something socially and economically interesting was occurring in the interior during Late Prehistory. Evidence from the Chief White Bird site shows that during Late Prehistory people used interior resources in seasons other than winter, lacked direct access to the coasts, and made ceramic stylistic choices not clearly linked to an expression of a coastal identity. The nature of the lithic assemblages from Late Archaic and Late Prehistoric period inland sites reflects two different social settings: one during the Late Archaic that was open and allowed travel between the inland and the coasts as well as even more widespread connections, and one during Late Prehistory where access across resource zones was circumscribed. Foraging communities using the High Plains found their access to coastal resources limited by coastal tribal alliances during Late Prehistory (ca. A.D. 1200–1600). Developing mobile rounds of seasonal subsistence activities focused on waterscapes, the most productive resources in the High Plains, would have been critical to compensate for reduced access to coastal zones. Also, interior foraging populations were surrounded by coastal tribal systems with a well-developed sense of identity and territoriality. Thus developing both ways to gain entry into these systems as well as some sense of community among locally dispersed populations to assert horizontal (segmental) differentiation from coastal tribal systems would have been important in the circumscribed milieu in which they found themselves.

These developments are not accounted for in any working model of Late Prehistory; but a discussion of figure 3.9 further highlights that something interesting, distinct, and parallel to developments on the northern Great Lakes coasts was happening in the interior. This figure shows a map of reported mounds and earthworks in the northern 20 counties of the Lower Peninsula digitized from the State Site Files.[6] Mounds and earthworks are widely distributed across the northern Lower Peninsula and occur in both coastal zones and the interior High Plains (fig. 3.9). Given that many of these sites were destroyed before they were ever reported (Halsey 2003), this map presents a reduced picture of how many sites were actually once present. Considering this, it is easy to suggest that these constructions did not simply dot but dominated the landscape.

Mound Distribution

The distribution of mound sites is particularly revealing of local interior developments. The normal-use mound in Michigan is a circular, mounded burial feature

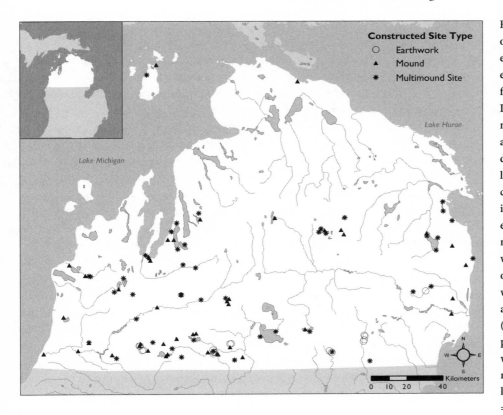

Figure 3.9. Distribution of reported and securely extant mounds and earthworks in 20 counties forming the northern Lower Peninsula. This map shows that mounds and earthworks are widely distributed across the landscape, occurring in coastal zones and in the interior High Plains. The evidence indicates that mounds are associated with inland lakes: (a) 50 of the 92 mound sites are within half a kilometer of an inland lake (54.34%); (b) inland lake size is positively correlated with the total number of mound sites found on a lake (Pearson's correlation = .506, p = .003); and (c) lake area is positively correlated with the presence of multimound sites (Pearson's correlation = .535, p = .002). In sum, larger lakes are more likely to have mound sites; the larger the lake, the more likely these are to be multimound sites.

(Halsey 2003). Burial mounds were not common in Michigan until the Middle Woodland period (A.D. 1–600). The Middle Woodland had a rich mound construction heritage in southern Michigan as communities participated in Hopewellian traditions (see chapter 2), which included elaborate mound complexes (the best example being the Norton Mounds). Northern Michigan did not see this same florescence of Hopewell, and mounds did not become commonplace until the Late Woodland period (Fitting 1975: 149).[7]

In these 20 northern counties, 92 mound sites are reported with some certainty of having existed. Of these, 44 are single-mound sites and 48 are multiple-mound sites (fig. 3.9). Figure 3.9 shows the location of mound site patterns with major water features in both coastal lake-effect zones and the interior High Plains. Indeed, 85 of the 92 mound sites are within half a kilometer of a river, a Great Lake, or an inland lake.

Most striking is the association of mound sites with inland lakes: 50 of the 92 sites are within half a kilometer of an inland lake (54.3%; fig. 3.9). Inland lake size (areal measurement in hectares) is positively correlated with the total number of mound sites found on a lake (Pearson's correlation = .506, p = .003). Moreover, inland lake area seems determinate not just for the presence of mound sites but for whether the sites are single-mound or multimound. That is, lake area is positively correlated with the presence of multimound sites (Pearson's correlation = .535, p = .002). Larger lakes are more likely to have mound sites; and the larger the lake (in hectares), the more likely these are to be multimound sites. Inland lakes would have been key resource locales for local communities throughout prehistory. It would have become particularly important to protect claims to the lakes as territorialism increased after A.D. 1200. These ceremonial constructions were purposefully used to mark inland lakes. Moreover, decisions about constructing mound sites or multimound sites were strategically made to claim larger resource features.

Figure 3.9 shows that this marking of resource features occurred in the coastal zones along Lake Michigan and Lake Huron where we know communities became restricted to defined territories and developed stronger senses of group identity, which were expressed through ceramic styles (see fig. 3.1). The distribution of mounds seen here indicates that groups demarcated key recourse zones like inland lakes and rivers as well as key positions on the Great Lakes (perhaps essential navigation points) within their tribal territories with these sacred structures.

Mounds are distributed across inland lakes in the interior of the northern Lower Peninsula as well, which suggests comparable cultural developments in this area. Small winter hunting parties who made their homes on the coasts of the Great Lakes would not have had reason to invest the time, energy, and labor in monument construction as they passed through the interior. This had to be done by people embedded in the interior landscape who wanted to write in an enduring way their presence on the landscape (Low and Lawrence-Zúñiga 2003: 13). Emerging evidence indicates that the Late Prehistoric communities using the south shore of Houghton Lake lacked direct access to the coasts (and were possibly even actively blocked) and did not use ceramics that clearly identified them with a coastal region. All this suggests that communities spent more time, were more connected to, and were more actively invested in the interior than has been appreciated to date.

Earthwork Distribution

As figure 3.9 also shows, mounds were not the only earthen constructions crosscutting both the coasts and interior of the northern landscape during Late Prehistory. Earthworks were built throughout the Great Lakes region. Some were constructed as early as the Early Woodland (Beld 1993), but almost all of them date to the centuries preceding European contact, during Late Prehistory (A.D. 1200–1600) (Fitting 1975: 149; Greenman 1927a). The majority of these constructions were located in southern Michigan, northern Indiana, and Ontario (see Hinsdale 1931; Lee 1958; Speth 1966; Zurel 1999; the majority of the over 100 enclosures that Hinsdale [1931] reported in Michigan were in this southern area). Earthworks, which are more substantial labor investments than mounds, share a common form of circular ditch and embankment enclosures with planned entryways. Depending on geographic and temporal factors, they range from 30 meters to 120 meters in diameter (Milner and O'Shea 1998: 198).

Despite their prominence on the landscape, earthen enclosure sites have received little systematic investigation. The enclosures themselves have been treated as isolated finds when studied, and work has focused inside them. This lack of systematic investigation has hindered current understandings of the place of earthworks in the broader socioeconomic context of Late Prehistory. The prevailing interpretation today, based on limited investigations at Late Prehistoric period earthwork sites, is that they all served as fortifications (e.g., Krakker 1999; Stothers 1995; Stothers et al. 1998; Zurel 1999).

Figure 3.10. Aerial view of one of the enclosures, 20OG1. This photo was taken during the lumber era and provides a uniquely clear view of this construction: today the region is reforested (image reproduced with permission from the University of Michigan Museum of Anthropology Great Lakes Range Files).

A fortification interpretation may be feasible for southern enclosures that have a large average size (closer to the 120 meters average diameter end of the size range) and when excavated are typically found to have palisades and dense living debris inside.[8] But I suggest that a fortification interpretation is weak for the series of Late Prehistoric circular earthwork enclosures spread from east to west across north-central Michigan (shown in fig. 3.9). These earthworks include at least 17 enclosures with some certainty of having existed (even if no longer extant).[9] Figure 3.10 provides an aerial view of one of these northern enclosures (20OG1) taken during the lumber era; this should help provide the reader with a better mental image of what these constructions look like.

While some are no longer present or locatable, almost all of these northern enclosures originally seem to have been intentionally paired (Moll et al. [1958] reports a twinning of the enclosures in Ogemaw County). Purposefully paired, these enclosures had an explicit design that was closely adhered to, which suggests that something other than expediencies and practicalities was considered in their construction. Also, several of these enclosures are associated with burial mounds (fig. 3.9). During work on enclosures in Ontario, Lee (1958) observed that association of such sacred structures with a fortification earthwork site is highly unusual. Rather than consider each enclosure an isolated find, I suggest that considering these features as complexes with a layout that was repeated across the landscape in monumental form is more appropriate. Six earthwork site complexes can be identified from these seventeen enclosures from west to east: the Boon Earthworks, Mosquito Creek (Boven/Falmouth) Earthworks, Missaukee Earthworks, Walters-Linsenman and Harcourt Swamp Earthworks, Rifle River Earthworks, and the Mikado Earthwork (these are the focus of chapters 5 and 6).[10]

Prior to my research program, limited archaeological research had occurred at these sites and none at the Boon Earthworks, now unlocatable (for the results of work on these enclosures, see Carruthers 1969; Cleland 1965; Cornelius and Moll 1961; Dustin 1932; Greenman 1926, 1927a; Moll et al. 1958). We know that all of these earthworks have breaches through their embankments and not all (none conclusively) have palisades. Excavations inside these enclosures have found light habitation debris, which is of course not what would be expected of intensively occupied fortified habitations. These findings highlight the problems with a fortification interpretation.

Further, the communities' positioning of these enclosures in the landscape is striking. Every enclosure complex is associated with some kind of water source, be it a small spring, a swamp, or a creek. But in stark contrast to mound sites, only one complex is within half a kilometer of a major water source: the Rifle River Earthworks (fig. 3.9). This positioning away from resources that could support a residential population further suggests that these enclosures were not intended as habitation sites.

It is interesting that this consistent location of complexes away from major water features appears to be a coordinated decision. Major water resource features were purposefully marked by mound sites. Earthworks, consistently placed away from these features, were obviously located to serve a different function than mound sites. Using contrasting constructions had to be important in filling different socioeconomic demands in Late Prehistory (fig. 3.9).

A closer look shows that the earthwork complexes tend to be positioned closer to (and some almost on) the border between the High Plains ecosystem and the lake-effect ameliorated coasts. No earthworks are present in the heart of the High Plains (where the large Higgins Lake and Houghton Lake are located), leaving a notable gap in the middle of the west-east spread of enclosures. As noted, Late Prehistory was a time when territorialism became pronounced along the coasts of the northern Great Lakes and parallel developments occurred in the interior among foragers cut off from the coasts. People in both the coastal and interior regions actively marked local resources with mounds. It is interesting that earthwork constructions are located in what seem to be neutral positions, away from resource features, which (if the mounds are any indication) were hotly contested in the territorial setting of Late Prehistory. These trends call for an explanation.

Ritual Gatherings, Ceremonial Monuments, and a New Model of Tribal Regional Organization for Late Prehistory

The milieu of Late Prehistory saw increasing territorialism along the coasts, which led to heightening social alterity between coastal horticulturalists and inland foragers. As the long-established socioeconomic system featuring high mobility, fluid social boundaries, and ready procurement of items across resource zones ended, the setting of Late Prehistory (A.D. 1200–1600) demanded creative social, economic, and ideological strategies from regional communities. I propose that this period saw the development of a multifaceted regional system enacted through monumentalism.

As territorialism became pronounced, local groups in the interior and on the coasts needed to inscribe their presence on the landscape. They used mounds to mark critical resource zones as their own; to protect resources against outsiders; and to create nexi or aggregation centers where people throughout the local area would come together for ritual and associated economic renewal. I postulate that burial mounds formed local, panresidential intratribal ceremonial centers that were used to fulfill internal tribal processes during Late Prehistory in northern Michigan.

Both inland and coastal groups occupied environmental settings riddled with risk and uncertainty, making regional interaction and access to outside resources important. Trade between coastal and inland communities would level out resource uncertainty across annual and interannual cycles and unpredictable resource failures typical of the northern Great Lakes. Resource pooling at periodic aggregations would offer opportunities to balance shortfalls in annual rounds, which trade within local territories alone could not always buffer. Because communities were living in a restricted social sphere with strong territoriality, formal contexts for regional intertribal interaction would be necessary. With their twinned blueprint repeated in monumental form across the landscape, earthwork complexes were designed to be interpretable and accessible (socially, ideologically, and physically) to multiple communities, serving as centers of intertribal ritual and exchange.

Late Prehistoric Anishinaabeg communities created rituals and constructed monuments with contrasting positions and roles in the landscape to facilitate local community coherence (mounds) and intersocietal exchange (earthworks) in a constantly evolving cultural landscape. By creating permanent, meaningful, easily interpreted, consistent, and predictable contexts for the enactment of liturgical orders, constructed monuments conferred their own distinct advantages for facilitating intra- and intertribal interaction. This system operated for hundreds of years before it was interrupted by European contact circa A.D. 1600.

CHAPTER 4

Staking Local Claims

MOUNDS AS INTRATRIBAL CEREMONIAL MONUMENTS

The exaggerated story of how a battle led to the production of the burial mound site at the confluence of the Cut River and Houghton Lake began this book. Even with its fallacies, the story emphasized facts that were important in the real history of the Cut River Mounds site (20RO1): it was an essential resource zone, had a deeply sacred nature, and was a place of deep memory, remembering, and legend-making.

People living today along Houghton Lake continue to tell sometimes equally speculative tales about the site. Why should it be so alive in modern dialogue? This continued local interest speaks to the staying power of the monument site in the landscape. This chapter shows that it was a marked, uniquely persistent place for much longer than the trajectory of modern storytelling surrounding it. This site was remembered and used for millennia by indigenous communities throughout the northern Great Lakes for its rich resources. At the onset of Late Prehistory (ca. A.D. 1200–1600) inland groups transformed it into a locally claimed place, developing an intratribal ceremonial monument center demanding ritual attention and facilitating key economic interactions in the changing socioeconomic setting.

Site Location, Cultural Features, Resource Offerings, and Archaeological Evaluation

The Cut River Mounds site (20RO1) is in Markey Township, Roscommon County, Michigan (23N03W). It is located at the confluence of the Cut River (which connects Higgins Lake and Houghton Lake) and Houghton Lake (fig. 4.1). The Cut River flows south from Higgins Lake toward Houghton. It enters the north side of Houghton Lake at a westward angle.

The mounds that gave the site its name are located on the north side of the confluence. Here the land rises roughly 2 meters from the river/lake shore, and the mounds are positioned on this elevated bank (fig. 4.2). The site, the first reported in Roscommon County, was originally recorded as having three mounds. Today only two are preserved: one large and one small, referred to herein as Mound A and Mound B, respectively (see fig. 4.3 for pictures of these two mounds as they exist today).

The property containing the two mounds is a large rectangular parcel encompassing a resort called the Mounds. The resort property runs east from the confluence point, almost 250 meters along the Cut River, and is roughly 100 meters wide from north to south. Boat docks and fishing piers ring the Cut River waterfront. The

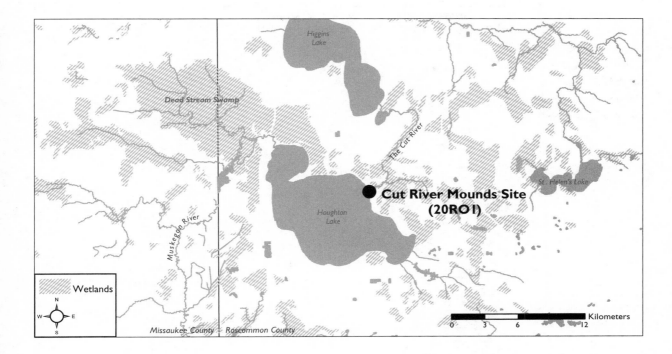

Figure 4.1. Location of the Cut River Mounds site (20RO1).

land of the resort contains 43 residential buildings, including the Old Hotel, cabins and trailers (one of which is parked on the edge of Mound A, as shown in fig. 4.3), a large tool garage, a restroom, a shuffleboard court, a large septic field, and a gravel road running north-south through the property (which cuts off the edge of Mound B). I did the first professional research at this site. The owners of the Mounds Resort kindly granted permission for all work. The archaeological site extends beyond this property, and many neighbors also generously allowed testing on their land, enabling a more thorough evaluation.

The bank that the mounds are on is extremely flat. The first notable rise in the landscape lies roughly 100 meters north of the confluence, where a small, 50-meter-long and 50-meter-wide shelf is elevated roughly 2 meters above the surrounding landscape. On this shelf (the closest elevated terrain to the mounds) a series of 30–40 cache pits was identified in a walk-over survey (fig. 4.2). These shallow surface depressions (generally reflecting storage pits) called cache pits are the most common archaeological feature in Michigan (Dunham 2000). If not from the historic period, they almost always date to circa A.D. 1000–1600 based on associated ceramics, as is the case at Cut River (Dunham 2000: 229).

Site Resource Profile

According to Vreeland's story of the battle, this locale's resources were worth fighting for. Even a cursory look at its resource profile confirms a notably rich locale. The confluence of the Cut River and Houghton Lake is a principal natural landmark in the interior High Plains. Cut River is the widest tributary on the largest and one of the shallowest inland lakes in Michigan, making it an obvious and critical locale

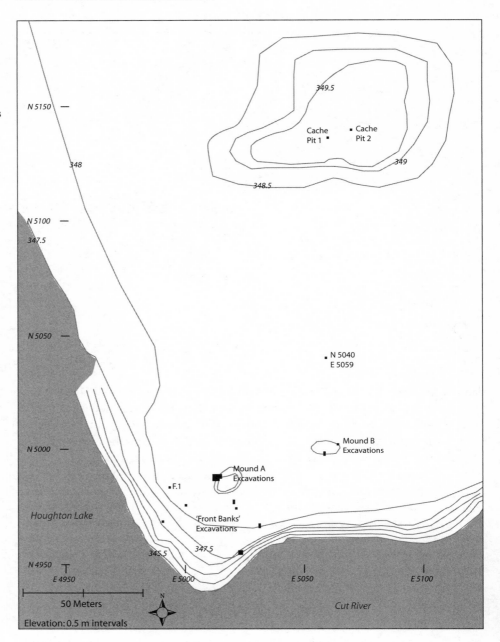

Figure 4.2. Topographic map of the Cut River Mounds site (20RO1), showing major site features and excavation areas.

for the fish spawning in Houghton Lake. Tributaries that flow into lakes in a shallow lacustrine habitat, where larvae can easily float to and feed from, are preferred spawning zones for inland lake fish. A riverine spawning ground and a shallow larvae nursery are the settings replicated in modern management practices for walleye in the Great Lakes region (see Eldridge et al. 2002; Jones et al. 2003).

Inland lake fish species thus would have been particularly dense resources during their spring-spawning runs as they swam up riverine tributaries of lakes (Bailey et al. 2004; Cleland 1982; Jones et al. 2003). Throughout prehistory, regional indigenous

Figure 4.3. Mound A and Mound B as they look today (with people for scale).

communities would have been able to mass-capture these fish, making the spawns in this locale a very dense, reliable, and seasonally predictable resource, critical and unique in the High Plains interior ecosystem. This locale is still renowned for its walleye runs; fishers come from all over on spring evenings, shining lights to find these spawners.

In addition to the dense resources supplied by spring-spawning fish, other diverse and abundant resources were available in the site's vicinity. The sandy soil on the north side of the confluence, where the mounds are situated today, hosted a beech–sugar maple–hemlock forest before development (Comer et al. 1995). On the other side of the river, the sandy soils supported a white pine–red pine forest (Comer et al. 1995). The mucks supported hardwood swamp and conifer swamp. The broader vicinity (5 kilometers) had a large diversity of land cover; conifer swamp and white pine–red pine forests were dominant, along with stands of beech–sugar maple–hemlock forests as well as aspen-birch and white pine–hemlock forests.

The vicinity of the Cut River confluence contained a multiplicity of wildlife and plant habitats, including open lake, riverine, tributary, wetland, coniferous forest, and hardwood forest. They held a high diversity and abundance of floral and faunal resources, in addition to the unique seasonal resource of spawning fish. The sandy soil forests contained a variety of blueberries, raspberries, and bunchberry plants. The beech–sugar maple–hemlock forests offered maple sugar, a carbohydrate-rich resource best harvested in early spring (Holman 1978). The wetlands served as a home for beavers, muskrats, and waterfowl. The low marshy areas along the shores provided turtles and tubers (Harding and Holman 1997). The forests hosted additional species of wildlife, including large terrestrial mammals like bears, deer, and elk (native to Michigan's Lower Peninsula prior to 1875) as well as smaller mammals like rabbits and woodchucks and a variety of birds.

Site Evaluation

Excavations occurred in five areas of the site: at the base of Mound A; at the base of Mound B; at Unit N5040 E5059; along the Front Banks; and in two cache pits, which were cross sectioned. These areas are designated in figure 4.2.

Analyses of lithic, ceramic, and subsistence remains found during excavations and radiometric dates demonstrate that Cut River Mounds (20RO1) was a multicomponent site dating from the Middle Woodland (radiocarbon date of 1570 ±60 B.P.,

TABLE 4.1. RADIOMETRIC DATES CITED IN DISCUSSION OF CUT RIVER MOUNDS
(IN CHRONOLOGICAL ORDER)

Dated item	Conventional radio-carbon date	Calibrated date
Charred Log, Feature 2, Mound B (Modern modifications)	190 ± 60 B.P.	A.D. 1630–1950
Bulk Charcoal, Burnt Layer, Mound A (Modern modifications)	190 ± 60 B.P.	A.D. 1630–1950
Zea mays, Flotation, Feature 7, Mound A (AMS) (Directly preceding mound construction)	890 ± 40 B.P.	A.D. 1030–1240
Ceramic Vessel Residue, Mound B (AMS) (Directly preceding mound construction)	930 ± 40 B.P.	A.D. 1020–1200
Bulk Charcoal, Flotation, Feature 7, Mound A (Directly preceding mound construction)	950 ± 80 B.P.	A.D. 960–1260
Bulk Charcoal, Flotation, Feature 6, Mound A	1090 ± 70 B.P.	A.D. 780–1040
Bulk Charcoal, Flotation, Level 2, N5040 E5059	1090 ± 70 B.P.	A.D. 780–1040
Bulk Charcoal, Flotation, Feature 4, Mound B	1570 ± 60 B.P.	A.D. 380–620

calibrated to A.D. 380–620) through the late Late Woodland/Late Prehistoric period (ca. A.D. 1200–1600) (table 4.1). Over the course of millennia regional communities took advantage of this interior resource hub.

The largest component recovered was a dense early Late Woodland occupation dated across the site to A.D. 780–1040 (table 4.1). The features and material remains show that during this time Cut River hosted seasonal aggregations that included groups from throughout Michigan; these communities had direct access to the coasts of the Great Lakes. Cut River was a regionally open resource aggregation and extraction locale.

Excavations at the base of both mounds show that (1) these were explicitly, even intricately, designed constructions; (2) they were constructed on top of the dense previous occupation; (3) ritual involving food consumption may have accompanied both of their constructions; and (4) they were added to this site contemporaneously around A.D. 1200, when the regional climate was changing to a more territorial and exclusive setting.[1]

When stronger tribal alliances developed on the coasts of the northern Great Lakes, this decisive interior resource spot was staked with a formal claim for the first time in its long history through the addition of burial mounds. The excavations of the cache pits suggest that these features were associated with the transformation of the site into a ritual center during Late Prehistory, constructed to provide storage in support of new ritual. A comparison of Late Prehistoric materials with early Late Woodland ones shows that the communities who added the mounds no longer had direct access to the coasts of the Great Lakes. While abundant seasonal resources had drawn communities from throughout a broad region to Cut River for a long time, during Late Prehistory the site was transformed into a local corporate ceremonial center.

Site Modifications

Before going any further, we must consider the limitations imposed on archaeological interpretations by the condition of the site. When the current owners bought the property in 1993, they made several changes to make the resort more user-friendly that were detrimental to the preservation of the archaeological site. The land's transition from the water of Cut River/Houghton Lake to the higher bank formerly was gradual and contained a marshy wetland. The wetland area was filled in, so that today the terrain goes from water to dry and grass-covered low land to grass-covered bank. On wet days, however, the water tries to reclaim its old marshy ground. The fill for this area came from the high ground, which leveled the land around the residential structures and filled in the wet marsh. A septic field was likewise filled with soil from across the resort. Unwanted vegetation was burnt off across the site and cleared from the property (see table 4.1 for two radiometric dates from this modern process from the edge of both mounds). Clean beach sand was laid down across much of the resort to complete the leveling process.

These changes disturbed a significant amount of in situ archaeological remains, with the Late Prehistoric occupation layers most impacted. Because the stratigraphic layers containing more recent cultural materials were higher, they were the ones pushed into areas needing fill. Thus it is not surprising that test excavations along the Front Banks of the site hit Late Prehistoric deposits (fig. 4.2). Unlike early Late Woodland deposits, which were more or less in situ, Late Prehistoric deposits were in disturbed contexts. While this was limiting, sufficient data were recovered from the Front Banks area, excavations at the base of the mounds, and the work on the cache pits to develop an understanding of the changes occurring and the role of this site in the Late Prehistoric regional network.

Practicing Monumentalism: Designing, Constructing, and Dedicating Mound A in Late Prehistory

Mound A is oriented on a north-west axis (see fig. 4.2). A 12 square meter (4 meters east-west by 3 meters north-south) excavation block was laid out on the northwestern face of the mound, with the top corner of the block cutting into the edge of the mound (fig. 4.4). The top 1 by 1 meter corner was omitted to avoid disturbing the mound itself. The excavations expanded outward from the mound, allowing an evaluation of the timing and process of mound construction.

A lens of modern burning (table 4.1; radiocarbon date of 190 ± 60 B.P., calibrated to A.D. 1630–1950) overlaid with a clean layer of beach sand from modern leveling covered almost the entire excavation block. It ended at the edge of the two units closest to the mound itself.

These modern activities overlay a dense occupation layer that ran across the entire excavation block. The layer contained dense cultural materials and features predating mound construction, including five overlapping pits, which filled the bulk of the excavation units. Charcoal from one of these pits (Feature 7) produced an early Late Woodland date (table 4.1; fig 4.5; radiocarbon date of 1090 ± 70 B.P., calibrated to A.D. 780–1040).

These features produced the majority of materials recovered at the base of Mound A in a relatively high density, indicating an intense occupation. The overlapping of these features suggests that the site was used repeatedly throughout the early Late Woodland period, indicating repeated seasonal aggregations.

Figure 4.4. Excavation block at the edge of Mound A.

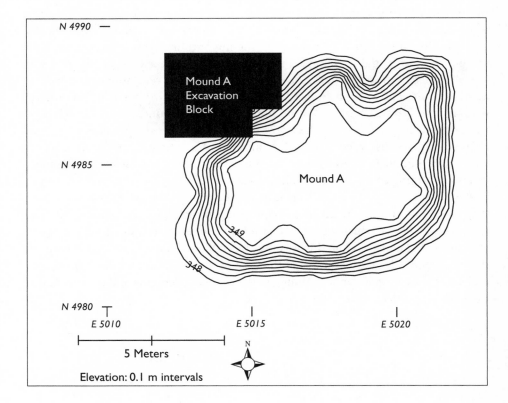

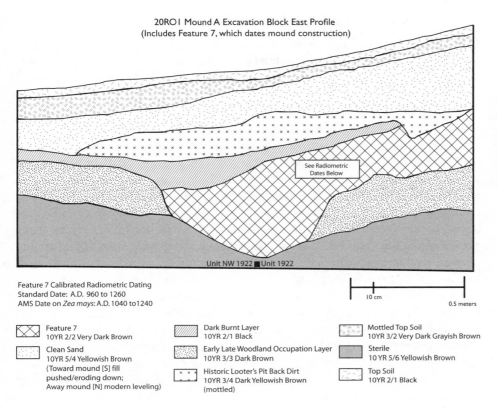

20RO1 Mound A Excavation Block East Profile
(Includes Feature 7, which dates mound construction)

See Radiometric
Dates Below

Unit NW 1922 ▪ Unit 1922

Figure 4.5. Mound A excavation block east profile, showing Feature 7 (indicates *Zea mays* association and radiometric dates).

Feature 7 Calibrated Radiometric Dating
Standard Date: A.D. 960 to 1260
AMS Date on *Zea mays*: A.D. 1040 to1240

10 cm   0.5 meters

Feature 7
10YR 2/2 Very Dark Brown

Clean Sand
10YR 5/4 Yellowish Brown
(Toward mound [S] fill
pushed/eroding down;
Away mound [N] modern leveling)

Dark Burnt Layer
10YR 2/1 Black

Early Late Woodland Occupation Layer
10YR 3/3 Dark Brown

Historic Looter's Pit Back Dirt
10YR 3/4 Dark Yellowish Brown
(mottled)

Mottled Top Soil
10YR 3/2 Very Dark Grayish Brown

Sterile
10 YR 5/6 Yellowish Brown

Top Soil
10YR 2/1 Black

A cultural feature (Feature 7) located in the eastern profile of the excavation block provides conclusive evidence that the mound was constructed after A.D. 1200, at the onset of the Late Prehistoric period (fig. 4.5).

Feature 7 is large and expansive. An increased density of burnt material and fire-cracked rock was noticed during excavation in the units containing it. This was not determined to be a separate cultural feature from the surrounding matrix, however, until it was seen in the eastern profile of the excavation block (fig. 4.5). It is clear that the northern portion of this feature has been truncated by the modern burning and land leveling and that backdirt from a historic looter's pit overlies the feature as well. While upper levels were disturbed, this feature postdates the main early Late Woodland occupation layer found across excavations at the base of the mound dated to A.D. 780–1040.

Feature 7 runs directly under the mound; no prehistoric occupation layers are found between it and mound construction (fig. 4.5). A 10-liter flotation sample was removed from the profile to provide a secure context for a radiometric date. One standard radiometric date was run on bulk charcoal from the flotation and produced a radiocarbon date of 950 ± 80 B.P., calibrated to A.D. 960–1260 (table 4.1). In the analysis of the ethnobotanical materials from this flotation, Kathryn Parker identified two carbonized cupules and one kernel of eight-row *Zea mays*. An AMS dating of the cupule produced a radiocarbon date of 890 ± 40 B.P., calibrated to A.D. 1030–1240. These two dates demonstrate that Mound A was built after A.D. 1200.

Mound A: Possible Maize Dedicatory Ritual

More than simply dating mound construction, the maize recovered in Feature 7 provides a glimpse into activities that may have surrounded construction during Late Prehistory. Readers familiar with contemporaneous Late Woodland/Late Prehistoric/Mississippian sites in the central and lower Midwest and the Southeast might consider the presence of a few fragments of corn an underwhelming find, but it must be put into the context of the research universe under consideration here. Simply put, food floral remains across Michigan are poorly represented in prehistoric archaeological flotation samples (Parker 1996: 308). Fewer than twenty sites in Michigan have securely dated remains of prehistoric domesticated crops; that in itself makes this find from Cut River significant (Parker 1996: 309).

Unique circumstances allowed excavators of the Late Woodland site 20SA1034 along the Flint River in Saginaw County to use a 100% flotation recovery at the site. Even so, they found that "except for wood charcoal, which was abundant and ubiquitous, botanical materials were neither uniformly distributed nor numerous" (Parker 1996: 316). Maize density across the site was 2.74 fragments/10 liters, which is of course lower than densities from most contemporaneous sites in the central and lower Midwest (Parker 1996: 324). Paleoethnobotanists working in Michigan believe that the low visibility of cultigens and other floral food remains reflects site formation processes and unfavorable preservation conditions (recovery strategies may also be a contributing factor). Recovery of floral food remains (especially of cultivated crops), even in low density, is significant in the research universe of Michigan's archaeological landscape.

At Cut River standard 10-liter flotation samples were taken from 18 contexts and all light fractions were examined by paleoethnobotanist Kathryn Parker. Only three contexts at the site produced edible plant remains (Feature 7 and Feature 5 from the base of Mound A and one of the cross-sectioned cache pits discussed below). Of these, only the two features at the base of Mound A produced maize, an association that is compelling and hard to explain as due to random chance or coincidence.

At the base of Mound A, the only other feature found in the excavation block away from the dense, overlapping early Late Woodland pits was a large, U-shaped pit in the northwestern corner (Feature 5, fig. 4.6). Feature 5, like Feature 7, has been truncated at its upper extent by modern burning and land leveling; but, also like Feature 7, it stratigraphically postdates the early Late Woodland occupation layer across the excavation block. This feature contained an extremely low density of cultural materials, but a 10-liter flotation from it produced the only other *Zea mays* found at the site: four cupules and one glume. Note that the maize densities for these features are respectively 3 fragments/10 liters for Feature 7 and 5 fragments/10 liters for Feature 5. Both features also produced seed remains (two huckleberry, one raspberry, and one unidentified seed at Feature 7 and three huckleberry and two unidentified seeds at Feature 5).

The recovery of *Zea mays* in these two features that are separate from and postdate early Late Woodland activities indicates that the species was exclusive to the Late Prehistoric use of the site. The carbonized maize suggests that it was cooked and deposited on site. Given the generally short growing season in the High Plains, the maize cooked here was most likely acquired through trade with coastal horticulturalists.[2]

20RO1 Mound A Excavation Block 2 Meters of North Profile (Feature 5 Extent)

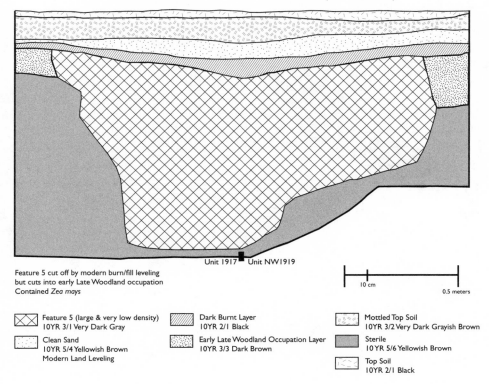

Figure 4.6. Mound A excavation block north profile, showing Feature 5 (indicates stratigraphic relationship and *Zea mays* association).

Unit 1917   Unit NW1919

Feature 5 cut off by modern burn/fill leveling
but cuts into early Late Woodland occupation
Contained *Zea mays*

10 cm   0.5 meters

Feature 5 (large & very low density) 10YR 3/1 Very Dark Gray	Dark Burnt Layer 10YR 2/1 Black	Mottled Top Soil 10YR 3/2 Very Dark Grayish Brown
Clean Sand 10YR 5/4 Yellowish Brown Modern Land Leveling	Early Late Woodland Occupation Layer 10YR 3/3 Dark Brown	Sterile 10YR 5/6 Yellowish Brown
		Top Soil 10YR 2/1 Black

Being found in Feature 7, a clear product of activities immediately preceding mound construction, suggests that *Zea mays* perhaps was used in ritual activities associated with the construction of the mound itself. We have seen that the communities responsible for construction at the Cut River Mounds site in Late Prehistory (after A.D. 1200) lived in a socioeconomic setting where maize was assuming an increasingly dominant role in coastal economies. Using this resource in symbolically charged dedication activities during mound construction may have been a way for inland foragers to connect their symbolic practices to increasingly powerful coastal horticulturalists, asserting their place at the regional table. Interpretive possibilities abound.

Mound A: Intentional Mound Design

A truly intriguing feature was identified in the excavations at the base of Mound A: a portion of a trench (Feature 10; fig. 4.7). This trench was roughly 25 centimeters wide and was oriented north to west, running parallel to the mound. While only a portion was uncovered, its orientation suggests that it encircled the entire circumference of the mound.

The trench demonstrates that a specific design layout went into the mound's construction. The groups building the mound marked out its location and then built the ceremonial structure within this enclosed space. Similar practices of staking out an

Figure 4.7. Mound A
Feature 10 plan. This
trench appears to encircle
Mound A, a unique
aspect of this mound's
construction process.
The trench indicates
that a specific plan was
laid out and followed in
constructing this mound.

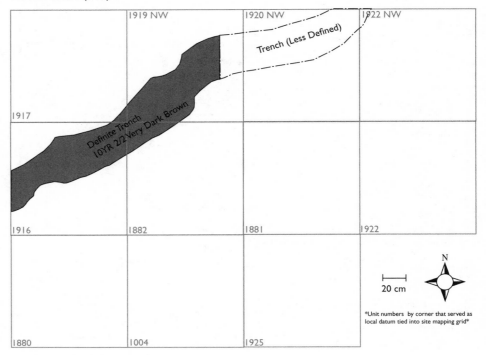

20RO1 Mound A Excavation Block
Trench Feature (F. 10)

earthen construction before building have deep antecedents in the prehistory of the
broader Midwest and Southeast, documented in Hopewell earthen constructions in
Ohio (cf. Greber 1979) and even deeper in time in Middle Archaic mound construction practices in Louisiana (see Saunders et al. 2005: 663). But this is a unique design
sequence for mounds in Michigan. Although mounds were common burial structures from the Middle Woodland onward in Michigan (Halsey 2003), this apparent
strategy of laying out the mound before construction has never been previously documented and appears distinctively related to the setting of Late Prehistory.

A Shared Logic of Intentional Mound Design

A similar strategy to the one found at Cut River was identified during salvage excavations conducted at the base of a Late Prehistoric mound, the Papineau Mound
(20AA17), located on Hubbard Lake in Juntunen tribal territory near Lake Huron
(the landowner was considering building a driveway that would have cut the edge of
the mound off). Excavation found that the mound form was outlined with cobbles
and then constructed on top of this physical outline (O'Shea and Howey 2003; given
the significance of this find, the landowner was convinced to redo his driveway plans
to avoid disturbing the unique design of the mound).[3]

While the outline is different in the cases of Mound A at Cut River and the
Papineau Mound, the design scheme is logically similar. This design strategy differ-
entiates Late Prehistoric northern mounds from earlier mounds across Michigan.
In addition to this unusual design practice, both mounds have an oval shape and a

flattened top, features that also distinguish them from normal-use Michigan burial mounds, which are circular/round. Late Prehistoric burial mounds have now been documented in both coastal and inland northern Michigan as having this new type of design and form, suggesting that mounds were repurposed during this time to have a new significance and functionality in the changing social, economic, and ideological milieu.

Practicing Monumentalism: Designing, Constructing, and Dedicating Mound B in Late Prehistory

Mound B is oriented almost due east-west (fig. 4.2). Today this mound is surrounded by the resort road, which has cut substantially into its eastern edge (fig. 4.3). This mound is surrounded by roads, so a broad excavation block like the one at the base of Mound A was not possible. To assess the timing and process of mound construction, two 1 by 1 meter units were dug on the southern edge of Mound B; a profile cut was done on the northeastern edge where the resort road has eroded the edge of the mound (fig. 4.2).

A pattern similar to that found at the base of Mound A was found at Mound B. As at Mound A, both units and the profile showed modern modifications, including burning and filling, which ended at the edge of the mound (a charred log found in profile cut of Mound B produced a radiocarbon date of 190 ± 60 B.P., calibrated to A.D. 1630–1950; table 4.1; fig. 4.8). Also as at Mound A, dense early Late Woodland occupation predated mound construction. Unlike Mound A, however, an amorphous pit feature was identified below the early Late Woodland occupation in the profile cut. The pit dated to the Middle Woodland (radiocarbon date of 1570 ± 60 B.P., calibrated to A.D. 380–620) and shows that the site was a known place in the landscape prior to the dense early Late Woodland occupation. Again, though, the dominant materials recovered were early Late Woodland materials.

While more restricted, the excavations at the base of Mound B were sufficient to provide evidence on the timing and process of this mound's construction. In the two units at the base of Mound B, a dark cultural layer was located between the early Late Woodland occupation layer and the mound construction (fig. 4.9). Like Feature 7 at the base of Mound A, this layer preceded mound construction. It contained the remains of a single pot break with dense charred residue AMS-dated to provide a date on the mound construction. The AMS date was 930 ± 40 B.P., calibrated to A.D. 1020–1200 (table 4.1; fig. 4.10). Corresponding to this date, this vessel does not fit with known early Late Woodland wares and instead shows a somewhat transitional decorative pattern, with a configuration band, which became common later on Juntunen pottery. This date shows a tight correspondence with the AMS date calibrated to A.D. 1030–1240 from the maize in Feature 7 under Mound A. Mound B was unquestionably added contemporaneously with Mound A (table 4.1).

Mound B: Possible Food Dedicatory Ritual

The dense residue on the vessel recovered immediately below mound construction suggests that it could have been used in cooking (Skibo 1992). Deposited during activity just prior to mound construction, this find highlights another shared

Figure 4.8. Mound B road-cut south profile. Two radiometric dates are noted, one from the modern burning/ modification that has occurred across the site and another from the Middle Woodland occupation of the site.

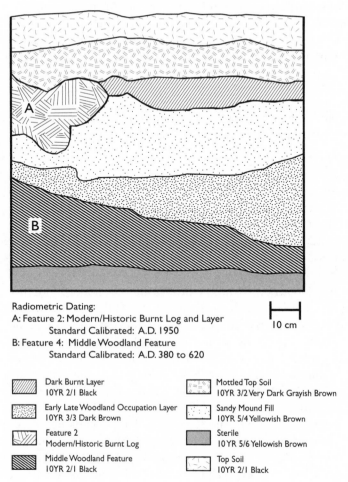

20RO1 Mound B Road Cut South Profile

Radiometric Dating:
A: Feature 2: Modern/Historic Burnt Log and Layer
        Standard Calibrated: A.D. 1950
B: Feature 4: Middle Woodland Feature
        Standard Calibrated: A.D. 380 to 620

10 cm

Dark Burnt Layer 10YR 2/1 Black		Mottled Top Soil 10YR 3/2 Very Dark Grayish Brown
Early Late Woodland Occupation Layer 10YR 3/3 Dark Brown		Sandy Mound Fill 10YR 5/4 Yellowish Brown
Feature 2 Modern/Historic Burnt Log		Sterile 10 YR 5/6 Yellowish Brown
Middle Woodland Feature 10YR 2/1 Black		Top Soil 10YR 2/1 Black

pattern with Mound A, where Features 5 and 7 preceding Mound A's construction also contained evidence of food preparation or consumption with maize remains. These finds suggest the possibility that food preparation/consumption was a key aspect of ritual preparations/dedications for the mound construction here.

Mound B: Intentional Mound Design

While excavations at the base of Mound A extended outward and picked up the unique trench feature indicating design layout (fig. 4.7), the excavation units at the base of Mound B went deeper into the mound. The north profile of the two 1 by 1 meter units at the base of Mound B reveals that the mound was built with alternating colored layers of fill (fig. 4.9). The first layer was clean beach sand, followed by gray soil, which was followed by another lens of clean sand fill and capped off by a brown soil lens. This was obviously designed and orchestrated construction. In particular, layers of clean sand fill could not have happened by happenstance. These clean soils were explicitly targeted for use in mound construction.

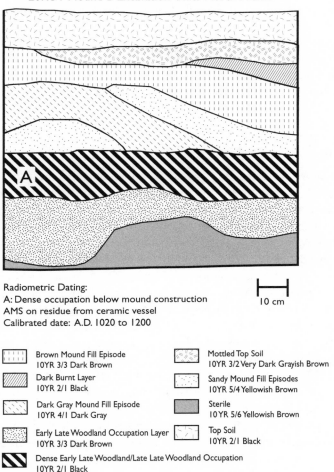

20RO1 Mound B Excavation Units North Profile

Radiometric Dating:
A: Dense occupation below mound construction
AMS on residue from ceramic vessel
Calibrated date: A.D. 1020 to 1200

10 cm

	Brown Mound Fill Episode 10YR 3/3 Dark Brown		Mottled Top Soil 10YR 3/2 Very Dark Grayish Brown
	Dark Burnt Layer 10YR 2/1 Black		Sandy Mound Fill Episodes 10YR 5/4 Yellowish Brown
	Dark Gray Mound Fill Episode 10YR 4/1 Dark Gray		Sterile 10 YR 5/6 Yellowish Brown
	Early Late Woodland Occupation Layer 10YR 3/3 Dark Brown		Top Soil 10YR 2/1 Black
	Dense Early Late Woodland/Late Late Woodland Occupation 10YR 2/1 Black		

Figure 4.9. Mound B excavation units north profile, showing the AMS date from ceramic residue from the dense occupation layer directly below mound construction. The alternating colored layers of soil used to build up the mound are also shown, indicating the planned/purposeful construction process (as for the trench in Mound A) that went into this mound construction.

Vessel Orifice Radius

a

Rim Profile

a

b

b

1 cm

Figure 4.10. Vessel from occupation directly below Mound B construction, AMS dated to A.D. 1020–1200 (see table 4.1 and fig. 4.9).

Whether this construction of alternating colors occurred at once or in sequential episodes throughout the Late Prehistoric period (from A.D. 1200 onward), color was clearly an important aspect of mound construction and use. This has precedents in other earthen constructions in the Midwest (see Sherwood and Kidder 2011). Like Mound A, Mound B is oval (loaflike: fig. 4.3) and built with a specific design plan. These features appear to be distinctive for northern mounds added to critical resource zones in Late Prehistory.

Supporting Monumentalism: Cache Pits and Ritual Storage during Late Prehistory

As noted above, 30–40 cache pits were identified in a walk-over survey on an undeveloped piece of land on the first rise in the landscape north of the confluence (fig. 4.2). At surface level, these cache pits were all circular and roughly 1 meter in diameter. Two of these cache pits were cross-sectioned and shared a similar profile (fig. 4.11). They were roughly 1 meter deep and narrowed inward considerably from their surface diameter, ending at roughly 40 centimeters wide.

The most common archaeological features found today in Michigan are these shallow surface depressions (generally reflecting storage pits) called cache pits (Dunham 2000). Although cache pits sometimes occur alone, more often they are in clusters, as is the case at the Cut River Mounds site. Clusters commonly range from 15 to 25 pits but sometimes occur in larger numbers, from 50 to 150. If not historic, cache pits almost always date to ca. A.D. 1000–1600, based on associated ceramics (Dunham 2000: 229). These subterranean food storage features are largely understood as important in creating a stable food supply in the northern Great Lakes (Holman and Krist 2001: 7).

While these features literally cover the region's archaeological landscape, they have been the subject of comparatively limited research. Only a few cache pits in Michigan have been systematically excavated by professional archaeologists. The excavation of two from Cut River, while admittedly only a start, is still a significant contribution to the extant knowledge base regarding these pits. The most powerful reason for the lack of work on cache pits is that they have not produced abundant (or any) material artifacts when excavated; their contents were removed during occupation, and they are considered "empty" (Dunham 2000; Dustin 1966; Greenman 1926; Hambacher et al. 1995; Holman and Krist 2001; Schneider 1942). In an early paper describing archaeology in Door County, Wisconsin, J. P. Schumacher (1918: 133) offers a snapshot of cache pit excavation: "investigations failed to disclose remains of any kind." Hence it is really striking that the two cross-sectioned cache pits at the Cut River Mounds site both produced cultural materials.

Cache Pit 2

Cache Pit 2 contained a few lithics and the remnants of an entire ceramic jar (table 4.2; fig. 4.12). This vessel was deposited whole in this cache pit, although over time it has been badly eroded by root damage and frost spalling. Its presence is significant because of its location in a cache pit, which is atypical. While extensive flotations

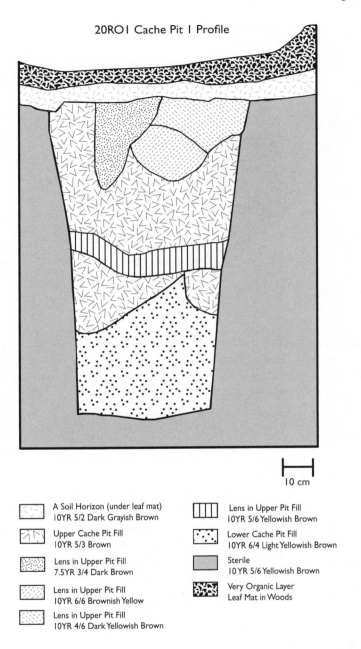

20RO1 Cache Pit 1 Profile

A Soil Horizon (under leaf mat) 10YR 5/2 Dark Grayish Brown	Lens in Upper Pit Fill 10YR 5/6 Yellowish Brown
Upper Cache Pit Fill 10YR 5/3 Brown	Lower Cache Pit Fill 10YR 6/4 Light Yellowish Brown
Lens in Upper Pit Fill 7.5YR 3/4 Dark Brown	Sterile 10YR 5/6 Yellowish Brown
Lens in Upper Pit Fill 10YR 6/6 Brownish Yellow	Very Organic Layer Leaf Mat in Woods
Lens in Upper Pit Fill 10YR 4/6 Dark Yellowish Brown	

10 cm

Figure 4.11. Cross section of Cut River Mounds (20RO1) Cache Pit 1.

were taken, no floral remains were recovered, which suggests that the vessel and pit may have been used for something other than food storage.

This vessel has stylistic and morphological features fitting the Late Prehistoric period, dating expected for nonhistoric period cache pits. This demonstrates that these cache pits were constructed during this later use of the site and were associated with the emergence of monumentalism at this locale. Although the jar shows late features, it does not fit well with any of the distinctive coastal wares of the Late Prehistoric period. This vessel of "White Bird ware" has a channel running along the

TABLE 4.2. CACHE PIT 2 CONTENTS

22 lithics	45.29 g
600+ ceramic sherds representing 1 almost complete vessel (figure)	300+ g

Figure 4.12. Ceramic vessel found in Cache Pit 2.

entire lip and retains a cord-marked exterior (fig. 4.12), similar in many ways to vessels recovered on the Late Prehistoric Chief White Bird site, also on Houghton Lake (see chapter 3). This jar seems to have been made and deposited by people who were not expressing strong material and social ties to the coasts.

Cache Pit 1

Cache Pit 1 contained a much wider diversity of materials than Cache Pit 2 (table 4.3). A few lithics and ceramics were recovered. Unlike Cache Pit 2, floral remains from edible wild resources were recovered in the flotation, including 9 seeds from berry plants. As illustrated above, these economic resources would have been plentiful around the site. Berries have their peak season in the summer and are readily storable. They were likely harvested on site and stored in this cache pit for later use. Feature 7 at the base of Mound A produced two huckleberry, one raspberry, and one unidentified seed, and Feature 5 produced three huckleberry and two unidentified seeds. Obviously a direct connection between these contexts cannot be made, but the presence of edible seeds in only these two places at Cut River suggests that these cache pits were crafted to facilitate/support activity at the site as the mounds were built during Late Prehistory.

Food storage, fascinatingly, was not the only or perhaps even primary function of this cache pit. A unique and important cultural item was recovered at the bottom of this pit: pieces of a bowl or other tool made from a skull. The recovered fragments of this single human cranium included elements deriving only from the lower portion of the skull (table 4.3). The tooth wear and size indicate that the skull was of an older male.[4] Its presence shows that communities used these cache pits to care for and curate sacred ritual paraphernalia. Just like the burial mounds, this ritual item was directly linked to mortuary symbolism, indicating that ancestor association was critical and distinctive of the ritual practices at this site.

TABLE 4.3. CACHE PIT 1 CONTENTS

9 lithics	4.33 g
40 ceramic sherds (minimum vessel count 1)	65.72 g
9 seeds (identified in 10 liter flotation sample)	3 huckleberry 4 blackberry/raspberry 2 unidentified berry plant
Fragments of a possible bowl or other tool made from the lower skull of an older male (based on molar size and wear). Human cranial fragments recovered include:	6 premolars/molars Right temporal bone (mastoid process) Portion of right zygomatic bone Portion of maxilla Portion of mandible

The tie to ancestors would have been particularly powerful in facilitating local corporate claims, transforming this space into a living place demanding attention from local communities (see chapter 1). These cache pits were more than simple subsistence storage facilities; they were integral in storing materials, including religious paraphernalia as well as food supplies, that were used to support the emerging ritual festivities at the site's ceremonial monuments after A.D. 1200.

Supporting Monumentalism: Subsistence Activities during Late Prehistory

Eight 1 by 1 meter excavation units were placed throughout the Front Banks of the site: the higher ground between the mounds and the east bank of the Cut River and a profile on the edge of this high ground abutting the river were excavated (see fig. 4.2). Because the most recent deposits have been pushed into this area through leveling and flattening of the septic field, getting a strong sense of Late Prehistoric activities in contexts separate from distinct cultural features has been difficult (even along the mounds later deposits were removed or disturbed as well).

These Front Banks units produced mixed temporal assemblages, but the ceramic assemblage indicates that the dominant component is from the Late Prehistoric period. Across these units, at least 13 jars were recovered. Of these vessels, 2 have a decorative technique, drag-and-jab, which occurs only on Late Prehistoric ceramics (cf. Milner 1998). The only vessel at the site with a collar, a distinctly Late Prehistoric stylistic feature, was recovered in these units. While disturbed, these units still provide viable information on the site's use during this later period.

One intact cultural feature was found in the Front Banks excavations: a large roasting pit with dense faunal remains and greasy cooking/roasting by-products (Feature 1; fig. 4.13). Feature 1 contains two dense roasting pits on top of each other. The top and bottom layers are dark black, very greasy, and dense with calcined bone.

Figure 4.13. Front Banks Feature 1, a multiuse roasting pit (upper layers possibly date to the Late Prehistoric).

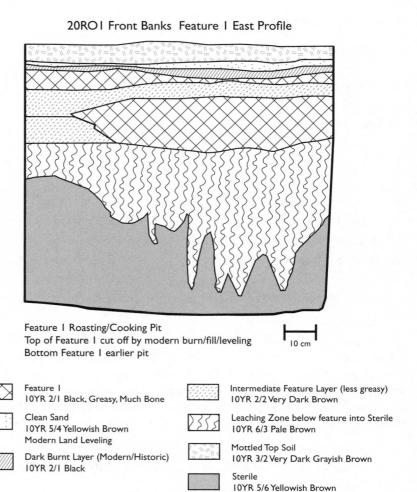

20RO1 Front Banks Feature 1 East Profile

Feature 1 Roasting/Cooking Pit
Top of Feature 1 cut off by modern burn/fill/leveling
Bottom Feature 1 earlier pit

10 cm

	Feature 1 10YR 2/1 Black, Greasy, Much Bone		Intermediate Feature Layer (less greasy) 10YR 2/2 Very Dark Brown
	Clean Sand 10YR 5/4 Yellowish Brown Modern Land Leveling		Leaching Zone below feature into Sterile 10YR 6/3 Pale Brown
	Dark Burnt Layer (Modern/Historic) 10YR 2/1 Black		Mottled Top Soil 10YR 3/2 Very Dark Grayish Brown
			Sterile 10YR 5/6 Yellowish Brown

Between these layers is intermittent feature fill/occupation debris. The top use of the roasting pit has been truncated by the modern leveling, and its high stratigraphic position suggests that the upper portion is late (although this is not conclusive).

Identifiable faunal remains included the calcined remains of a large ungulate, most likely an elk (native in Michigan's Lower Peninsula until 1875), turtles, and catfish.[5] These remains indicate that groups using the site capitalized on the fish and wetland faunal resources as well as the resources in surrounding forests (the berries in the cache pits also show this).

An interesting group of artifacts was recovered in the profile cut along the bank of the Cut River: a pile of fishing net weights. Seine nets, requiring stone sinkers, were commonly used to catch spring-spawning fish species from the Middle Woodland throughout the Late Woodland (Smith 2004: 78; fig. 4.14). No date can be securely assigned to the weights, but their location in the predominantly Late Prehistoric Front Banks region suggests that they may date to this period. Regardless of date, their presence demonstrates that groups using the site harvested the rich spawning fish resources offered at this Cut River confluence.

1 cm

Figure 4.14. Selected
net weights from pile
recovered in Front Banks
profile cut.

Before Monumentalism: Early Late Woodland Occupation

The largest component recovered at this site came from the early Late Woodland period. Dense overlapping remains from repeated aggregations were found to precede the construction of both mounds. The characteristics of the early Late Woodland remains demonstrate that the communities aggregating at the site in the early Late Woodland came from a wide geographic range.

The early Late Woodland ceramic assemblage from the base of Mound A consists of 18 jars. These vessels fit early Late Woodland wares from both northern (Mackinac wares) and southern (Wayne ware) Michigan (Brashler 1981; Holman 1978; Lovis 1973), reflecting the wide geographic draw of the site in this period. The ceramic assemblage from the base of Mound B produced a minimum of 7 ceramic jar vessels. Of these, 6 were represented by rim pieces less than 3 by 3 centimeters in size, making it impossible to assign each to a distinct ware (the other vessel is discussed above).

The early Late Woodland lithic assemblages from Mounds A and B include 540 lithics recovered securely from early Late Woodland occupation at the base

TABLE 4.4. COMPARISON OF LITHIC RAW MATERIALS BY EXCAVATION CONTEXT

	Early Late Woodland			Later	
	Base Mound A	Base Mound B	N5040 E5059	Front banks	Cache pits
Bayport	170	16	40	127	7
	31.5%	35.6%	5.1%	36.8%	22.6%
Norwood	251	6	591	54	6
	46.5%	13.3%	76.1%	15.7%	19.4%
Northern Gray	30	3	50	0	0
	5.6%	6.7%	6.4%	0%	0%
Glacial	49	4	71	157	15
	9.1%	8.9%	9.1%	45.5%	48.4%
Mercer	29	13	25	0	0
	5.4%	28.9%	3.2%	0%	0%
Indiana	8	0	0	0	0
Hornstone	1.5%	0%	0%	0%	0%
Quartzite/	3	3	0	7	3
Argillite	0.6%	6.7%	0%	2.0%	9.7%
TOTAL	**540**	**45**	**777**	**345**	**31**
	100%	**100%**	**100%**	**100%**	**100%**

of Mound A (61 were found at the base of Mound A from unsecured provenience) and 45 lithics from the excavations at the base of Mound B. Table 4.4 shows that both of these assemblages are dominated by two coastal primary cherts, Bayport and Norwood. Northern Gray is present in a small amount. Interestingly, the highly exotic Mercer chert, from 650 kilometers south in Ohio, has a notable presence in both. The even more exotic Indiana hornstone, from 800 kilometers south in Indiana, composes a minor but noteworthy portion of the Mound A assemblage. In both Mound A and Mound B locally available glacial till forms only 9% of the assemblage.

Like the ceramics, this raw material profile speaks of people who were embedded in an open and extensive regional system, where they moved freely across resource zones and made use of this interior resource hub as well as the Great Lakes coasts where these lithic materials outcropped. They had open trade relationships that resulted in exotic materials. These finds are not surprising, because the early Late Woodland is believed to have been distinguished by a moderately diffuse social network (see Brashler 1981).

A Separate Northern Michigan Contingent?

An additional perspective on early Late Woodland life at this site comes from excavations in a 1 by 1 meter unit located in flat land north of both mounds, which uncovered a single-component (table 4.1; radiocarbon date 1090 ± 70 B.P., calibrated to A.D. 780–1040) lithic production area and possible structure.

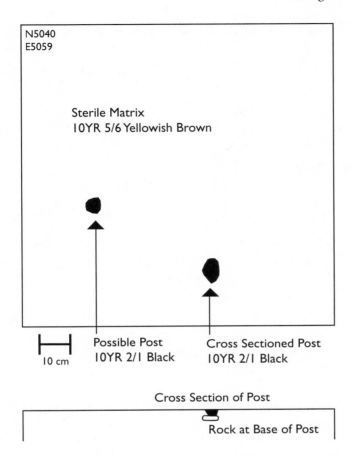

**Figure 4.15. Plan of unit
N5040 E5059, showing
post holes from early Late
Woodland structure (dated
A.D. 780–1040).**

Unit N5040 E5059 had a single-component dense occupation layer. The activities in this unit were contemporary with the early Late Woodland activity at the base of Mound A. Identical radiocarbon dates were produced on charcoal recovered in this occupation debris and that from the early Late Woodland Feature 6 under Mound A (radiocarbon date 1090 ± 70 B.P., calibrated to A.D. 780–1040; table 4.1). Two post molds were found once sterile soil was hit, indicating that some kind of structure stood here (fig. 4.15). When one post was cross-sectioned, it held its shape; a rock was found at its base, suggesting construction techniques or repair of the structure. This structure's function could not be determined from a single unit, but it is important to mention it, because no other definite post molds were recovered.

The ceramic assemblage from Unit N5040 E5059 consists of a minimum count of 6 jars. Every one of these vessels fits early Late Woodland wares from northern (Mackinac wares) Michigan (see Holman 1978). This unit produced by far the highest density of lithics at this site, and this assemblage mirrors the ceramic assemblage. Like the early Late Woodland lithic raw materials from the base of both mounds, the assemblage from this lithic production area is dominated by nonlocal materials (table 4.4). Unlike the assemblages at the bases of Mounds A and B, however, this lithic assemblage has less diversity of nonlocal materials; it is dominated by one high-quality, nonlocal chert: Norwood, which composes 76.1% of the assemblage.

TABLE 4.5. COMPARISON OF BIPOLAR REDUCTION BY EARLY LATE WOODLAND EXCAVATION AREA

	Base Mound A	Base Mound B	N5040 E5059
Bipolar	99	8	59
	18.8%	18.6%	8.4%
Not bipolar	429	35	643
	81.3%	81.4%	91.6%
Pearson Chi-Square	$X^2 = 29.66$ $df = 2$	**p-value < .001**	

Note: This table includes only lithics where bipolar reduction or lack of bipolar reduction could be determined.

TABLE 4.6. COMPARISON OF CORTEX BY EXCAVATION AREA

	Early Late Woodland			Later	
	Base Mound A	Base Mound B	N5040 E5059	Front banks	Cache pits
Cortex	60	6	153	49	4
	11.1%	13.3%	19.7%	14.2 %	12.9%
Not cortex	480	39	624	296	27
	88.9%	86.7%	80.3%	85.8%	87.1%
Pearson Chi-Square	$X^2 = 18.95$ $df = 4$ **p-value < .001**				

While bipolar reduction occurs in a low proportion across all three early Late Woodland contexts at the site, the bipolar reduction of Unit N5040 E5059 is significantly lower than the others (table 4.5). This unit also has the highest proportion of lithics with cortex (19.7%), a significantly higher proportion than in the other excavation contexts (table 4.6). The amount of cortex from raw materials in an assemblage is a useful initial indicator of core reduction (see chapter 3). Generally speaking, the reduction of unworked nodules produces more cortical flakes than the reduction of already partially reduced cores or preforms, although raw material geometry can influence this (Dibble et al. 2005). The higher abundance of cortex paired with the low abundance of bipolar reduction suggests that primary reduction of raw material nodules occurred in this locale.

More telling than this abundance of cortex is its distribution across different kinds of raw materials from N 5040 E 5059 (table 4.7). Norwood composes an overwhelming 81.7% of the cortex recovered. These data indicate that lithic production occurred on unworked Norwood that the early Late Woodland groups using the site brought with them.

Considering that the ceramic and lithic assemblages are dominated by northern/northwestern Michigan materials, most likely the structure and activity in this unit represents a spatially segregated area at the Cut River Mound site occupied by a group from the north/northwest coastal geographic area. As groups came for regional aggregations during the spawning runs in the early Late Woodland (A.D. 780–1040), some created a segregated space for their activities. While this interior region was open and accessible to people from throughout the northern Great Lakes and people interacted with distant neighbors, some also stuck close to their familiar community members.

TABLE 4.7. LITHIC RAW MATERIAL OF CORTEX IN N5040 E5059T

Lithic raw material	No. and % of cortex lithics
Bayport	7
	4.6%
Norwood	125
	81.7%
Northern Gray	8
	5.2%
Glacial	13
	8.5%
Total cortex lithics	**153**
	100%

This unity perhaps signaled the regional changes on the horizon when group exclusivity became much more pronounced after A.D. 1000/1100.

Lithic Changes: Indexing Social Changes in Access and Use of the Site

An expanded comparison of the lithic assemblages from these early contexts to those from likely later contexts at the site sheds more light on the accessibility and use of Cut River before and after the addition of the mounds. In total, 1,799 lithic items were recovered across all five excavation contexts. The lithics from early Late Woodland contexts include 540 items recovered securely from the base of Mound A (plus 61 from unsecured provenience); 45 lithics from the excavations at the base of Mound B; and 777 lithics, composing 43.2% of the site's total lithic assemblage, from the early Late Woodland occupation in the 1 by 1 meter unit N5040 E5059 (table 4.4). The materials recovered from later contexts include the 31 lithics from the two cache pits and 345 lithics in the eight units along the Front Banks.

The overwhelming majority of lithic materials recovered were flakes and shatter. Only 64 tools, composing 3.6% of the assemblage, were recovered; the majority of these were retouched flakes. Cores were the second most common tool. Only two projectile points were recovered. Both were early Late Woodland side-notched points and came from the base of Mound A. Lithic objects were evenly distributed across the excavation areas.

Raw Materials

When the lithic raw material profile is broken down by excavation area, differences between the early Late Woodland and Late Prehistoric contexts are immediately noticeable. The three early Late Woodland contexts contain more nonlocal cherts, including primary coastal cherts as well as exotic materials (table 4.4). The later contexts contain less coastal cherts, more local glacial material, and no exotic materials. These differences are statistically significant (table 4.8).

TABLE 4.8. COMPARISON OF COASTAL CHERT VERSUS GLACIAL
CHERT IN EARLY LATE WOODLAND AND LATER CONTEXTS

	Early Late Woodland (Mounds A and B and N5040 E5059)	Later (Front Banks and cache pits)
Coastal cherts (Norwood, Northern Gray, and Bayport)	1,157 84.9%	194 51.6%
Glacial chert	124 9.1%	172 45.7%
Other lithic material	81 5.9%	10 2.7%
Pearson Chi-Square	$X^2 = 280.2$ $df = 2$	**p-value < .001**

Michigan's coastal cherts (which at this site include Norwood, Northern Gray, and Bayport chert) compose 85% of the early Late Woodland assemblage recovered at the Cut River Mound site, a significantly higher proportion than from the two later contexts (table 4.8). The Late Prehistoric contexts, with almost half their assemblage (45.7%) made of local glacial materials, have a significantly higher proportion than the early Late Woodland contexts, where glacial materials make up less than 10% of the assemblage.

These differences highlight some kind of shift between periods. While there was an overall significant decrease in the amount of coastal cherts between periods, however, the change was not homogeneous across the three kinds of chert (Norwood and Northern Gray from northern coastal zones and Bayport from the southeast in the Saginaw Bay area: table 4.9). Bayport chert forms 35.6% of the likely Late Prehistoric assemblage at the site. So the overall reduction in coastal cherts seen between the early and late periods is caused by drastic reductions in the two northern coastal cherts. Norwood forms 62.3% of the early Late Woodland assemblage and only 16% of the likely Late Prehistoric assemblage, a significant difference. Northern Gray occurs in low frequency in the early Late Woodland assemblage (only 6%) but still represents significantly more in this assemblage than in later contexts, where it is completely absent.

The patterns and shifts among these coastal cherts between the early and later assemblages from Cut River are extraordinarily similar to the patterns found in the comparison between the Meade's Bridge Late Archaic assemblage and the domestic inland Late Prehistoric Chief White Bird (20RO50) site (see chapter 3). Likewise, the later period has higher than expected proportions of Bayport, an extremely limited amount of Norwood chert, a complete absence of Northern Gray, and an absence of highly exotic materials.

The shared patterns demonstrate that Late Prehistoric Anishinaabeg communities using these High Plains sites had very limited or no access to northern coastal farming community territories. This highlights a circumscription of foragers in the interior during the Late Prehistoric that was not present in earlier periods. The

TABLE 4.9. DISTRIBUTION OF COASTAL CHERT BY TYPE IN EARLY LATE WOODLAND VERSUS LATER CONTEXTS

	EARLY LATE WOODLAND (MOUNDS A AND B AND N5040 E5059)		LATER (FRONT BANKS AND CACHE PITS)		
	No.	%	No.	%	p-value[a]
Bayport chert vs. other material					
Bayport	226	16.6	134	35.6	< .001
Other raw materiaL	1,136	83.4	242	64.4	
Norwood chert vs. other material					
Norwood	848	62.3	60	16.0	< .001
Other raw material	514	37.7	316	84.0	
Northern Gray vs. other material					
Northern Gray	83	6.1	0	0	< .001
Other raw material	1,269	93.0	376	100	

[a] Fisher's Exact Test.

abundance of Bayport at both of these sites seems to substantiate that a preferred axis of exchange developed that was directed toward the southeast, where Bayport outcrops. The raw material patterns from these two late inland sites, rather than reflecting the passive effects of distance or tribal marking (cf. Luedtke 1976; O'Shea and Milner 2002), seem to reflect indirect trade arrangements *actively* established and maintained between inland communities and coastal groups to the east-southeast. This access, and the possibility that it involved an active relationship, should be investigated further.[6]

Lithic Production/Transport

Bipolar reduction, which indicates that a tool producer tried to maximize a core of material, occurs significantly less frequently on lithics from early Late Woodland contexts than in likely Late Prehistoric contexts at Cut River (table 4.10). This difference indicates that in general the groups using the site in the early Late Woodland period did not have to maximize their lithic raw materials as much as later groups did. Earlier groups using the site apparently did not have to practice as much expedient and maximizing production, because they had ready access to an array of high-quality primary coastal chert sources.

The distribution of bipolar reduction from the Front Banks Late Prehistoric assemblage varies significantly by raw material type and in ways that seem to reflect the differential access to coastal cherts outlined above (table 4.11). Glacial pebbles can be small and thus subject to bipolar reduction to get the most out of them as chert sources, so glacial material might be expected to represent the highest proportion of bipolar reduction. Local glacial material shows the lowest proportion, however: less than 10% in this late assemblage. Norwood chert shows significantly more bipolar reduction (over half). This highlights just how inaccessible this northern coastal chert material was to late inland groups, because much of the Norwood present was subject to maximizing bipolar reduction. Bayport shows the second highest

TABLE 4.10. BIPOLAR REDUCTION IN EARLY LATE WOODLAND VERSUS LATER CONTEXTS

	Early Late Woodland (Mounds A and B and N5040 E5059)	Later (Front Banks and cache pits)
Bipolar	166	79
	13.0%	22.9%
Not bipolar	1,109	266
	87.0%	77.1%
Fisher's Exact Test	p-value = .0001	

Note: This table includes only lithics where bipolar reduction or lack of bipolar reduction could be determined.

TABLE 4.11. COMPARISON OF BIPOLAR REDUCTION IN THE FRONT BANKS ASSEMBLAGE BY RAW MATERIAL

	Bayport	Norwood	Glacial
Bipolar	30	27	14
	25.6%	50.9%	9.9%
Not bipolar	87	26	128
	74.4%	49.1%	90.1%
Pearson Chi-Square	$X^2 = 37.95$ $df = 2$	p-value < .001	

Note: This table includes only lithics where bipolar reduction or lack of bipolar reduction could be determined.

proportion, which suggests that it was less rare than Norwood but, with access being indirect, was still maximized to some extent.

I have discussed the evidence from Unit N5040 E5059 showing that groups brought this coastal chert material in unworked forms to Cut River in the early Late Woodland period. The change in the use of the site over time is even more striking when we consider that communities using the Cut River site in the early Late Woodland period were able to bring whole unworked nodules of Norwood with them. Just a short time later, in the Late Prehistoric period, the groups using the site had almost no access to Norwood, and the little Norwood they did have was subject to heavy bipolar reduction.

The raw material proportions, cortex patterns, and bipolar reduction trends in the lithic materials recovered across the Front Banks units offer strong evidence of a notable change in who was using the site between the early Late Woodland and Late Prehistoric periods (changes mirrored in the lithic comparison presented in chapter 3). During the early Late Woodland period the site was used by communities moving throughout Michigan in a diffuse social sphere. As the regional setting changed during Late Prehistory (after ca. A.D. 1200), the site was used by communities increasingly circumscribed to the interior.

A New Story for an Ancient Place

It seems fitting to conclude this chapter with a revisioning or rewriting of Vreeland's 1924 story of the Cut River Mounds site (20RO1). This site is still frequently the subject of legend for area residents. I hope that developing a systematic understanding of the site will further the persistence of this place in ways that more appropriately reflect the true dynamism and indigenous histories that played out there.

Through excavations, analysis of lithic, ceramic, and subsistence remains, and radiometric dates, it is clear that the Cut River Mounds site was a multicomponent site dating from the Middle Woodland (radiocarbon date of 1570 ± 60 B.P., calibrated to A.D. 380–620) through the Late Prehistoric period (ca. A.D. 1200–1600). It was a key locale in the regional landscape for centuries, heavily used for its seasonal spawning runs by diverse groups through the early Late Woodland period. As developments along the northern coasts of the Great Lakes began changing the region from an open setting to a more closed setting around A.D. 1000/1100, this once open resource zone was transformed into an intratribal ceremonial monument center by communities circumscribed to interior Michigan.

While the site is multicomponent, the major component recovered in excavations was a dense early Late Woodland occupation (dated across the site with two radiocarbon dates of 1090 ± 70 B.P., calibrated to A.D. 780–1040). The work at the site shows that in this early Late Woodland period the rich spawning runs drew and supported large aggregations of communities from throughout Michigan. These large aggregations produced dense material remains.

The excavations demonstrate that both mounds were added after A.D. 1200 on top of dense early Late Woodland debris; the social and economic sphere was changing at this time, with the rise in the dominance of maize along the coasts and emerging exclusive tribal systems. The addition of the mounds was an imperative move given the economic, social, and ideological milieu of this later period. By commemorating the site through the addition of ceremonial monuments, local ancestral Anishinaabeg communities were able to mark and claim this critical interior resource zone as an exclusive part of their territory. The monuments also created a formal space for panresidential interaction, which was increasingly essential for balancing the resource uncertainty faced by groups restricted to the interior during their annual rounds. Within the circumscribed social setting of Late Prehistory, strategies previously relied on to balance resource shortfalls were no longer options.

The inland communities using the site in the Late Prehistoric period intricately embedded this resource zone in the sacred and the ancestral, which not only let them stake claim to this locale but also made it a living place demanding that community members pay attention to it, come to it, and maintain their interaction with it. The burial mounds associated this site with ancestors, staking corporate claims to the space. These were purposefully planned constructions, designed in ways never seen before in the region. These mounds may also have been dedicated with what seems to be food-related ritual, perhaps even symbolically charged maize consumption to provide a direct link to regional developments, where this resource was gaining prominence. Furthermore, groups transformed the high ground near the site into a storage complex, developed to store food resources but also to hold, curate, and protect sacred ancestral ritual paraphernalia for use in ritual events, which made this an intimately familial place in the landscape of Late Prehistory.

Burial mounds across northern Michigan are strongly correlated with major resource features and were used as markers of local resource zones (see chapter 3). The findings presented here show that Late Prehistoric burial mounds in both coastal and inland northern Michigan had new purposeful designs and forms. In the changing social, economic, and ideological milieu of Late Prehistory, mounds were repurposed with a new significance and functionality. The evidence indicates that this new purpose was to serve as locally salient intratribal ceremonial monument centers.[7]

CHAPTER 5

Coming Together

THE MISSAUKEE EARTHWORKS AND BEAR'S JOURNEY

As the last two chapters illustrate, within the restricted social and economic context of Late Prehistory, communities in both coastal and inland areas shifted their local resource efforts to specialized economies based on Great Lakes fish spawns and maize horticulture along the coasts and intensified use of the waterscapes in the interior. They also staked claims to resource zones with burial mounds, transforming them into sacred locales for panresidential, intracommunity interaction. In this chapter I move beyond the local scale and consider regional interaction between inland and coastal communities that offered opportunities for resource pooling and exchange, activities critical to the prosperity of groups across northern Michigan.

Chapter 3 introduces a series of earthwork enclosures spread from east to west across northern Michigan. The locations of these complexes are shown in figure 5.1. A lack of systematic investigation has hindered understandings of these enclosures. The prevailing interpretation is that they served as fortifications, but the fit between the limited extant data from these sites and that interpretation is problematic. My alternate hypothesis is that earthwork complexes were ceremonial monument centers used to ensure regional and external cultural processes.

A multiyear research program at one of these enclosure complexes, the Missaukee Earthworks site (20MA11–12) (fig. 5.1), demonstrates that it was a purposefully designed and constructed and coherent ritual precinct that served as a regionally important ceremonial monument center, drawing together disparate communities during Late Prehistory (site dated to ca. A.D. 1200–1420). The ritual practices at Missaukee left patterned material traces that were readily interpretable as ritual in origin because ritual has a practiced component, according to theorists from multiple and disparate schools of thought (from Durkheim [1976 (1912)] to Tambiah [1985: 128], to Geertz [1973: 90], to Rappaport [1999: 24] to Grimes [1982], formalized by Bell [1992]). Connections with Anishinaabeg ethnohistory enhance interpretation of the site, but a good understanding of its ritual use was obtained first from material remains.

The systematic research program at the Missaukee Earthworks (20MA11–12) opens new avenues for understanding the role that this entire cluster of enclosures played in the regional network of Late Prehistory. Drawing on systematic material and ethnohistoric investigations at Missaukee, I position all of these northern earthworks in their regional ritual context (see chapter 6). First, however, we visit a site located on top of a glacial esker in Missaukee County, Michigan. Today most would consider this the middle of nowhere, yet this place held profound social and spiritual significance in the centuries preceding European contact.

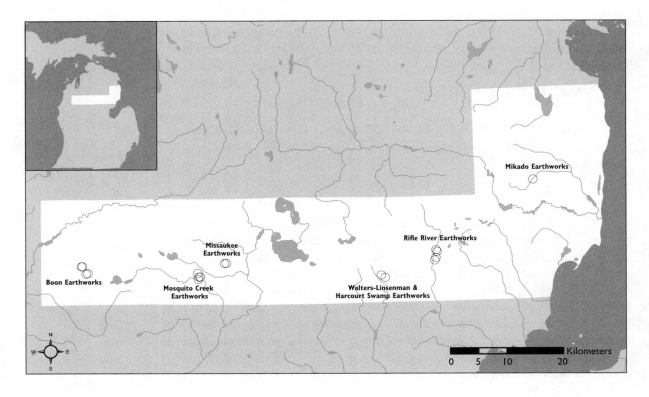

Figure 5.1. The series of six earthwork site complexes in the northern landscape. From west to east: the Boon Earthworks, Mosquito Creek (Boven/Falmouth) Earthworks, Missaukee Earthworks, Walters-Linsenman and Harcourt Swamp Earthworks, Rifle River Earthworks, and Mikado Earthwork.

Situating the Missaukee Earthworks Site (20MA11–12)
Site Location, Limited Resource Profile, and Cultural Features

The Missaukee Earthworks site consists of a pair of circular ditch and bank structures in Aetna Township, Missaukee County, Michigan (22NR06W) (fig. 5.2). The site is located in the High Plains of the Lower Peninsula and removed from all major waterscapes, 20 kilometers southwest of Michigan's largest inland lake system, Houghton Lake (80 square kilometers) and Higgins Lake (39 square kilometers), and 8 kilometers west of the Muskegon River. No major aquatic resources are in the site's proximate resource profile.

State Soil Geographic Database (STATSGO) identifies the soil at the Missaukee Earthworks site as Rubicon-Graycalm-Montcalm (these are excessively drained sandy soils that occur on glacial features). With such soils, at a site located far from any major water source and unsheltered from the High Plains' short growing season, maize agriculture would not have been a viable activity. The sandy soils of this glacial esker hosted a white pine–mixed hardwood forest prior to historic lumbering (Comer et al. 1995). The broader vicinity of the site (5 kilometers) contained beech-sugar maple-hemlock forest and conifer swamp (Comer et al. 1995). With no large stands of nut-bearing trees documented, the resource offerings of these forests would have been limited to large terrestrial mammals like bears, deer, and elk and smaller mammals like rabbits and woodchucks and a variety of birds.

The limited resource profile for the Missaukee Earthworks (20MA11–12) stands in sharp contrast to the Cut River Mounds site (20RO1) discussed in chapter 4. Unlike Cut River, the Missaukee Earthworks site is in an area with a low diversity

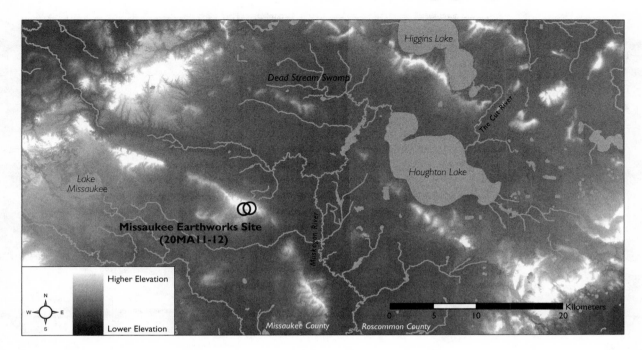

of resource offerings and lacks a seasonally abundant resource base. That location probably would not have been a prime focus of any community's seasonal procurement. This contrast suggests that these earthworks served a different role in the landscape of Late Prehistory.

The position of the earthworks in the landscape has other distinguishing characteristics. Figure 5.2 shows the area's Digital Elevation Model (DEM), indicating that the site was on top of one of the landscape's highest features, a glacial esker. At the top of this esker is a shallow, basin-shaped area (fig. 5.3). The circular ditch and embankment earthen enclosures here were constructed 653.5 meters apart on an east-west line. An unusual upland spring and adjoining wetland lie in this basin immediately southwest of the eastern earthwork.

Each enclosure featured two planned entryways composed of an approximately two-meter-wide breach in the embankment and a raised platform running from the breach across the ditch onto flat land outside the enclosure. One opening on each enclosure roughly aligns with the other, and the second opening on each aligns in the same northwest direction (the azimuth of the western one is 336 degrees and of the eastern one 334 degrees; Marshall 1990; fig. 5.3). The westernmost earthwork was assigned state site number 20MA11 and has a diameter of 48 meters. A large boulder sits in the center of this enclosure. The easternmost earthwork, assigned state site number 20MA12, has a diameter of 53 meters. Although they enclose a similar amount of space, the ditch and embankment of this eastern enclosure (20MA12) are both higher and wider than those of the western enclosure (20MA11).

The site includes addition components. Small, circular burial mounds are located symmetrically at opposite ends of the site: two northeast of the eastern earthwork and one south of the western earthwork (Greenman 1927b; fig. 5.3).[1] The area also contains hundreds of abandoned subterranean cache (storage) pits. Some occur in

Figure 5.2. Position of the Missaukee Earthworks in the landscape shown on a Digital Elevation Model. Note that the site is positioned away from major water resource features as well as built atop of one of the highest features in the landscape, a glacial esker.

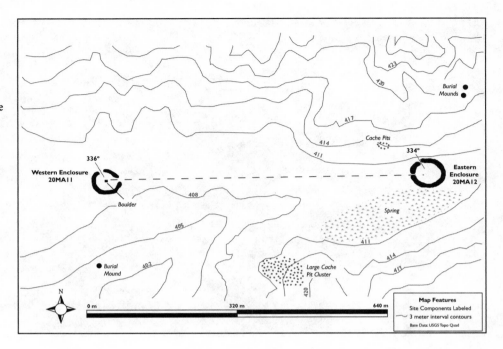

Figure 5.3. Topographic details of the Missaukee Earthworks site on the glacial esker and major site components.

small clusters of 4 to 10 pits, while a large concentration of more than 100 pits is located in the central portion of the site (Greenman 1926: 2).

Looking Inside: Previous Investigations

Two professional archaeology teams worked at the Missaukee Earthwork site prior to the recent multiyear investigation that I co-led through the University of Michigan Museum of Anthropology (UMMA). Emerson Greenman, leading a UMMA expedition, worked at the site in 1925 and 1926. Charles Cleland, leading a Michigan State University field school, worked at Missaukee in 1965. Both teams focused their investigations inside the two enclosures. Their excavations revealed no palisade and only light debris. No habitation structures were found inside either enclosure.[2]

In his 1926 season Greenman found an inverted ceramic vessel in the east gate of the western enclosure (20MA11) (Greenman 1926: 5–6, fig. 5.4). He also excavated the conical mound located southwest of the western earthwork (Greenman 1927b). He found a single cremated body buried with a bundle that contained a layer of bark about half an inch (1.25 centimeters) thick encasing a copper ceremonial axe.[3] Materials collected during Greenman's mound excavation were dated when radiometric dating was invented in the 1950s, producing a date of 750 ± 150 B.P., reported by Fitting (1975) as 1200 ± A.D. (M-790; the calibrated range of this date using the intcal04 curve is A.D. 1070–1320; table 5.1). Greenman also excavated some of the cache pits in the large concentration. All of these were empty (Greenman 1926: 2).

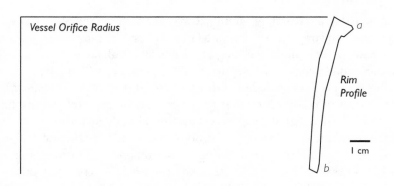

Figure 5.4. Ceramic vessel (Greenman 1926) found inverted in the east entrance to 20MA11.

TABLE 5.1. RADIOMETRIC DATES CITED IN DISCUSSION OF MISSAUKEE EARTHWORKS (20MA11–12)

Dated item	Conventional radiocarbon date	Calibrated date
Bulk Charcoal, Burial Mound southwest of 20MA11, collected by Greenman, reported by Fitting (1975), date number M-790	750 ± 150 B.P.	A.D. 1200 ± 75
Ceramic Vessel Residue, Station B (east of 20MA12) AMS	600 ± 40 B.P.	A.D. 1290–1420

Thinking Outside the Circle: Recent Investigations

Although the Missaukee Earthworks site was built on a larger, more permanent, and more elaborate scale than other sites in northern Michigan, previous excavations showed only what Missaukee was not—a defensive or habitation site—and failed to produce any strong conclusions about its function. The ceremonial copper axe and the inverted ceramic vessel are tidbits of evidence that point to a different explanation: ritual use. The multiyear investigation that I co-ran broadened the focus of inquiry and examined the space outside of the earthwork circles. This was the first time that a research program had systematically examined the space surrounding any earthwork enclosure in the Great Lakes. The purpose of this program was to develop a fresh understanding of the site and evaluate its role in the social, economic, and ideological developments of the period in which it was created.

Our field program included a cross section of the western enclosure to understand the process of construction and to confirm previous investigations' findings. Our work involved systematic shovel testing around both enclosures to evaluate the use of the space and to follow up excavations in areas with positive shovel tests.

The information recovered through this multiphased research program indicates that the Missaukee Earthworks site was a structured ritual precinct for periodic aggregations of coastal fisher-horticulturalists and inland foragers during Late Prehistory (ca. A.D. 1200–1420; table 5.1). The following discussion presents these findings (additional details can be found in Howey 2006 and Howey and O'Shea 2006).

The Enclosures: Ceremonial Constructions

The most prominent features at the Missaukee Earthworks site are obviously the two circular enclosures, mounded embankments ringed on the outside by a ditch. As discussed above, the previous excavations inside the enclosures demonstrated that they were not fortifications or habitation structures. These attributes point to a unique, nonroutine role for these constructions. A further analysis of their location, design, and construction suggests that these structures were ceremonial monuments. A comparison of ceramic vessels from inside and outside the enclosures indicates that these constructions defined a specific ritual space. The inside of the enclosures appears to be the locus of distinct ritual activities.

Enclosure Location

Evidence indicates that the location of these enclosures was intentional. The limited resource profile discussed above would have made this locale a neutral space, not claimed by one group or another and thus suitable for a regional crowd in the territorial setting of Late Prehistory. Other physical traits made it an ideal location for a significant regional ceremonial precinct. The shallow basin–shaped area on top of this esker offered an isolated, protected space well suited for the construction of a coherently organized site (fig. 5.3). While the basin provided isolation, the esker's general topographic prominence in the landscape would also have made it easy to remember and relocate, suggesting that it had a special and significant function in the regional landscape (fig. 5.2).

The easternmost enclosure was built next to the spring (fig. 5.3) that occurs in an upland area where it would not be expected. This location suggests that this was not an arbitrary decision. Springs have been widely documented as important natural features within Anishinaabeg mythology, viewed as portals between the dangerous underworld and living world (Copway 1980 [1851]: 133; see also Cleland 1992: 71; Hoffman 1891: 166; Landes 1968; fig. 5.5). The position of one of the enclosures next to this spring highlights the ritual character of these enclosures and their surrounding landscape. The large boulder in the center of the western enclosure appears to be another intentional aspect of this location (fig. 5.3).[4]

Bad spring under earth.

Figure 5.5. Image of a spring from Anishinaabeg pictographs, showing their association with danger recorded by Ojibwa scholar George Copway (1980 [1851]: 133).

The alignment of each enclosure's two planned entryways indicates that they were purposefully designed to link the two enclosures together and orient them both to something important lying to the northwest at 334–36 degrees (fig. 5.3).

Enclosure Construction

These enclosures were built on a larger and more elaborate scale than anything else in the landscape. Previous excavations inside the enclosures suggested that they were not built to serve as fortifications. To confirm this and understand the process of enclosure construction, we excavated a cross section on the western enclosure (20MA11). This cross section ran 10 meters from inside the enclosure to a location beyond the ditch. To minimize damage to the enclosure, the cross section was done by cutting back an existing cut in the enclosure, a trench from Greenman's 1926 excavations (backdirt from this trench still lies on top of the earthwork embankment).

The cross section confirms that this enclosure is a ditch-and-embankment structure. The embankment is 4 meters wide and 0.5 meters high at its maximum. Dirt was removed from a ditch, piled upon the extant ground beside it, and mounded and spread to form a humped embankment. The ditch has a shallow U shape, being 2 meters wide and 1 meter deep at its maximum depth. This construction process indicates that the enclosure was built in a single episode rather than accumulatively.

No palisade was found on top of this enclosure, which corresponds with Greenman's findings (Greenman 1926). Thus the enclosures were not defensive structures.

During the cross-sectioning excavations, all removed dirt was screened. Only one artifact, a single ceramic sherd, was recovered. It came from the ditch and indicates two important things: (1) the earthwork was not constructed upon or with previous occupation debris; and (2) the ditch was not a repository for trash. These were clean constructions both during the process, when clean materials were used, and after, when the ditch was explicitly maintained.

Together the enclosures' topographic location and the cross-sectional data demonstrate that Late Prehistoric communities selected the glacial esker location for its favorable natural and topographic elements. The material evidence indicates that a large amount of planning, design, labor, and maintenance went into the enclosures themselves, showing that these enclosures had a definite and special purpose. Further, these precisely oriented circular enclosures were a distinctive referent of some kind, because this form was repeated across the regional landscape (fig. 5.1;

see also chapter 6). These facts strongly suggest that the enclosures were designed to be ceremonial monuments.

Ceramics Inside versus Outside Enclosures: Material Evidence of a Division in Ritual Space

Comparison of ceramic vessels used and deposited inside the enclosure space (both enclosures) with those used and deposited outside the enclosures (all vessels recovered in shovel testing and excavations outside enclosures) adds a new dimension to the assertion that these were ritual constructions. This comparison indicates that the enclosures divided space at the site: different activities occurred inside and outside them.[5]

Through a minimum count based on diagnostic ceramics from the three professional excavation projects at the Missaukee Earthworks site (20MA11–12) 85 vessels were identified. All of the ceramic vessels from inside the two enclosures came from Greenman and Cleland's excavations, while all of the vessels outside the enclosures came from the work by UMMA. Minimum vessel count was based on diagnostics and provenience. At least 16 vessels were recovered inside the eastern enclosure (20MA12) and 20 vessels from inside the western enclosure (20MA11). Although 3 vessels from inside excavations were identified and analyzed, their specific enclosure provenience has been lost. The remaining 46 vessels were recovered in our recent work outside the enclosures.

Ceramic Wares Before proceeding with the comparison of the functional and decorative attributes of vessels from inside and outside the enclosures, we need to examine the spread of ceramic wares in the assemblage. Table 5.2 shows that the ceramic vessels recovered across the site can be divided into (1) distinctly known Late Prehistoric coastal wares; (2) Late Prehistoric import wares; (3) vessels fitting "White Bird ware," distinguished by Late Prehistoric traits observed on vessels from interior sites (discussed in chapter 3; see also table 5.3); and (4) vessels not fitting into any known category but showing some admixture of Late Prehistoric ceramic traits. This mix of vessel wares and decorative attributes indicates that Missaukee drew coastal groups as well as interior groups.

Distinct coastal wares recovered across Missaukee are predominantly from one region: Traverse ware from northwestern Michigan around present-day Traverse City (table 5.2; see also Hambacher 1992). Juntunen ware, well-defined along Lake Huron, occurs much less frequently. The trend of one specific coastal ware forming the majority of represented coastal wares is repeated at the other enclosure sites in this northern earthwork cluster and varies based on geography: Missaukee, which is closer to the tribal territory of Traverse ware producers, has more Traverse ware, while sites closer to Lake Huron and the tribal territory of Juntunen producers have more Juntunen wares (see chapter 6 for more on this geographic patterning).

Ceramic Function All but one of the vessels recovered at the site were jars, and the average orifice diameter did not significantly differ between those found inside and outside the enclosure. The exception was a small undecorated bowl or cup recovered by Cleland (1965) inside the western enclosure (20MA11). While only one has

TABLE 5.2. SUMMARY OF MISSAUKEE (20MA11–12) DESIGNATED WARES

	Traverse ware	Juntunen ware	Other wares (imports)	"White Bird Ware" (Interior late traits)	Mixture late traits (not securely one ware)
Number of jars	17	3	2	15	48
% of jars	20%	3.5%	2.4%	17.6%	56.5%

TABLE 5.3. SUMMARY OF 15 VESSELS SHOWING "WHITE BIRD WARE" INTERIOR TRAITS

	Channel	Protruding lip	Finger decoration	Cord-Marked exterior surface
Number of jars	6	11	5	4

Note: These traits are increasingly observed on Late Prehistoric vessels from interior sites (see chapter 3).

been recovered, the presence of this unique vessel form (typically used in serving rather than in food preparation or storage) inside an enclosure suggests that activities occurred in this space that did not occur outside.

The presence or absence of residues on Late Prehistoric vessels has been shown to relate to their functions (Milner 1998: 178). Jars were typically used for two main functions: storage and food preparation (O'Shea and Milner 2002: 214). While vessels can be used in a multitude of functions over time (see Skibo 1992), the presence of charred residues suggests involvement in food preparation or consumption. The observed pattern of residues indicates that ceramics used and deposited inside the enclosures were involved in one or both of these functions (table 5.4).

Considering these patterns and the presence of a serving vessel (a bowl/cup) from inside 20MA11, perhaps food consumption rather than preparation occurred inside the enclosures. This suggestion, as well as all conclusions about activities related to food, must be considered tentative, because no floral or faunal remains were recovered inside the enclosures (Cleland 1965; Greenman 1926) and only a handful of faunal remains were recovered outside. Nonetheless, the residue patterns reflect a difference in the way ceramics deposited inside and outside the enclosures were used.

Ceramic Decoration Explicit differences in decoration marked the ceramics used and deposited inside and outside the enclosures at the Missaukee Earthworks site.

TABLE 5.4. RESIDUE ON CERAMIC VESSELS INSIDE VERSUS OUTSIDE ENCLOSURES

	Inside enclosures	Outside enclosures
Residue	19	6
	48.7%	13.0%
No residue	20	40
	51.3%	87%
Fisher's Exact Test	p-value = .001	

Specifically, vessels inside the enclosures had more overall decoration than those recovered outside. Certain decorative techniques were utilized primarily, and in some cases exclusively, for vessels employed in activities or disposed of inside the enclosures. In contrast, no decorative technique was exclusive to vessels outside the enclosures.

The proportion of vessels with exterior decoration is much greater inside the enclosures; 48.7% of vessels from inside have exterior decoration, compared with only 30.4% of vessels found outside (table 5.5). All of the vessels with exterior decoration recovered outside have only simple (one element) decoration. In comparison, 10.5% of the decorated vessels inside enclosures have complex (more than one element) decoration. While neither of these distinctions is significant at the .05 level, they seem suggestive of more decoration being acceptable (or required) for vessels involved in activities inside the enclosures.

The proportions of exterior decorative element spacing are significantly different: 73.7% of the exteriorly decorated vessels recovered inside the enclosures and 35.7% of those recovered outside have wide element spacing (table 5.5). One interesting technique of exterior decoration is present only on vessels from inside the enclosures: punctates made from a bunched cord. The punctate impression on the exterior of the vessel was made by crumpling a single cord between the fingers and pushing it into the clay. This technique is noticeably different from other punctate techniques because it creates a textured mark from the ridged, wound nature of the cord rather than a plain, smooth punctate.

Overall, punctates are a more common decorative technique on vessels from inside the enclosures. Around three-quarters of exterior decorated vessels from inside are decorated with punctates, while only a little more than a third from outside have punctates (table 5.5). Of vessels with punctates from inside the enclosures, 50% were punctated with bunched cord. None of the punctated vessels outside the enclosures were made with this technique. The exclusive presence of bunched cord punctates inside the enclosures is statistically significant.

Lip decoration is more frequent on vessels inside the enclosures. Over three-quarters of these vessels have lip decoration, while over half of vessels found outside have lip decoration (table 5.5). Significantly more vessels from inside have both lip and exterior decoration: 39.5% compared with 11.1% of vessels outside. The ceramics found inside and outside the enclosures differed significantly in the frequency of combined lip and exterior decoration on a vessel.

Discussion of Ceramics from Inside and Outside Enclosures The decorative analysis did not find a rigid distinction between the kinds of elements on ceramics used and deposited inside and outside the enclosures. But when the patterns in decorative differences are considered collectively, these elements would have had a significant impact on the visual appearance of vessels being used inside and outside. The inside vessels produce an impression of fanciness that is lacking on those recovered outside. The difference would have been perceptible to the participants in the distinct activities in these two spheres and must have been appreciated and chosen in the ritual production process. Certain decorative patterns were acceptable primarily for vessels used and deposited inside the enclosures. This provides evidence of a

TABLE 5.5. DECORATIVE FEATURES ON CERAMIC VESSELS INSIDE VERSUS OUTSIDE ENCLOSURES

	Inside enclosures		Outside enclosures		
	No.	%	No.	%	p-value[a]
Exterior decoration	19	48.7	14	30.4	.118
No exterior decoration	20	51.3	32	69.6	
Complex exterior decoration (2+ elements)	2	10.5	0	0.496[b]	
Simple exterior decoration (1 element)	17	89.5	14	100	
Wide spacing	14	73.7	5	35.7	.029[b]
Not wide spacing	5	26.3	9	64.3	
Exterior decorated with punctates	14	73.7	5	35.7	.148[b]
Exterior decorated not with punctates	5	26.3	9	64.3	
Cord punctates	7	50	0	0.013[c]	
No cord punctates	7	50	6	100	
Lip decoration	29	76.3	25	55.6	.065
No lip decoration	9	23.7	20	44.4	
Lip and exterior decoration	15	39.5	5	11.1	.004
No lip and exterior decoration	23	60.5	40	88.9	

[a] Fisher's Exact Test.
[b] On vessels with exterior decoration.
[c] On vessels with punctate exterior decoration.

formality and set of rules applied to the amount and type of decoration appropriate for them and demonstrates that the enclosures created a distinction in ritual space.

It is conceivable that ritual space inside the enclosures was distinct from the space outside because these vessels were involved in formal presentation and consumption events inside. The functional differences between the vessels used and deposited inside and outside the enclosures indicate that the serving/consumption of food may have been an aspect of the activity inside the enclosures.

Discussion of the Enclosures

The enclosures themselves, their location, their construction, and the ceramic vessels used and deposited inside them indicate that these structures were precisely designed, carefully maintained, and linked ceremonial constructions that created a large division in the ritual space at the site. They enclosed one distinct ritual space inside and defined another outside. Our investigation of the space outside the enclosures (discussed below) suggests that these structures anchored a larger ritual precinct around them. The work outside the enclosures reveals in more detail the regional draw of the site. Not only the enclosures but also the entire site were precisely planned and highly structured. Outside ritual space was further divided, prescribing different rituals in spatially segregated locales.

Outside the Enclosures: A Prescribed Use of Space

To evaluate the space outside the Missaukee enclosures, a 100 by 100 meter grid system was defined around both enclosures. A systematic stratified unaligned sampling scheme was used to place one shovel test in every 10 by 10 meter square in each 100 by 100 meter grid or sampling stratum (fig. 5.6). Strata inside and on the enclosures were excluded. Around the eastern earthwork (20MA12), four complete 100 by 100 meter grids and one 50 by 100 meter grid were tested. Around the western earthwork (20MA11), four complete 100 by 100 meter grids were tested.

This extensive shovel testing revealed a pattern of concentrated and localized activity (fig. 5.6). Small clusters of dense cultural debris were separated by extensive areas with no debris. This pattern of discrete dense cultural debris areas, separated by large areas devoid of material, demonstrates a structured and prescribed use of space in the area outside of the earthworks.

Excavations were conducted in two locations high in cultural debris outside of the eastern enclosure (20MA12): one on a rise to the northwest of the earthwork (A) and another west of the entrance to the earthwork and near the upland spring (B) (fig. 5.6). Excavations were also conducted in two locations high in cultural debris outside of the western enclosure (20MA11): one south of the enclosure (C) and another on a rise to the northwest (D), in a position similar to excavation area A outside of the eastern enclosure.

Figure 5.6. Shovel test survey grids and excavations outside the enclosures at the Missaukee Earthworks site (20MA11–12). A, B, C, and D represent the location of excavations conducted in high-density cultural material zones identified during shovel testing (note: these are not scalar representations of excavated areas).

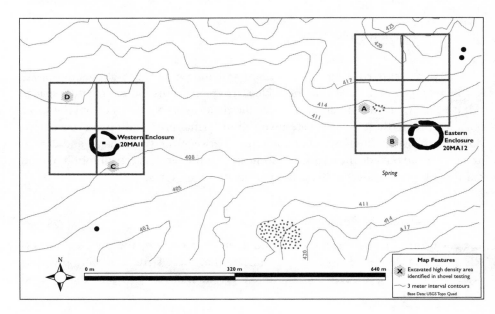

A new radiometric date was run on materials recovered in these excavations, which dated the activities outside the enclosures to Late Prehistory, 600 ± 40 B.P., calibrated to A.D. 1290–1420 (table 5.1; this corresponds with the date from Greenman's 1926 excavations). The excavation data and analyses of cultural materials from these four dense debris loci (see the discussion below) indicate that these spatially bounded activity areas outside the earthworks had distinctive functions as well. They were discrete activity-specific stations.

Excavations at Four Outside Stations

Station A Station A is located on the rise northwest of the eastern earthwork (fig. 5.6). In all 50 square meters were excavated here. The excavations revealed an abrupt falloff in the scatter of cultural remains, with debris limited to an area of 6 by 7 meters. This limited distribution suggests the presence of a small structure or enclosed space.

No floral or faunal remains were recovered. No cultural features indicative of cooking were found. The ceramic assemblage recovered had a minimum vessel count of 20 jars, none with residue. No artifacts (such as grinding stones) indicative of food preparation were recovered. This station shows no evidence of food preparation or consumption. It is unique among the other stations, however, because it is clearly linked with storage features. A cluster of cache pits is located immediately east of the cultural debris area (fig. 5.6).

Station B Station B is located west of the entrance to the eastern earthwork, near the unusual upland spring (fig. 5.6). In all 60 square meters were excavated here. While less abrupt and striking than at Station A, cultural debris here also had a tight distribution and distinct fall-off, restricted to an area of 8 by 7 meters.

This was the only outside station to produce an in situ cultural feature, a series of reused hearths. The hearths themselves were superimposed, resulting in the loss of their individual form, but it is clear that abundant fire cracked rock (FCR) associated with different hearth use episodes had been removed and placed to the north-northwest of the burnt hearth pit (fig. 5.7).

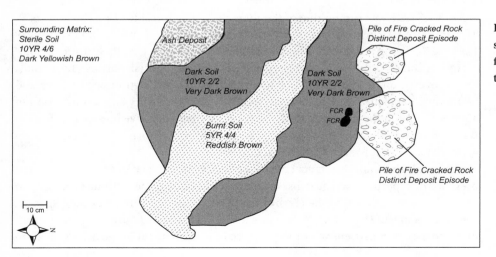

Surrounding Matrix:
Sterile Soil
10YR 4/6
Dark Yellowish Brown

Ash Deposit

Pile of Fire Cracked Rock
Distinct Deposit Episode

Dark Soil
10YR 2/2
Very Dark Brown

Dark Soil
10YR 2/2
Very Dark Brown

Burnt Soil
5YR 4/4
Reddish Brown

FCR
FCR

Pile of Fire Cracked Rock
Distinct Deposit Episode

10 cm

N

Figure 5.7. Plan of superimposed hearths found in Station B outside the eastern enclosure.

TABLE 5.6. COMPARISON OF FCR DENSITIES AT OUTSIDE STATIONS A, B, AND C

	Station A	Station B	Station C
FCR weight density	.061 kg/liter	.073 kg/liter	.008 kg/liter
Avg. weight per piece of FCR	94.3 g	47.06 g	156.34 g
FCR count density	.065 pieces/liter	.156 pieces/liter	.005 pieces/liter

TABLE 5.7. COMPARISON OF CERAMIC RESIDUE AT OUTSIDE STATIONS A, B, AND C

	Station A	Station B	Station C
Residue	0	3	3
	0%	15.0%	100%
No residue	20	17	0
	100%	85.0%	0%

Note: Too many cells with expected values less than 5 to run significance test.

The density of FCR across Station B is 0.073 kg/liter, 0.012 kg/liter higher than at Station A and 0.065 kg/liter higher than in the excavation area south of the western enclosure, Area C (table 5.6). In addition to the higher weight density, Station B has notably more pieces of FCR per liter of excavated soil than Station A, and the average weight of the FCR is much lower in area B (47.06 g). These data suggest that FCR was important to the activity conducted in Station B and that it was used in multiple firing events (FCR shrinks with reuse). This evidence suggesting multiple firings fits with the presence of the superimposed hearths (fig. 5.7).

The remains of a single white mussel shell were recovered, but no other faunal or floral remains were associated with these hearths (or elsewhere in the station). Further, the ceramic assemblage recovered in Station B represents a minimum count of 20 jars, and only 3 (15%) have residue (table 5.7). Again, residue indicates that a vessel was involved in food preparation or consumption. These patterns suggest that the main function of these hearths was not cooking food and that this shell was not a food deposit.

An AMS date was run on one of the three vessels with residue (fig. 5.8; table 5.1). This produced a conventional radiocarbon date of 600 ± 40 B.P., calibrated to A.D. 1290–1420, dating the activities in the outside stations to the Late Prehistoric period.

Station B also produced a category of nonstandard, special-purpose lithic tools not recovered anywhere else at the site: modified blades. Two utilized blades and two retouched blades were recovered. While these form a very small proportion of all tools found in the outside station excavations, their exclusive presence in Station B is noteworthy. These blades are a unique, specialized tool form; their presence suggests that a nonroutine activity occurred there.

The small, abundant fire-cracked rock at Station B, the lack of food remains, the presence of superimposed hearths, specialized lithics, and the station's proximity to the spring and entrance to the earthwork suggest a function that was both specialized and recurrent (fig. 5.6). While no clear evidence of a structure was observed, all our evidence is consistent with the presence of a small sweat lodge at this location

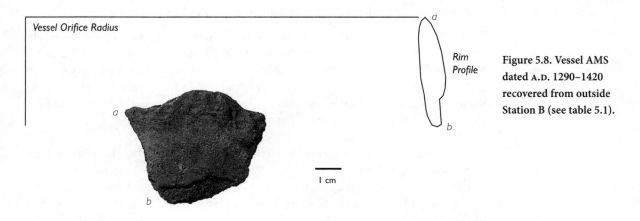

Figure 5.8. Vessel AMS dated A.D. 1290–1420 recovered from outside Station B (see table 5.1).

(these finds adhere closely to the archaeological expectations for a sweat lodge developed in Mehta [2008]). Considering its position outside the entrance to one of the enclosures and near the spring (which, as noted above, has a connotation of danger in Anishinaabeg mythology), the presence of a purification station perhaps used as people entered or exited from the activities in the enclosure is plausible.

Station C Station C is located south of the western enclosure (fig. 5.6). While 25 square meters were excavated here, cultural materials were restricted to only five units in a space 2 meters wide and 3 meters long. Although no food remains were recovered, the cultural materials suggest that cooking may have occurred there.

Ceramic density at Station C (0.027 kg/liter) is five times higher than around the eastern enclosure (A and B, both 0.005 kg/liter). At least three jars were recovered at this station. Both jars with a measurable orifice diameter had a diameter of 34 centimeters. These jars have a higher average and a larger orifice diameter than any jar recovered in Station A and B. All three of the vessels recovered at Station C had residue (table 5.7). While limited, this pattern of 100% of the vessels with residue is still notably different than at the other stations, where no vessels have residue (Station A) or only 15% have residue (Station B).

A possible grinding stone (an artifact type that is directly associated with food preparation) was recovered. Even though we conducted more extensive excavations in Station A and B, no grinding stones were found. Also, no lithics were recovered at Station C. The evidence suggests that this station was used for cooking, although no food remains were encountered.

Station D Station D is located on a rise northwest of the western earthwork (D), in a position similar to Station A outside of the eastern enclosure (fig. 5.6). Only seven 1 by 1 meter units were excavated here, because we discovered that this area had been damaged by historic plowing. Thus little can be said about it. But the lithics, while few, have a raw material profile (discussed below) indicating that the events in this area were distinct from those at the other outside stations. This further highlights that these spatially discrete areas outside the enclosures indeed formed distinct activity-specific stations within the ritual precinct.

Perspectives from the Lithic Assemblage of the Stations

The lithic assemblage recovered across the systematic excavations outside the enclosures offers further insights into the regional draw and specialized use of the Missaukee Earthworks site. In all 1,358 lithics were recovered in the four outside stations. Of these, 784 were recovered from Station A; 544 from Station B; and 30 from Station D. Station C produced no lithics. Most of the lithic materials were flakes and shatter. Lithic objects were evenly distributed across the stations.

Overall Trends in Raw Materials and Lithic Production Overall, the lithic assemblage is dominated by local glacial material (table 5.8), but three primary cherts from coastal regions are also present in notable proportions. Norwood, Bayport, and Northern Gray occur in roughly equal proportions and together form over 30% of the assemblage (see fig. 3.2 for their outcrop locations). The lithic production data (tool distribution and cortex patterns) discussed below show that these coastal cherts entered the site predominantly in an already processed form, often as finished tools. Considered in this light, 30% becomes an even more substantial figure: it was not produced from the reduction of large chunks of unworked nodules but through maintenance of already crafted lithic tools. The presence of these materials, which were transported a considerable distance from three distinct coastal regions (Norwood about 120 kilometers from northwestern Michigan, Northern Gray a similar distance from northeastern Michigan, and Bayport about 100 kilometers from the southeast), suggests that the Missaukee Earthworks site drew people from the coastal regions. The patterns of raw material transport and lithic production are further evidence of the geographic draw and specialized use of the site.[6]

A total of 141 modified lithic objects, forming 10.4% of the outside station assemblage, were recovered, and these tools were only found in Stations A and B. The majority of the tools were utilized or retouched flakes (table 5.9). Cores formed 23.4% of the tool assemblage; finished tools, including projectile points, other bifaces, and unifaces, composed 16.2%. All projectile points ($n = 14$) recovered were small and triangular, diagnostic of the Late Prehistoric (cf. Shott 1990).

The majority of the finished tools recovered outside the enclosures at Missaukee were made on the Great Lakes coastal primary cherts (table 5.10). Comparatively, over 80% of the cores, which are the by-products of tool production, were made on

TABLE 5.8. GROUPED RAW MATERIAL PROPORTIONS OF MISSAUKEE OUTSIDE STATIONS

Lithic raw material	Count	Percentage of assemblage
Bayport	164	12.1
Norwood	136	10.0
Northern Gray	121	8.9
Glacial	893	65.8
Mercer	1	0.1
Indiana Hornstone	3	0.2
Other	40	2.9
TOTAL	**1,358**	**100**

TABLE 5.9. GROUPED LITHIC ASSEMBLAGE TOOLS OF OUTSIDE STATIONS

Tool type	Count	Percentage of tools
Projectile point	14	9.9
Biface	5	3.6
Uniface	4	2.8
Utilized flake	60	42.6
Retouched flake	16	11.3
Utilized blade	2	1.4
Retouched blade	2	1.4
Core	33	23.4
Core rejuvenation flake	5	3.6
TOTAL	**141**	**100**

glacial material. This difference indicates that coastal cherts were generally not transported to Missaukee in an unworked form. Rather, they were brought as finished tools or in a nearly finished form. Lithic production on these coastal cherts was not primary but was the final stage of tool finishing and retouching maintenance. The pattern of primarily cores of glacial material but few formal, finished tools suggests that local glacial chert (abundant on this esker) was exploited on an as-needed basis.

Patterns in the amount of cortex from outside the stations further support these trends. The amount of cortex from raw materials present in an assemblage is a useful initial indicator of core reduction (Andrefsky 1998; see also chapter 3). Reduction of unworked nodules usually produces more cortical flakes than reduction of partially worked cores or preforms, although raw material geometry can have some influence (Dibble et al. 2005).

Among all the lithics recovered in the outside stations, 33.6% have cortex (table 5.11). When this is considered by material, however, only 12.8% of the primary coastal chert (Bayport, Norwood, and Northern Gray) lithics had cortex; in comparison, 43.8% of glacial raw material lithics had cortex (table 5.12). The higher abundance of glacial cortex paired with the lower abundance of coastal cortex, like the tool data, suggests that primary reduction of glacial raw material nodules occurred on site, while reduction of primary coastal cherts did not.

TABLE 5.10. RAW MATERIAL OF FINISHED TOOLS VERSUS CORES AT OUTSIDE STATIONS

	Finished tools (Projectile points, other bifaces, and unifaces)	**Cores**
Glacial material	8	27
	34.8%	81.8%
Coastal chert	15	6
(Bayport, Norwood, and	65.2%	18.2%
Northern Gray)		
Fisher's Exact Test **p-value < .001**		

TABLE 5.11. GROUPED LITHIC ASSEMBLAGE CORTEX AT OUTSIDE STATIONS

	Count	Percentage of assemblage
Cortex	456	33.6
No cortex	902	66.4
TOTAL	**1,358**	**100**

TABLE 5.12. CORTEX ON GLACIAL VERSUS COASTAL RAW MATERIALS AT OUTSIDE STATIONS

	Cortex	Not cortex
Glacial material	391	502
	43.8%	56.2%
Coastal chert	54	367
(Bayport, Norwood, and Northern Gray)	12.8%	87.2%
Other raw material	11	33
	25%	75%
Pearson Chi-Square $X^2 = 560.33$ $df = 2$ **p-value < .001**		

The evidence that coastal cherts came to the site primarily as formal tools combined with the lower abundance of formal tools on glacial material shows that the tools made on higher-quality coastal materials were designed and selected for specific purposes, such as trade items and important ritual paraphernalia. The overall high proportion of glacial material (and specifically glacial cortex) indicates that locally abundant glacial chert sources were used in the lithic production occurring on site, which consisted predominantly of informal, expedient tool production to fulfill needs arising during activities at the site.

Comparing Lithic Assemblages at Outside Stations The overall outside lithic assemblage at Missaukee contains important information on the regional draw of the site. A comparison of assemblages at each of the outside stations sheds further light on the site attraction as well as the distinctive functions of the stations.

First, the lithic raw material profiles of the three lithic-producing stations A, B, and D differ significantly (table 5.13).[7] Analysis of the two areas excavated around the eastern enclosure (20MA12), Station A and Station B, shows significant differences in the proportion of lithics made on two distinct Michigan chert sources, Bayport chert and Norwood chert (table 5.14; for chert locations, see fig. 3.2). These sources are important, because both varieties are of high quality and were transported a considerable distance (about 120 kilometers for Norwood and about 100 kilometers for Bayport). Station B contains significantly more Bayport chert and less Norwood than Station A. That is, Bayport and Norwood chert occur in inverse proportions in these two stations.

The inverse relationship of these two coastal cherts that outcrop in separate coastal tribal systems, Bayport chert from the Saginaw Bay area and Norwood chert

TABLE 5.13. COMPARISON OF LITHIC RAW MATERIAL PROPORTIONS OF MATERIALS
RECOVERED AT OUTSIDE STATIONS

Lithic raw material	Station A	Station B	Station D
Bayport	65	92	7
	8.6%	17.4%	23.3%
Norwood	112	16	8
	14.8%	3.0%	26.7%
Northern Gray	69	48	4
	9.1%	9.1%	13.3%
Glacial	510	372	11
	67.5%	70.5%	36.7%
TOTAL	**756**	**528**	**30**
	100%	**100%**	**100%**
Pearson Chi-Square	$X^2 = 77.31$ $df = 6$	**p-value < .001**	

Note: Lithic materials recovered at all three stations.

TABLE 5.14. COMPARISON OF BAYPORT VERSUS NORWOOD CHERT AT OUTSIDE
STATIONS A AND B

	Station A	Station B
Bayport chert	65	77
	36.7%	82.8%
Norwood chert	112	16
	63.3%	17.2%
Fisher's Exact Test p-value < .0001		

from northwestern Michigan along northern Lake Michigan, suggests the possibility of some degree of spatial segregation of groups from different regions during ritual activities. This is only speculation, but it opens an interesting line for further research. At the very least, it emphasizes that these stations were the locus of different activities.

As noted above, Station B produced a category of nonstandard, special-purpose lithic tools not recovered anywhere else at the site: modified blades. Station B also shows a significantly higher percentage of bipolar reduction than Station A (table 5.15). The difference could be related to the production of the modified blades. In any case, the difference in tool production strategies again indicates that distinct activities occurred in the outside stations.

While only 30 lithics were recovered from Station D, this assemblage is distinct from that of Stations A and B (table 5.13). It has the lowest proportion of glacial material of the stations, with only 36.7% of the assemblage made on locally abundant glacial till. The rest of the assemblage (63.3%) is composed of Bayport, Norwood, and Northern Gray cherts. This dominance of coastal cherts is significantly different than at Stations A and B. Further, Bayport and Norwood are almost evenly

TABLE 5.15. COMPARISON OF BIPOLAR REDUCTION AT OUTSIDE STATIONS A AND B

	Station A	Station B
Bipolar reduction	109	96
	17.0%	21.8%
No bipolar reduction	533	344
	83.0%	78.2%
Fisher's Exact Test p-value = .049		

Note: On lithics where bipolar reduction or lack of bipolar reduction could be determined.

distributed. While few lithics were recovered overall from Station D, its raw material profile is significantly different than at Stations A and B, which indicates that it was a locus of distinct activity in the ritual precinct.

The Missaukee Earthworks Ritual Precinct

When the information from the enclosures themselves is combined with the data from outside of them, it becomes apparent that the Missaukee Earthworks site was a ritual precinct with a formal, designed, and structured layout. The earthworks, the discrete stations outside of them, the nearby mounds, and the clusters of cache pits were all incorporated into one coherent ritual precinct (fig. 5.9).

As noted above, ritual has a practiced component. Ritual activity typically involves distinctive attributes such as formalism, traditionalism, invariance, rule-governance, sacral symbolism, and performance (Bell 1997: 138). These characteristics, while not exclusive, provide an initial lexicon for considering the ways in which people materially or physically inscribed ritual activities on the landscape at Missaukee.

The cross section of the Missaukee enclosures confirmed that they were not fortifications. Rather, these enclosures were deliberately paired, formally planned, precisely oriented, and actively maintained ceremonial constructions. Formality is the use of a restricted code of behavior. It contrasts with a more open or elaborated code of behavior (Bell 1997: 139). Ritual activity is more formal and more restrictive than other activities. Rule-governance as an attribute of ritual entails complex regulations for the orchestration of activity (Bell 1997: 153). The rule-governance of the ritual practices at the Missaukee site caused the enclosures to be constructed and maintained free from trash, an activity that was readily detectable in the material record. Furthermore, rule-governance and formality were also materialized in decorative differences in the ceramics used inside and outside the enclosures. The comparison of ceramics recovered in the previous excavations inside these enclosures with the vessels recovered in the recent work outside confirmed that the open space inside was the locus of distinct ritual activities, perhaps related to formal consumption and presentation events.

The testing program outside the enclosures revealed a formally structured use of this space as well. Spatially segregated locations with dense cultural debris were separated by areas with absolutely no cultural materials. The excavation of four of these locations and the analysis of the material remains recovered demonstrate that distinct activities occurred in each location. This pattern indicates that these locations formed distinct activity-specific stations within the ritual precinct (fig. 5.9).

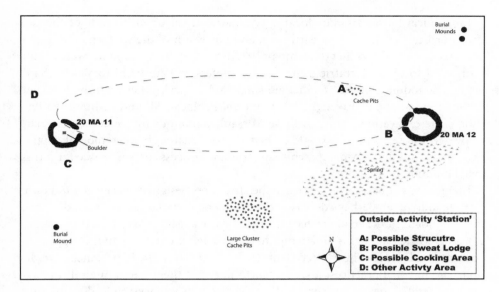

Figure 5.9. Schematic of the coherent ritual precinct of the Missaukee Earthworks site (20MA11–12) developed from the recent archaeological research program.

Invariance, another major attribute of ritual activity, entails a disciplined set of actions marked by precise repetition and control (Bell 1997). Station B, the possible purification station associated with the spring and eastern earthwork, could be interpreted from material remains as a ritual space because of invariance. The repeated use of the hearths and the deposition of FCR in the same direction from the hearths show precise repetition and control of activities. As people moved in or out of the enclosure and past the dangerous spring, they practiced an invariant sequence of actions to ensure personal purification as well as the shared continuation of the liturgical events at the site.

Station C had an almost opposite profile from Station B; the routine activity of cooking seems to have occurred in a restrained space and possibly only once here. Station A had its own unique cultural material patterns and was the only station directly associated with storage features (a cluster of cache pits). This suggests that activities here did not occur at the other stations. Station D has been damaged by historic plowing; but even the limited materials recovered there show that it was distinct from the other three stations.

The precise orientation of the planned entrances to the earthwork enclosures combined with the fixed locations of the outside stations constrained and ordered the cycle of movement throughout the ritual precinct (fig. 5.9). A formal code for movement and a rule-abiding order for the location of ritual activity produced this prescribed arrangement. Movement through the precinct was restricted and explicitly orchestrated. The ritual rounds at the precinct flowed between the two enclosures. People moved into and out of the enclosures through the planned entryways and visited the intervening stations that formed defined stops within the cycle of movement.

The inverted ceramic vessel that Greenman found in the east gate of the western enclosure (20MA11) can now be understood as an important remnant of ritual activity at the site (Greenman 1926: 5–6; fig. 5.4). The pot's placement blocked the flow of the cycle between the two earthworks for either permanent or temporary cessation of the ritual activity.

The conical burial mounds located symmetrically at opposite ends of the site (two northeast of the eastern earthwork and one south of the western earthwork) bounded the ritual precinct (Greenman 1927b; fig. 5.9). Burial mounds were a built form used to create intratribal monument centers in Late Prehistory (see chapter 4). The mounds in the precinct are small and conical rather than the oval, flat mounds found at Cut River (20RO1) and the Papineau Mound in Juntunen territory. The excavation of one of these Missaukee mounds by Greenman (1927b) recovered the remains of a single cremated individual with a ceremonial copper axe. He did not find any comparable construction process such as we see for intratribal mounds.

The mounds at Missaukee appear to be structures designed specifically to house a single individual, perhaps deceased ritual leaders. As testaments to an individual, they bounded (rather than created) the ritual space at Missaukee. Traditionalism as a characteristic of ritual is an attempt to make a set of current activities appear to be linked with older cultural precedents (Bell 1997). Given the importance of traditionalism in ritual practices, it seems fair to interpret these burial mounds as having been built alongside the earthworks to evoke links to ancestral leaders in order to legitimate current activities.

The material remains document the intertribal nature of the site. The presence of coastal wares and ceramics with common interior stylistic attributes reflects Missaukee's role in drawing groups from coastal and inland areas together. The geographic draw of the site was illuminated through a consideration of the lithics recovered outside the enclosures, which showed that coastal groups brought formal tools with them. This suggests that these tools were designed for activities at Missaukee, serving as trade items or important ritual paraphernalia.

The cluster of well over 100 pits on a rise between the earthworks may have been constructed to hold the items that different communities brought to be traded, consumed, or used in the ritual activities (fig. 5.9). All cache pits excavated were empty, so whatever was stored in them was used up or taken away. An obvious explanation is that these storage features held things like foodstuffs and ritual paraphernalia that were used in the ritual practices or served as items for trade as well as provisions used to support the atypical influx of people in this resource-poor setting. It is possible that materials were stored for longer durations, providing a kind of sanctified storage place on the landscape. These storage pits perhaps could have been an emergency reserve for the communities involved in the ritual practices when they faced unexpected and intense moments of resource stress in their annual rounds. Or they could have been off-limit spaces designed to ensure that the appropriate ritual items would be at the site when rites were held. The exact role of these cache pits is not clear at present, but this large cluster again supports the finding that this ritual precinct had to support a large body of people (fig. 5.9).

Missaukee's location in an empty resource zone, its conspicuous position on a glacial esker in the flat landscape (fig. 5.2), the effort and design that went into the construction and orientation of the enclosures, the lack of evidence supporting a habitation/fortification use, and the evidence of ritual activity found in previous excavations originally piqued my interest in evaluating Missaukee's role in the Late Prehistoric. Considering these features in light of the new information from UMMA's research program leads to the conclusion that the Missaukee Earthworks site (20MA11–12) served as a detached intertribal ceremonial monument center for periodic liturgical and trade events between coastal and inland communities in the Late Prehistoric regional network. The ritual order was political, and the economic order and shared ritual inscribed there helped to ensure the continuance of this complicated egalitarian social system.

This constructed ritual center provided a defined, durable, and formal context for periodic aggregations of inland and coastal tribal systems during the Late Prehistoric period (fig. 5.9). Entrenching intersocietal interaction, which provided critical opportunities for resource pooling and exchange, in shared communal ritual or liturgy ensured formality and order. The interaction affirmed that this was a space where individuals could not aggrandize themselves and reduced the potential for hostilities between different communities. A connection with Anishinaabeg ethnohistory (discussed below) suggests that the liturgical events there were not just important but fundamental in the social, economic, and ideological systems of Late Prehistoric ancestral Anishinaabeg communities throughout northern Michigan (Howey and O'Shea 2006).

Bear's Journey and the Missaukee Earthworks Site

The understanding of the Missaukee Earthworks just presented was developed from archaeological data alone. But the serendipitous discovery of a linkage involving ethnohistoric data, the Midewiwin origin tale of Bear's Journey, and the layout of the Missaukee Earthworks site confirms the site's ritual nature and indicates the tremendous significance of the shared religious practices embedded in it. While the details of the argument are available elsewhere (Howey and O'Shea 2006, 2009), a concise description of this linkage is important.

The Midewiwin Ceremonial Complex

The Midewiwin is a ceremonial complex whose importance among the Algonquin-speaking people of the Great Lakes Region was noted frequently throughout the historical era (cf. Copway 1980 [1851]; Densmore 1929; Hoffman 1891; Kidder 1994 [1910]; Kinietz 1947; Landes 1968; Warren 1984 [1885]). The historical Midewiwin was "more than just another ceremony, for it provided an institutional setting for the teaching of the world view (religious beliefs) of the Ojibwa people" (Angel 2002: 48). The Midewiwin ceremony had two main elements: an initiation rite and a healing ritual (Angel 2002: 14).

The Midewiwin Society (Grand Medicine Society) as observed at the end of the nineteenth century consisted of an indefinite number of members (Midé) of both sexes (Hoffman 1891: 164). The society was graded into four or eight distinct degrees (depending on local custom), and members were initiated into and passed through these degrees at semiannual meetings (Densmore 1929).

The Midewiwin ceremonial meetings lasted several days and were directed by "priests" (Mideg), who did most of the singing and speaking. The Mideg had been blessed by the Mide Manidoog (spirits) and were highly educated in Midewiwin origin narratives, sacred teachings, and medicinal practices (Angel 2002: 181). Meetings included both public and private components. The entire community participated in dancing, feasting, and the construction of the Midé Lodge. The execution of religious rituals for Midé candidates was directed by the Mideg and occurred inside the lodge to maintain privacy and exclude noninitiates (Kidder 1994 [1910]: 56).

While these ceremonies within the Midé Lodge were private, a sense of their nature does emerge in the ethnographic and historic accounts. Candidates advanced from one degree to another by giving gifts to older members and by undergoing an initiation involving moral instructions as well as learning the names and uses of medicinal plants and the narratives of the origin and development of the Midé rites (Kidder 1994 [1910]; Landes 1968). Each degree had a specific kind of medicine bag; during the initiation a spirit power was "shot" at a candidate by other Midé members from medicine bags with white shells (mi'gis) (Densmore 1929). Through the power of the mi'gis shot into candidates they became blessed by the Mide Manidoog (spirits) (Angel 2002: 181).

The Mideg kept birch-bark scrolls with diagrams for the conduct of Midewiwin rites and songs as well as the records of the society (Densmore 1929; Hoffman 1891; Landes 1968; Warren 1984 [1885]). These scrolls were critical to the practice and persistence of the Midewiwin and were considered sacred and powerful by the Ojibwas (Landes 1968: 223). Origin narratives were also kept on birch-bark scrolls and were a critical component of the Midewiwin ceremonial complex. The telling of the Midewiwin origin was required at every Midewiwin ceremony. A common account of the origin details Bear as the servant who delivered the great mystery of the Midewiwin (Densmore 1929; Dewdney 1975; Hoffman 1891; Kinietz 1947; Landes 1968; Warren 1984 [1885]).

The Convergence of Ethnohistory and Prehistory

The Bear origin narrative told to Ruth Landes by Will Rogers (Hole-in-the-Sky) at Red Lake reservation near Bemjim, Minnesota, in 1932–33 and the associated sketch of Bear's travels with the Midé pack (Landes 1968: 107; fig. 5.10) provide a detailed comparative ethnohistorical source for the prehistoric Missaukee Earthworks site (Howey and O'Shea 2006). The narrative is as follows:

> Here [A] is where Bear emerged from the Earth's center. Then he went down under the water and came out here [B] at a place called "Big Earth." This is somewhere in the east, where he saw the daylight [eastern quarter of the] world. He reared up [at C] and went down to the ocean [at D]. There he looked north. He saw whitecaps and didn't dare cross. He saw the Point, looked out from it, but discerned nothing. He went to the south Point, saw nothing, and returned to here [D] at the ocean. He touched the water with his right hand, but noticed no effect [on the water's behavior]. He tried his left hand, but it too made no difference. The Great Lion [an evil mighty water monster] happened to be ashore in the south. Bear asked him, "Will you help me? I can't get across." [Lion, characteristically jealous and touchy, was especially so with Bear, resenting his appointment as the Supernatural's emissary.] "Oh, you do want help! You, so brave, so strong!" He touched the water with one hand, and [for he was the great water spirit] it became calm and smooth as glass. Bear said, "Thank you!" He made four steps, and the water did not bend. He thought, "I will go under," and walked along the ocean

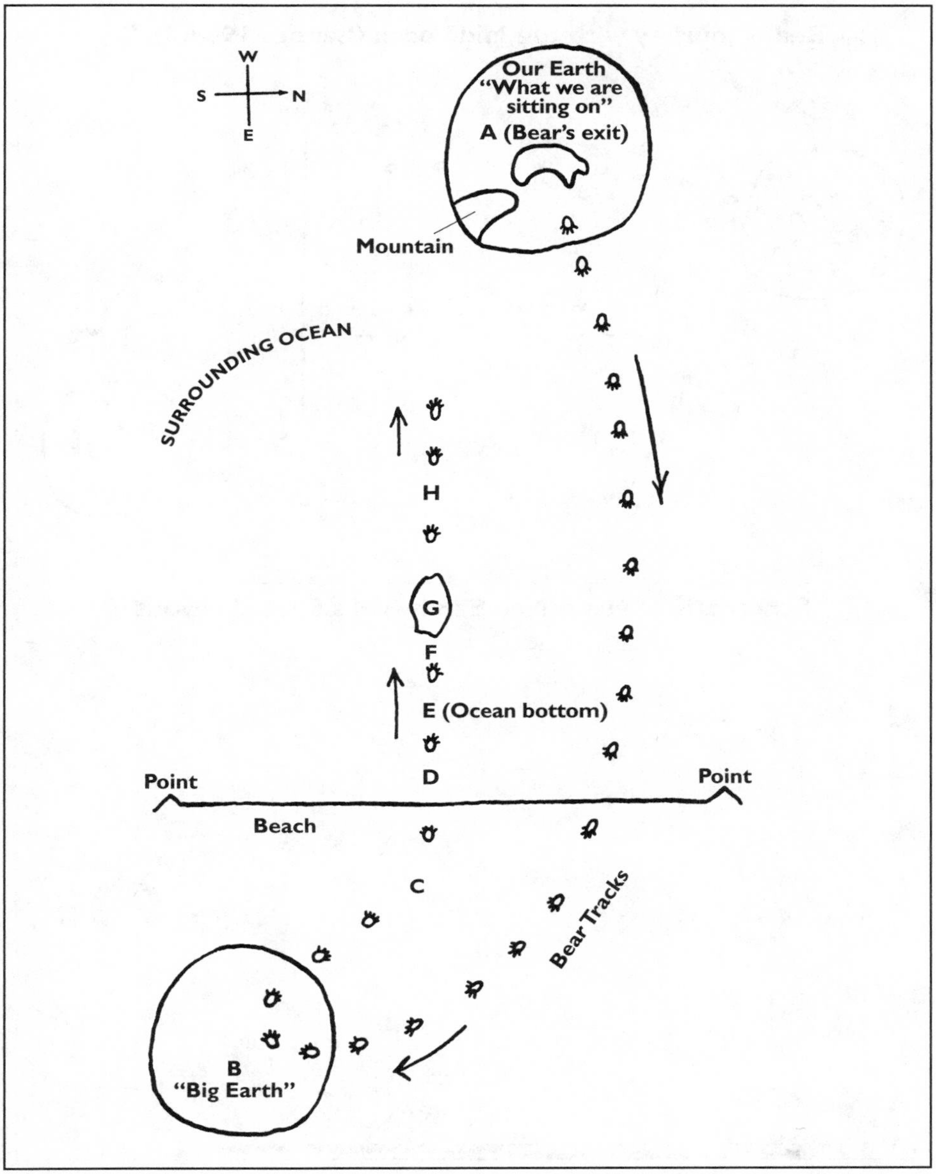
W
S
N
E
Our Earth
"What we are sitting on"
A (Bear's exit)
Mountain
SURROUNDING OCEAN
H
G
F
E (Ocean bottom)
D
Point
Point
Beach
C
Bear Tracks
B
"Big Earth"

Figure 5.10. Diagram of Bear's Journey with the Midé pack used during the teaching of the Midé origin myth as recounted by Will Rogers or Hole-in-the Sky (Landes 1968: 107). It is presented here as it was oriented in the original publication. The original labeling is annotated to facilitate reading (reproduced from Howey and O'Shea 2006).

> bottom [toward E]. After a distance, it looked light so he rose [at F] and saw that it was calm. He saw [G] and took it for a rocky island. Close up, he saw it was manito mig'is [the mystic shell]. He climbed out on it and rolled about and finally stood up. It sounded then as though icicles were clinking on him. [At H] he continued west, swimming atop the ocean. (Landes 1968: 108)

What is particularly striking about the Rogers drawing is the way in which the journey is represented; it encompasses two large circles, with a circular path between them dotted by a series of prescribed stops or locations at which particular events are enacted or recounted (fig. 5.10). The drawing is also a map with a definite axis

Figure 5.11. Comparison of the diagram of Bear's Journey with the Midé pack and a topographically situated schematic of the Missaukee Earthworks ritual precinct site layout. Both figures are oriented north-south. To facilitate reading, the original labeling has been deleted and retyped verbatim (reproduced from Howey and O'Shea 2006).

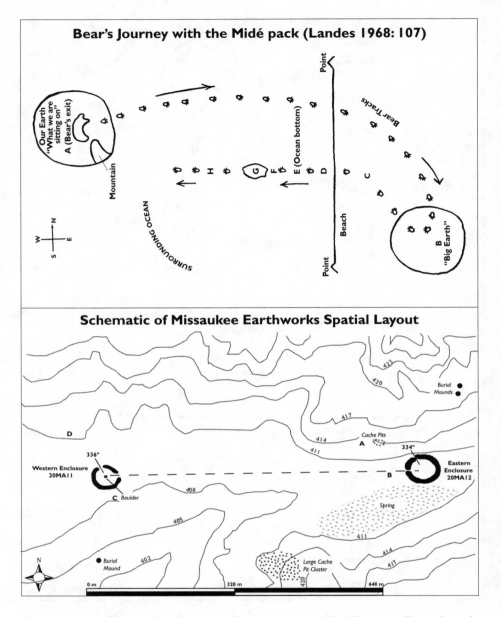

of orientation. This map's role is significant: it is reproduced on scrolls and on the ground for the teaching of the Midewiwin origin narrative, inscribing sacred space for a reenactment of Bear's original journey.

When the Missaukee precinct's plan is compared to the Rogers diagram (fig. 5.11), the similarities are remarkable. The respective size of the circles and the route of travel between them, the location of water, the topographic setting, and even the directional orientation of the features all match. Along the projected pathway between the enclosures are specific activity areas or stations that appear to have been used repeatedly.

The Rogers travel narrative and drawing have other similarities with the layout of the Missaukee Earthworks. Bear begins his travels in a large circle labeled "Our

Earth," "what we are sitting on." Within this sphere is a drawing of a mountain. Bear exits east and travels clockwise to the Big Earth, sketched as another large sphere. At Missaukee a western earthwork (20MA11) has a large boulder in its center (fig. 5.11). The boulder brings a physicality to the enclosure and is possibly an emblem of Our Earth; it is the counterpart of the mountain in the ethnographic drawing. This enclosure has an eastern exit, just as Bear exited east when he left Our Earth. Bear then traveled east to "Big Earth." At Missaukee another enclosure (20MA12) is located east of the western one (20MA11). While the two are similar in diameter, the eastern enclosure is larger, with a diameter of 53 meters versus 48 meters for the western enclosure (Marshall 1990). Moreover, the ditch and embankment of the eastern enclosure is more substantial in both height and width than at the western enclosure. This corresponds with Big Earth lying east of Our Earth, "what we are sitting on," in the ethnohistoric diagram.

Bear's travel continues as he leaves Big Earth to the west and looks into the Surrounding Ocean. He travels to lookout "points" to the north and south of the Surrounding Ocean. Seeing nothing, he returns to the ocean and, with Lion's help, continues west into the Surrounding Ocean. Outside the entrance of the eastern enclosure are the upland spring and the wetland area, which correspond to the location of the Surrounding Ocean. Furthermore, the ground notably rises north and south of the eastern enclosure and the spring (see the topographic detail in fig. 5.11), paralleling the location of the lookout points and the Surrounding Ocean in Bear's Journey.

Throughout Bear's travels from Our Earth, "what we are sitting on," to Big Earth and through the Surrounding Ocean, he stops at specific activity areas or stations, including the ocean bottom. He repeatedly returns to some of these areas. Outside the enclosures we found dispersed activity areas (stations) in a pattern that matches the discrete stops on Bear's Journey (fig. 5.11). We also have archaeological evidence that at least one and probably all of these stations were used repeatedly.

The Missaukee Earthworks site is probably a materialization of the tale of the origin and delivery of the Midewiwin great mystery by the servitor Bear. The Missaukee enclosure precinct was a physical representation of Bear's Journey, rendered on a monumental scale. This archaeologically and ethnohistorically informed understanding of Missaukee opens new avenues for situating the other sites in the cluster of Late Prehistoric earthworks in north-central Michigan.[8]

CHAPTER 6

Pairs and Precincts

Contextualizing the Regional Ritual Landscape of Late Prehistory

The results of the research program at the Missaukee Earthworks for the first time provide a reliable comparative base that archaeologists can use to place other sites in the cluster of Late Prehistoric earthworks spread across the northern Michigan landscape (see fig. 5.1 in the preceding chapter). I believe that these enclosures were interconnected anchors of an intertribal regional ritual circuit inscribed in monumental form across the landscape.

External interaction provides tribal societies with an essential means of resource risk buffering and social vitality (see chapter 1), and intertribal exchange networks are well documented cross-culturally. When economies become more specialized, local social identity develops and resources become overtly claimed (as was happening during Late Prehistory), creating opportunities for aggrandizement or open hostility between disparate communities. These local processes can radically shift egalitarian tribal social orders and threaten the physical and social well-being of communities typically ensured through external interaction. In settings of increasing social difference (alterity), ensuring intertribal interaction can become difficult. During Late Prehistory in the northern Great Lakes, monumental renditions of Bear's Journey in the form of earthwork enclosures with fundamentally important and widely salient symbolism provided the framework for external interaction in the face of growing tribal territoriality across the region.

The comparison between the other northern enclosure sites and Missaukee begins with a summary of previous work at the other enclosures, exploring their shared spatial similarities and comparing ceramic collections from the Missaukee Earthworks, the Rifle River Earthworks, and the Mikado Earthwork. The lack of investigations outside any other enclosure site and the frequently unsystematic and poorly documented nature of the investigations inside enclosures (when conducted) make the emergence of several similarities all the more striking and reinforce my argument that they shared a role.

Situating and Connecting the Northern Earthwork Complexes

Six earthwork complexes are found in northern Michigan. From west to east these are the Boon Earthworks, Mosquito Creek (Boven/Falmouth) Earthworks, Missaukee Earthworks, Walters-Linsenman/Harcourt Swamp Earthworks, Rifle River Earthworks, and Mikado Earthwork (see fig. 5.1).

The Boon Earthworks includes two sets of paired enclosures (four enclosures in all) and at least one burial mound associated with the northern pair in Wexford County. The southern pair includes the Hardy Earthwork (20WX155), which was reported to be in the shape of a horseshoe. The site is located on a topographic prominence called Boon's Lookout, roughly 1,200–1,400 meters from Slagle Creek, which flows into the Manistee River. No professional archaeological work has occurred at these enclosures, so it is unclear whether they are still extant. Although they were reported several times in State Site Files (suggesting that they were once extant), they should be considered tentative members of the cluster of enclosures (the files also indicate that the Hardy Earthwork has been destroyed).[1]

The Mosquito Creek (Boven/Falmouth) Earthworks complex includes four enclosures that possibly represent two sets of pairs, with at least one associated burial mound along Mosquito Creek in Reeder Township, Missaukee County. Mosquito Creek is in the Muskegon River watershed. Professional archaeologists conducted two projects at the Mosquito Creek enclosures. Emerson Greenman (1927a) worked inside one enclosure in 1926, which he referred to as the Falmouth Inclosure (and sometimes as Missaukee III, because it was the third enclosure he worked at in Missaukee County). Charles Cleland (1965), leading a Michigan State University field school in 1965, worked inside an earthwork on Mosquito Creek named the Boven Earthworks (after the landowners) and assigned the site number 20MA19. From all available evidence, it seems that these are two enclosures in this set of four reported along Mosquito Creek. Excavations inside both enclosures revealed light habitation debris and no palisade. Boven was documented as having at least two breaches in its embankment that may have served as entrances. A radiocarbon date was run on materials from the Boven enclosure. Sample M-1768 dated to 480 ± 100 B.P., which calibrates using the intcal04 curve to A.D. 1340–1560, placing it in the Late Prehistoric period (Milner and O'Shea 1998: 186).[2]

For information on the Missaukee Earthworks, see chapter 5.

The Walters-Linsenman and Harcourt Swamp Earthworks likely consisted of two enclosures and an associated burial mound. The Walters-Linsenman enclosure (20OG7) is located in Ogemaw County with an associated burial mound. All work here was conducted by Harold Moll, an amateur archaeologist, in the 1950s (Cornelius and Moll 1961; Moll et al. 1958). All materials from this work reside in private hands and are unavailable for analysis. Moll found light habitation debris inside the enclosure. He claimed to have found evidence of a palisade, but no supporting data have ever been presented. Moll documented two formal entrances to this enclosure (Moll et al. 1958: 6). A radiocarbon date was run on bulk charcoal recovered inside the enclosure, which dated to A.D. 1350 ± 75 (Cornelius and Moll 1961; the calibration curve and the uncalibrated date are not known). Moll reported another enclosure less than 1 kilometer northwest on a rise in the landscape next to the Harcourt Swamp (20OG11). This enclosure unfortunately has been destroyed since Moll's work in the 1950s but probably formed the second enclosure in a pair.

The Rifle River Earthworks consists of two sets of paired enclosures (four enclosures in all) along the Rifle River in Churchill Township, Ogemaw County. Sites 20OG2 and 20OG3 occur together as the northern pair; 20OG1 and 20OG4 are the southern pair. These pairs are located 5 kilometers apart from north to south along the Rifle River. Much like the Boon Earthworks, one of the enclosures in the southern pair is in the shape of a horseshoe (20OG4 being an unfinished circle). The only archaeological work done on these enclosures (aside from ongoing pot hunting) was conducted by Fred Dustin (1932), who mapped them and conducted sporadic excavations inside all of them. His maps of the enclosures themselves were drawn with great detail and precision.[3] They show no known associated burial mounds, but Dustin indicated that he found "bones" on a path to the river from 20OG4, which we might infer came from a destroyed mound. Sites 20OG4 and 20OG3 (in the northern pair) are both associated with springs. Each enclosure has breaches through its embankment; both enclosures in the northern pair and the finished circle of the southern pair (20OG1) have two entryways. The northern pair has one much larger enclosure (20OG2), with a boulder located outside it. The excavations by Dustin (1932) showed no palisade on any of the enclosures and light habitation debris in all. No radiocarbon dates are available, but ceramic remains (housed at UMMA) show a clear Late Prehistoric association.

The Mikado Earthwork site (20AA5) is located in Alcona County on a bluff above a tributary of the south branch of the Pine River. Of all these enclosures, Mikado is the closest to a Great Lake, located roughly 25 kilometers west of Lake Huron. No mounds are associated with this site. This enclosure seems to be the only one that was not paired. Another enclosure (named the Glennie enclosure) was reported a few kilometers west of Mikado in the early 1900s. It has never been located since that time, however, and we have no other reports of its existence, so it has to be considered suspect. Mikado has been the subject of three substantial investigations, all of which focused inside the enclosure. The study by Greenman (1927a) in 1926 was followed by amateur tests in 1957 (Moll et al. 1958) and UMMA investigations in 1966 (Carruthers 1969). Excavation has shown evidence of a possible palisade but a low intensity of occupation. Corn and bean fragments were found. One of the corn fragments produced a radiocarbon date of A.D. 1450 ± 100, placing Mikado in Late Prehistory.

Shared Features of the Earthwork Complexes

Even with limited information from inside-only excavations, these other northern enclosures share a remarkable number of features with the Missaukee Earthworks site and with each other. The existence of so many similarities even with limited information makes these overlaps all the more striking and suggestive. Some of the major similarities are synthesized below.

Dating A comparison of dates shows that the other northern enclosures were single-component Late Prehistoric sites, like Missaukee. The radiometric dates available from the Boven enclosure, the Walters-Linsenman enclosure, and Mikado (even when the exact calibration curve is not known) all fall in the Late Prehistoric period (ca. A.D. 1200–600). Likewise, the available ceramic assemblages show a Late Prehistoric association (see the discussion below).

Landscape Position Only one complex (the Rifle River Earthworks) was located near a major water feature. Thus these sites are not in prime resource zones. As discussed in chapter 3 in relation to mounds, this is a notable contrast. These enclosures, like

Missaukee, seem intentionally placed in locations that would not have been explicitly claimed by single tribal groups, making them accessible to territorially disparate communities. Also, the Boon Earthworks complex is located on a topographic prominence, similar to Missaukee.

Earthwork Construction While no information is available from these other enclosures to confirm their construction process, all have embankments surrounded by a ditch. This suggests that they were constructed with the single-episode ditch-embankment process confirmed for 20MA11 at Missaukee.

Every enclosure has some kind of breach through its embankment, and many seem to have two original entryways like the enclosures at Missaukee. Mikado has a possible palisade, and Walters-Linsenman has a marginally possible palisade. But the rest of the enclosures, like Missaukee, do not offer conclusive evidence of palisades, suggesting that they also were not defensive structures.

Habitation Evidence The excavations inside all enclosures found light habitation debris, which of course is not what would be expected of habitation sites (Milner and O'Shea 1998). No habitation sites were in the immediate vicinity of any of these earthworks. While they were not all in locations as sparse as Missaukee, these enclosures were still not built in dense-resource areas, such as at the confluence points of rivers and lakes. These data suggest that, like Missaukee, these other enclosures were not habitation sites.

Pairing It is critical to emphasize that archaeological work at Missaukee showed that the two enclosures were intentionally coupled to form a single ritual precinct. The convergence with Bear's Journey showed that these monuments were constructed to represent two earths. As noted, the other earthwork sites all seem originally to have been paired, except perhaps Mikado. This lone singular enclosure, interestingly, is the only enclosure within a Great Lakes lake-effect coastal zone and perhaps played a unique role (see the discussion below).

Other Precinct Components All of these enclosures were constructed near a water feature, paralleling Missaukee, where the eastern enclosure was constructed directly next to the unusual upland spring. Both pairs of Rifle River enclosures, even though they were along a river, were still associated with a spring. The spring at Missaukee served a symbolic role, representing the surrounding ocean in the story of Bear's Journey (see chapter 5). The location of the Rifle River Earthworks near springs even though fresh water was available in the river adds support to this idea.

The Boon Earthworks, the Mosquito Creek Earthworks, and the Walters-Linsenman enclosure were each associated with a burial mound (as noted above, the Rifle River Earthworks was associated with "bones" outside 20OG4, which may suggest that a mound was once in the vicinity). At Walters-Linsenman, where we have more details on the mound location, the burial mound was located northeast of the enclosure. This corresponds with the location of the mound northeast of the eastern enclosure at Missaukee (Moll et al. 1958).

The eastern enclosure (20OG2) in the northern pair of Rifle River enclosures is substantially larger, which parallels Missaukee, where the eastern enclosure is slightly larger in diameter and much larger in height and width. Outside of the enclosure at Rifle River is a large boulder (Dustin 1932: 8). While this feature is not exactly the same as at Missaukee (where a boulder sits in the center of the western enclosure), it is another similarity in spatial design and adds coherence to the Bear's Journey pattern.

Outside Stations No exterior work has been conducted at any of the other northern enclosures, so the presence of stations (or Bear's stops) at these sites cannot be confirmed. Based on abundant similarities in location and internal aspects, however, systematic work outside these enclosures would likely reveal the presence of such stations. The research program at Missaukee provides a template for future fieldwork outside these other northern enclosures.

Monumentalization and Imbrication of the Intertribal Ceremonial Regional Circuit

The shared lack of palisades, light habitation debris, lack of proximate habitation sites, and location in resource-poor areas are evidence that a fortification or habitation interpretation is unsuitable for this cluster of enclosures (see also Milner and O'Shea 1998). With so many commonalities in design, the idea that these enclosure complexes were all built with a distinct referent in mind and to serve a shared purpose is compelling. Based on the work at Missaukee, we know that the shared referent is most likely the rendition of Bear's Journey. At the design level these complexes share pairing (two earths; at Rifle River, where detailed information on the paired enclosures is available, one enclosure is larger than another); many have two planned entryways (the exit and entrance for Bear); all are associated with water and many with springs (the ocean); one has an associated boulder (the mountain); and most are associated with mounds (traditionalism tying new regional ritual with older practices).

As noted, almost all of these enclosures are located away from major and claimed resources, creating a neutral positioning within the territorial regional setting. This also indicates a shared function as intertribally accessible ceremonial centers rendered on a monumental scale. The brief comparison of material assemblages from the Missaukee Earthworks site, the Rifle River enclosures, and Mikado presented below confirms that these enclosures had regional draws, crossing coastal and inland areas. The ceramic comparison indicates that these enclosures reflected their unique positions within the regional landscape. The enclosures were not simply linked; they formed an imbricated circuit for intertribal events, in which their use seems to have been orchestrated geographically.

Ceramic Comparison

Only three earthwork sites within the cluster, the Missaukee Earthworks site (20MA11–12), the Rifle River Earthworks (20OG1, 20OG2, 20OG3, 20OG4), and the Mikado Earthwork (20AA5), had sufficient extant ceramic assemblages available for analysis.[4] Excavations occurred only inside the enclosures at Rifle River and Mikado, so comparisons were only made between the ceramic vessels from these

TABLE 6.1. SUMMARY OF MISSAUKEE, RIFLE RIVER, AND MIKADO DESIGNATED WARES

	Traverse ware	Juntunen ware	Other wares (imports)	"White Bird Ware" (Interior late traits)	Mixture late traits (not securely one ware)
Missaukee inside enclosure ceramic vessels					
Number of jars	5	1	1	9	23
% of jars	12.8%	2.6%	2.6%	23.1%	59.0%
Rifle River inside enclosure ceramic vessels					
Number of jars	2	6	1	8	21
% of jars	5.3%	15.8%	2.6%	21.1%	55.3%
Mikado inside enclosure ceramic vessels					
Number of jars	0	14	3	7	7
% of jars	0%	45.2%	9.7%	22.6%	22.6%

inside spaces and those recovered during previous excavations inside the enclosures at Missaukee. Analysis involved a minimum vessel count based on diagnostics and provenience for each assemblage, followed by coding of vessels.

The minimum vessel count identified 39 vessels recovered from inside the enclosures at Missaukee (see chapter 5). Of these, 5 were Traverse ware from northwestern Michigan around present-day Traverse City, 9 had characteristics of "White Bird ware" with strong Late Prehistoric interior stylistic elements, and, interestingly, only 1 vessel was clearly Juntunen, the well-defined ceramic ware from along Lake Huron (table 6.1).

The minimum vessel count identified 38 vessels recovered from inside the Rifle River enclosures. Of these, 2 were Traverse ware; 8 had the characteristics of "White Bird ware," with strong Late Prehistoric interior stylistic elements; and 6 were clearly Juntunen ware (table 6.1).

A minimum of 31 vessels were identified in the available assemblage from Mikado. Of these, none were Traverse ware; 7 had characteristics of "White Bird ware," with strong Late Prehistoric interior stylistic elements; 3 were clear imports, likely Iroquoian (Carruthers 1969; Milner 1998); and 14 were Juntunen ware (table 6.1).

These ceramic ware trends indicate that the use of these enclosures varied geographically. Missaukee, closest to the tribal territory of Traverse ware producers, has the most Traverse ware. Mikado, closest to the Juntunen tribal territory, is dominated by Juntunen ware. Rifle River, in an intermediary geographic position, had more Juntunen than Missaukee but less than Mikado and had less Traverse ware than Missaukee but more than Mikado (where there is none). All of these sites show a similar amount of ceramics fitting "White Bird ware," with late interior traits (around 20% at all three) (table 6.1).

This comparison suggests a geographic arrangement in the use of these enclosures. Both Missaukee and Rifle River have a stronger presence of wares from coastal groups that they were closer to geographically (Lake Michigan and Lake Huron, respectively), showing at some level that they preferentially served or were used by more proximate constituencies. Both Missaukee and Rifle River have a mixed ceramic assemblage, however, showing that they drew other coastal communities as well. The lithics from Missaukee substantiate a mixed geographic draw with raw materials that outcrop in both eastern and western coastal regions in Michigan (Bayport, Northern Gray, and Norwood chert; see chapter 5). These finds seem to reflect the geographic positioning of Missaukee and Rifle River in boundary areas between the High Plains and coastal lake-effect zones, spaces likely to be unclaimed or somewhat neutral (fig. 5.1).

The ceramics from Mikado, in contrast, reflect a more exclusive use of this enclosure site. The ceramic assemblage suggests the presence of inland and Juntunen coastal groups, yet the site did not draw or was not open to northern coastal horticulturalists along Lake Michigan. Mikado is located firmly within the Lake Huron lake-effect zone. Many features of Mikado confirm its more targeted, unique role in the intertribal regional ritual system.

Mikado's Unique Role

The Mikado Earthwork site (20AA5) differs in a variety of ways from the other enclosure sites. Mikado's position in the landscape is distinct. The sites in Wexford County (Boon Earthworks), Missaukee County (Mosquito Creek and Missaukee), and Ogemaw County (Walters-Linsenman/Harcourt Swamp and Rifle River) are removed from Great Lakes lake-effect coastal zones, where territorial horticulturalist tribal systems emerged during Late Prehistory. But Mikado lies in close proximity to a Great Lake. It is only 25 kilometers west of Lake Huron on the border of a very homogeneous, strongly identified coastal tribal territory: the Juntunen tribal system discussed in chapter 3 (Milner and O'Shea 1998).

Materials from the site reflect its localized position near Juntunen territory. As outlined above, Juntunen ceramics dominate the assemblage, which excludes ceramic wares from other coastal communities (table 6.1). The lithics follow this same pattern. A sample of 264 lithics from excavations by Carruthers in 1966 (Carruthers 1969) was available for analysis in the UMMA Great Lakes Laboratory collections (analyzed by John O'Shea). This lithic assemblage is dominated by Bayport chert, which forms over 70% of the collection (table 6.2). Glacial material forms the next largest percentage, and the assemblage is rounded out with a small amount of Northern Gray. No Norwood chert is present. Like the ceramics, the lithics indicate an abundance of material linked with Lake Huron coastal communities and an exclusion of northwestern Michigan coastal groups. The ceramics also suggest an openness to even more distant farming tribal communities, possibly including Iroquoian groups (Milner and O'Shea 1998).

Unlike Mikado, the other northern enclosure complexes were not so close to coastal tribal territory. Thus any visiting inland or coastal group would have had to travel considerable distances for the ritual aggregations. Mikado, in contrast, is located in preferential position for access by Juntunen communities (fig. 5.1).

These differences at Mikado, however, do not mean that this site was not part of the larger intertribal ritual system; rather, they indicate that this enclosure was a specific kind of hub in the system. Recall that Mikado was the only enclosure site where the interior excavations recovered food remains, which included domesticated food remains such as corn and beans (Carruthers 1969). It is possible that Mikado, clearly the most accessible enclosure for Juntunen communities, was constructed

TABLE 6.2. LITHIC RAW MATERIAL PROPORTIONS AT MIKADO

Lithic raw material	No./%
Bayport	189
	71.6%
Norwood	0
	0%
Northern Gray	12
	4.5%
Glacial	58
	22.0%
Other	5
	1.9%
TOTAL	**264**
	100%

specifically as a place where Juntunen communities could trade domesticated crops with various regional communities, including inland groups (the ceramics show a strong southern connection, including Iroquoian styles). Such trade of bulk crop products from Juntunen territory would have been more difficult at the other enclosures farther away. Hence Mikado, on the border of the larger tribal territory, served as an important and specified place for this trade. While enmeshed in Juntunen territory and dominated by Juntunen material remains, Mikado (constructed as an earthwork enclosure ritual precinct) remained symbolically linked with the larger Late Prehistoric regional organization.

Macroregional Trends: Multicriteria Cost Surface Analysis, Michigan, A.D. 1200–1600

As Late Prehistoric intertribal aggregation centers, these northern earthwork complexes must have been accessible to diverse communities from widespread territories. An understanding of the varying costs that communities would have accumulated as they traveled throughout Michigan to access earthwork sites offers us the opportunity to gain further insight into the regional dynamics of Late Prehistory (A.D. 1200–1600).

To accomplish this modeling, I focused on the accessibility of the Missaukee Earthworks (20MA11–12) to groups living throughout Michigan. The accessibility trends and patterns observed in this modeling of Missaukee, the only enclosure site that has been systematically investigated and documented as a ritual intertribal center, provide a means for contextualizing regional patterns. A realistic Geographic Information Systems (GIS) model of the cost of prehistoric movement, which was limited to pedestrian and water travel, was established for the entire state of Michigan. Optimal routes from important Late Prehistoric sites distributed through High Plains interior areas, northern coastal lake-effect zones, and southern Michigan to the Missaukee Earthworks were calculated.[5]

Criteria Selection

Three criteria critical to prehistoric movement in Michigan were selected for the production of the cost-surface model: vegetation land cover, waterways, and slope. Slope is a critical element for all pedestrian travel. Vegetation affects the ability of an individual to travel through the landscape (Llobera 2000: 67). Canoe travel along Michigan's major rivers and the shores of the Great Lakes enabled people to transport themselves and goods long distances. Andrew Blackbird recounted the importance and feasibility of canoe travel among the Ottawas of Michigan during the nineteenth century: "in navigating Lake Michigan they used long bark canoes in which they carried their whole families and enough provisions to last them all winter," and "in one day they could sail quite a long distance along the coast of Lake Michigan" (Blackbird 1887: 33). Waterways and canoe travel were a significant aspect of life in precontact Michigan because of such transport and navigation benefits (Cleland 1992).

The projection, extent, and resolution of each criterion input raster were the same as the Michigan 90-meter Digital Elevation Model (DEM) (Michigan CGI 2006). Michigan GeoRef was the projection, using 90-meter cells as the resolution for final grids.

Criteria 1 and 2: Vegetation Land Cover and Waterways

Vegetation land cover and waterways were two related criteria in this analysis. The final input raster for these criteria was created from a Land Cover circa 1800 vector file acquired from the Michigan Department of Natural Resources (DNR). This map was created by biologists working for the Michigan Natural Features Inventory who translated the notes of the General Land Office surveys conducted in Michigan from 1816 to 1856 into a digital map (Comer et al. 1995). Roughly 80 different land cover types and their locations were established and digitized in the final map format (Comer et al. 1995). The map provides an approximation of Michigan's landscape prior to widespread European settlement (Comer et al. 1995). It was critical in this analysis because it provided an estimation of the landscape that tribal communities inhabited in the Late Prehistoric period (ca. A.D. 1200–1600). This map provided information on precontact vegetation features and river locations.

To make this analysis possible, a new field was added to a copy of the original Land Cover circa 1800 information. All of the polygons assigned to the 80 plus land cover codes in the original map were reassigned to eight major land cover categories determined to be relevant to prehistoric movement: Major River, Lake, Forested Wetland, Nonforested Wetland, Forested, Nonforested, Sparsely Vegetated, and Natural Disturbance (table 6.3). The coverage was then dissolved on this grouped variable. Dissolving is a topological procedure that involves removing boundaries between adjacent polygons having the same value for a specific attribute. Thus the result of dissolving in this situation was the removal of boundaries between adjacent polygons with the same values in the new grouped land-cover field.

In addition to the categories, a 5-mile (8,050-meter) buffer along the coasts of the Great Lakes was created. American Indian groups living throughout Michigan traveled to and through the Great Lakes, as shown by numerous prehistoric and historic

TABLE 6.3. DESCRIPTION OF GROUPED LAND COVER IN ANALYSIS

Grouped land cover	Description
Major river	Major rivers
Lake	Inland lakes
Great Lakes (created category)	5-mile buffer along Great Lakes shoreline
Forested wetland	Hardwood and conifer wetlands
Nonforested wetland	Marshes, marl flats, bogs, peatland, muskeg
Forested	Hardwoods, conifers, mixed forested
Nonforested	Grasslands and savannas
Sparsely vegetated	Beaches, sand dunes, exposed bedrock
Natural disturbance	Beaver flooding, windthrows, wildfire, thickets

sites on islands and documented historical travel routes (Hinsdale 1931). The distance of 5 miles was selected because it incorporated islands with known sites into the analysis. To create this space for travel, a variable indicating "state" or "not state" was added to a copy of the Land Cover circa 1800 map, which was then dissolved on this variable. A 5-mile buffer was computed around the state, creating a 5-mile Great Lakes shoreline buffer. This new Great Lakes category was added to the grouped land cover map by unioning (unioning is a *topological overlay* of two coverages or spatial data sets, where all *features* from both *coverages* are retained).

The result of these modifications was a single vector map with nine major land cover categories: Major River, Lake, Great Lakes, Forested Wetland, Nonforested Wetland, Forested, Nonforested, Sparsely Vegetated, and Natural Disturbance (table 6.3). The vegetation cover information and waterways input were derived from this map.

Waterways

The goal of the water criteria input map was to create an input with connected pre-dam water features. In order to connect waterways, Forested Wetland had to be included. Each water category was assigned a unique value, calibrated to the range 1–100, where the base value 1 represents crossing a cell with no barriers and 100 is a prohibitive friction value (cf. Jaga et al. 1993), determined to be the relative associated cost of travel in each water category in an unfrozen travel scenario (table 6.4).

This water-feature vector map was converted into a 30-meter raster grid based on these values. By converting to a 30-meter grid first then aggregating the 30-meter cells and resampling the grid into a 90-meter raster based on majority, the waterways remained connected. The final water grid had 90-meter cells and connected waterways.

Vegetation Land Cover

To create the vegetation land cover map, a unique value was assigned to each of the nine major land cover categories. As with waterways, values were calibrated between 1 and 100 to represent the associated cost of travel for each land cover category

TABLE 6.4. ASSIGNED COST VALUES OF GROUPED LAND COVER

Grouped land cover	Final assigned cost value	Reasoning
Major river	5	Canoe travel occurred up major waterways
Lake	65	Avoid "puddle-jumping"[a]
Great Lakes	10	Canoe travel occurred along shoreline
Forested wetland	25	Part of waterways—not as easy as unobstructed river
Nonforested wetland	70	Impassable wetlands with canoe, wet walking
Forested	40	Vegetation but openings
Nonforested	30	Easy to walk/see through
Sparsely vegetated	60	Includes sand and rocks, want to avoid scrambling
Natural disturbance	100	Random, unpredictable occurrences

[a] Lake was assigned a high cost value in order to avoid "puddle jumping." When assigned a low value, least-cost paths would go in and out of small lakes even though they were not following any other water features. This is not the way real travel would have occurred. Jumping in and out of small lakes when not on an otherwise water-based route would be an illogical and time-consuming decision. The qualitative comparison with major historic trails supports this decision to eliminate puddle jumping: historic routes themselves skirt around inland lake features when they are not following a water route.

in an unfrozen travel scenario (table 6.4). These values were determined through informed consideration of travel in vegetation classes relative to one another. To maintain consistency with the production of the water input grid, this vector map was converted to a grid in the same manner.

Combining Vegetation Land Cover and Waterways Grids

The grid created in this second process had water features as well as vegetation land cover categories. The production of a separate water input was necessary: during conversion from the vector map with all nine categories into a grid, the vegetation land cover types overwhelmed water features like rivers, creating a grid without connected waterways.

To eliminate the redundancy of the water features in the two maps, the connected waterways and the vegetation land cover grids were combined. The connected waterways were maintained in the final output by the construction of a conditional (CON) function in ARCInfo, which created an output grid with connected waterways and unique costs for each of the nine land cover categories (table 6.4).

Criterion 3: Slope

The slope input map was derived from the 90-meter Michigan Digital Elevation Model (DEM). Slope was calculated in degrees. Because the relationship between slope and the effort required to traverse it is not linear and the relative cost increases steeply with slope angle, modifications were made (following Bell and Lock [2000: 89]) to create a relative nonlinear slope cost grid. The tangent of the slope was

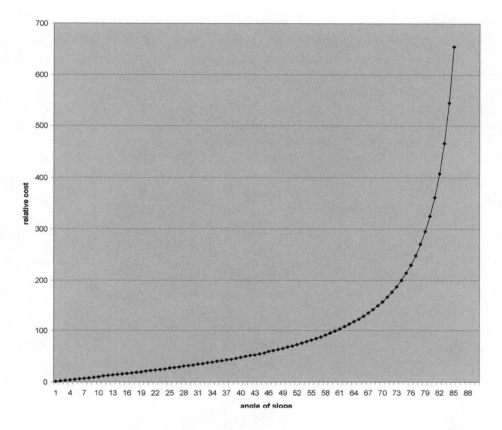

Figure 6.1. Modified slope calculation for a more accurate reflection of the effect of slope on pedestrian travel (reproduced from Bell and Lock 2000: 98).

divided by the tangent of 1 degree (0.007145), which more accurately reflects how someone on foot experiences slope (Bell and Lock 2000: 89; fig. 6.1).

To calibrate the cost values for all criteria, the values of this grid were stretched to range from 1 to 100. The entire modified slope grid was multiplied by 100 and divided by the maximum value of that grid.

Total Cost Surface and Least-Cost Paths

The grids reflecting the three criteria relevant to prehistoric movement (vegetation land cover, waterways, and modified slope) were combined to create the total cost grid. Each final criteria grid had the same projection (Michigan GeoRef), extent (the same as the Michigan 90-meter DEM), calibrated values ranging from 1 to 100, and 90-meter cells. Input grids were weighted equally and added together.

The total cost grid was used to calculate the accumulated cost distance to the Missaukee Earthworks for the entire state of Michigan. The locations of other earthwork enclosures from the northern series and significant Late Prehistoric sites (A.D. 1200–1600) representing interior areas, northern coastal horticulturalist-fisher tribal territories, and southern farming tribal territories were digitized to the nearest quarter section (site locations were derived from State Bureau of History [BOH] files).[6] Least-cost paths from the other enclosure sites and 23 significant Late

Figure 6.2. Accumulated cost grid for cost to Missaukee Earthworks (20MA11–12) computed from total cost grid with calculated least-cost paths (showing 30 sites).

Prehistoric sites (a total of 30 sites) to Missaukee were computed on the accumulated cost distance grid. The result was 30 paths representing the least-cost routes within the modeled cost-surface (fig. 6.2).

Historic American Indian Trails Note that these generated least-cost paths are generic relative least-cost evaluations (Whitley and Hicks 2001: 6). They suggest possible travel routes. The qualitative fit of these routes with a sample of major historic American Indian trails in Michigan, however, indicates that the modeled routes indeed have a probable basis in reality. I conducted this comparison after travel routes for Late Prehistory were modeled.

A sample of major historic trails from Michigan's Lower Peninsula was manually digitized from Wilbert B. Hinsdale's rendering of their locations (Hinsdale 1931; fig. 6.3). It is important to note that Hinsdale's renderings give only a general (fuzzy) location of the trails and show only trails that the original surveyors of the state of Michigan noted in their work. Furthermore, the destination of these historic trails was not the Missaukee Earthworks site (20MA11–12). They were positioned

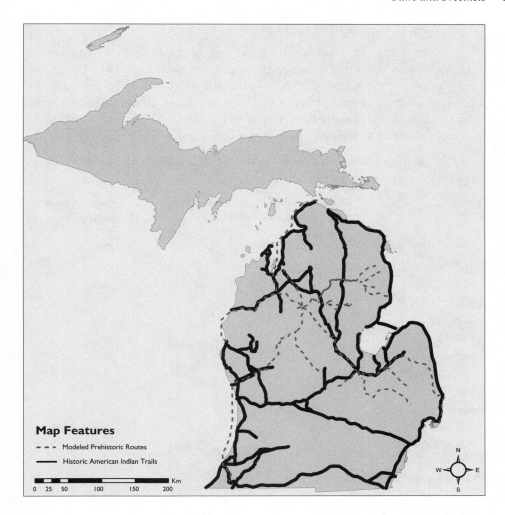

Figure 6.3. Sample of historic American Indian trails digitized from Hinsdale (1931) compared to modeled routes.

for historic circumstances: optimizing access to prime resources and the fur trade (White 1991).

Despite these concerns, a qualitative comparison of the modeled least cost paths with historic American Indian trails indicates that the trails overlap in some locations and share a similar placement logic with the historic routes (fig. 6.3). The historic trails frequently follow major river networks, run along the shoreline of the Great Lakes, and avoid steep slopes, as the modeled trails do. These congruencies support the predictive strength of the modeled least-cost paths, suggesting that the modeled cost-surface does approximate the landscape and that the least-cost paths approximate the route choices that people would have made to reach the Missaukee Earthworks. This qualitative assessment supports the GIS model and strengthens the results of the analysis.

Results: Accessibility of the Missaukee Earthworks

Using zonal statistics, the cost and length of each of the 30 paths were calculated. These scores were converted to distance rank and cost rank among the 30 sites (table 6.5).[7] To evaluate the accessibility of Missaukee from each site, the cost rank was subtracted from the distance rank of each site. A positive difference indicates that travel to Missaukee was easier than the distance implies, while a negative difference indicates that travel to Missaukee was harder than the distance implies.

TABLE 6.5. SITE RANK IN PATH LENGTH AND COST AND THE DIFFERENCE BETWEEN THE DISTANCE AND COST RANKS

Site	Least-cost path length rank (Distance)	Least-cost path cost rank	Distance rank minus cost rank
Boven Enclosure (20MA19)	1	1	0
Meade's Bridge (20RO5)	2	2	0
Cut River Mounds (20RO1)	3	3	0
Townsend (20RO8)	4	4	0
Lake St. Helen's Site 1 (20RO40)	5	5	0
Lake St. Helen's Site 2 (20RO19)	6	6	0
Skegemog Point (20GT2)	7	8	−1
Walters-Linsenman Enclosure (20OG7)	8	7	1
Rifle River Enclosure 1 (20OG1)	9	10	−1
Rifle River Enclosure 4 (20OG4)	10	9	1
Rifle River Enclosure 3 (20OG3)	11	12	−1
Rifle River Enclosure 2 (20OG2)	12	11	1
Midland Nature Center (20GR91)	13	14	−1
	14	13	1
Stotlmeyer	15	15	0
Mikado (20AA5)	16	18	−2
Gaging Station (20AA27)	17	19	−2
Gordon-McVeigh (20AA143)	18	20	−2
Scott (20AA22)	19	21	−2

TABLE 6.5. *CONTINUED*

Site	Least-cost path length rank (Distance)	Least-cost path cost rank	Distance rank minus cost rank
Malone	20	22	−2
Van Ettan Creek	21	25	−4
Aldrich (20GR220)	22	24	−2
South Flats Enclosure (20MU2)	23	16	7
Spring Creek (20MU3)	24	17	7
Dumaw Creek (20OA5)	25	23	2
Juntunen (20MK1)	26	26	0
Younge (20LP1)	27	27	0
20MB78	28	28	0
Moccasin Bluff (20BE8)	29	29	0
Wolf (20MB1)	30	30	0

Note: Positive difference indicates that travel to Missaukee is easier than distance implies; negative difference indicates that travel to Missaukee is harder than distance implies.

Table 6.5 shows that distance from the Missaukee Earthworks is a major determinant of the cost of travel to it (12 sites rank the same in distance and cost, and 15 sites have an absolute difference between distance and cost of 2 or less). This is not a uniform pattern, however: 3 sites have absolute discrepancies between cost and distance of greater than 2. The cases with notable discrepancies (which transcend the possibility that they are simply the result of noise in the analysis) have the potential to reveal important information about the social dynamics behind the accessibility of Missaukee to coastal and inland communities.

The most striking discrepancy between travel distance to Missaukee and the cost of travel comes from two neighboring sites along a small tributary (Spring Creek) of the Muskegon River near its confluence with Lake Michigan. These sites fall in Lake Michigan's coastal farming zone. The South Flats Enclosure (20MU2), another circular site, and the Spring Creek site (20MU3) have, respectively, the twenty-third and twenty-fourth longest travel routes to Missaukee of the 30 sites in the analysis. But they have the sixteenth and seventeenth ranked cost of travel to Missaukee (a positive difference in distance and cost rank of 7; table 6.5, fig. 6.3). Travel to the Missaukee Earthworks was easier from these sites than from others geographically closer to Missaukee because of their position on the Muskegon River. These results raise questions about social interaction between groups from different resource zones within the Muskegon River watershed, connections that have gone unnoticed and uninvestigated until this analysis.[8] Perhaps interaction among groups up and down the Muskegon River was fruitful and necessary in this period, an idea that merits further consideration.

Results: Macroregional Imbrication

It is striking in this case of cost and distance discrepancy that one of these sites is another Late Prehistoric circular enclosure like Missaukee, the South Flats Enclosure. The switch in distance and cost rank suggests a connection between Missaukee and South Flats that was incorporated into and reflected by their positioning in the landscape.

As noted above, I suggest that northern enclosures complexes served as integrative ceremonial centers like Missaukee. The discrepancy in distance and cost of travel between Missaukee and the South Flats Enclosure indicates that South Flats should be considered part of the proposed earthwork system (fig. 6.4).

Like Mikado, the South Flats enclosure is located in a Great Lakes lake-effect coastal zone. This enclosure, which would have been reached easily by Lake Michigan coastal farming communities, possibly served a similar role as Mikado did for Lake Huron: being constructed as a place where coastal groups could bring domesticated crops in bulk for trade with inland groups, who could readily access the site using the Muskegon River. Such trade would have been more difficult at other enclosures farther from local farming territories. Thus South Flats may have served as Mikado's western equivalent. Of course, expanded systematic investigations at South Flats (which Grand Valley State University began as a research project in the summer of 2006) are necessary to confirm this proposed pattern.

Adding support to this proposed pattern, the South Flats is a single enclosure, like Mikado (Quimby 1965). These two sites are the only single-enclosure sites in the northern landscape and are the only ones built in Great Lakes coastal lake-effect

Figure 6.4. Imbricated northern earthwork enclosure series (refined after GIS analysis).

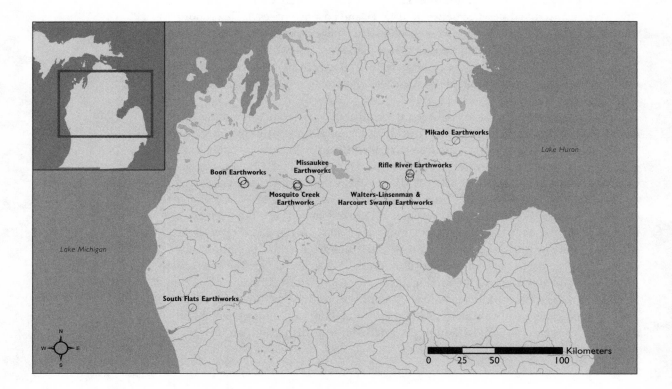

zones (fig. 6.4). As enclosures they were symbolically linked into the larger circuit; yet these features distinguish them from the others, likely a sign of their unique role. Is it possible that these two enclosures were in fact the bookend western and eastern pairs of the entire intertribal regional system? That is, are they a pair around which the entire system was imbricated? This idea is highly speculative, of course. But if all of the enclosures grounded a major regional organizational system that was purposefully orchestrated, it is not outlandish to suggest that the pattern was planned on a macroregional scale (and it is interesting food for thought).

Results: Tribal Territoriality

According to the working model of Late Prehistory in this book, through major resource shifts (including the widespread adoption of maize in lake-effect coastal zones) newly horticulturalist communities created stronger local connections, which precipitated the emergence of defined tribal systems with distinct social identities and spatially demarcated territories. The emergence of homogeneous ceramic styles along the shores of the Great Lakes in the Late Prehistoric period reflects this tribalization. As evidence in previous chapters indicates, foragers living inland had to respond to this new exclusivity on the coasts. They reformulated their seasonal rounds, created ceramic stylistic features distinct from the coastal wares, and, most vividly, used burial mounds to stake claims to their local resource zones, suggesting a concurrent or at least emergent process of inland tribalization.

As figure 6.5 highlights, least-cost paths from sites in distinct resource zones and different regional locations converge. These patterns illustrate the importance of local connections in tribal territoriality, which was a major aspect of social organization throughout Michigan. The patterns of path convergence deserve some discussion.

Least-cost paths from known Great Lakes coastal ceramic style zones and resource areas converge in the mobility analysis. The paths from sites in Juntunen territory in the northern Lake Huron coastal horticulturalist zone (Mikado, Gaging Station, Gordon-McVeigh, Scott, and Van Ettan Creek) converge (fig. 6.5). The paths from sites in southwestern Michigan's coastal horticulturist zone (Moccasin Bluff, Spring Creek, and South Flats Enclosure) converge. And the paths running from sites in the Saginaw Valley, which forms a unique resource zone, converge en route to Missaukee (Malone, Stotlmeyer, and Aldrich). The convergence of paths suggests that in these areas connections between local places were cost efficient and thus feasible. The results of the mobility analysis add support to the proposal that the Late Prehistoric period saw the emergence of strong localized connections between horticulturalist communities and the formation of spatially and socially distinct tribal territories and cultural affiliations.

In addition to converging, all of the sites in Juntunen territory have negative difference in their travel costs (Van Ettan Creek has −4, so this set includes the highest negative value of the 30 sites; table 6.5), which indicates that travel to Missaukee was harder than the distance implies. These trends indicate how important the localized focus on the Lake Huron shoreline was during Late Prehistory but also mirror the regional draw seen in the ceramics from Missaukee, where Juntunen ware occurs infrequently. Included in this site mix is Mikado, which was made to be particularly

Figure 6.5. Path
convergence patterns
highlighting local
connections in tribal
territorial systems of the
Late Prehistoric period
(A.D. 1200–1600).

accessible by Juntunen communities. Missaukee was less accessible than distance implies, which supports a purposeful geographic arrangement of these enclosure sites: this indicates a need for a locally embedded site like Mikado in Juntunen territory.

The least-cost paths running from sites in the interior High Plains (Lake St. Helen's sites 1 and 2, Rifle River Enclosures 1–4, and the Walters-Linsenman enclosure) converge at the Cut River Mounds (20RO1), located at the confluence of the Cut River and Houghton Lake (fig. 6.5). These paths converge in a manner similar to paths from distinct coastal tribal territories, which provides an additional layer of support for my suggestion that interior communities experienced parallel developments in strong local connections and emergent tribal identity.

It is even more significant that the point of interior site path convergence is the Cut River Mounds site (20RO1). Evidence from the site (see chapter 4) indicates that it was transformed into an intratribal ceremonial monument center for local pan-residential liturgical events as the social setting changed circa A.D. 1200. The convergence of these paths at the Cut River Mounds adds evidence to my working model of this period, showing that this site was indeed a unique focal point or hub in the interior landscape.

Perspectives from the Macroregional Spatial Modeling

The multicriteria mobility analysis helps to confirm that tribal territoriality and intertribal social interaction were critical during Late Prehistory (A.D. 1200–1600) in Michigan. The GIS study shows that patterns of local connections and territoriality were important in coastal tribal horticulturalist-fisher communities. It provides evidence of congruent local tribal developments in the interior, an area of Michigan whose archaeology has only recently begun to be considered systematically. The inland least-cost path convergences at Cut River Mounds further support the emerging evidence that this site had a unique role in the landscape.

The shifts in the accessibility of Missaukee from sites along the Muskegon River suggest an interaction pattern between interior communities and coastal groups along this river that probably would not have been recognized without this analysis. The substantial positive difference in the rank of distance and travel cost from the South Flats enclosure site to Missaukee adds a new dimension to my proposal that a Late Prehistoric intertribal regional ritual circuit was formed by enclosure sites. The South Flats Enclosure (20MU2) was located relatively far from Missaukee in a coastal zone; yet it was positioned along the Muskegon River, which made the Missaukee earthworks site (and the interior) highly accessible.

The results of this GIS spatial modeling and the earthwork feature and ceramic comparison indicate that during Late Prehistory communities purposefully distributed enclosure sites across the cultural and physical landscape. Each enclosure center filled the needs of different communities (including sometimes very targeted communities, as seems to be the case with Mikado and possibly South Flats). But each site was still connected to a larger whole, in an imbricated cluster of ritual precincts. Built across the landscape, this cluster of enclosures was planned and assembled on a monumental scale, with an imbrication that ultimately filled panregional needs for external interaction (fig. 6.4). This analysis for the first time provides a means of understanding the nature of interactions between tribal communities in coastal regions and the interior and reveals that these interactions were so important they had to be secured on a monumental scale.

CHAPTER 7

Breaking Out of the "Savage Slot"

Monuments, Ritual, and the Archaeology of Pre-Columbian Native North America

Despite the myths, impressions, and legacies that we have inherited as a country and a discipline, the North American continent before Europeans was not occupied by isolated peoples lacking the full spectrum of human ability, diversity, and complexity. It was full of ongoing and widespread social, ideological, political, and economic interactions. In this book I try to impress upon the reader that the northern Great Lakes region was a vital part of this extensive indigenous space. It was a place where active and dynamic ancestral Anishinaabeg communities, formed with soul-spirit as "spontaneous beings" by Sky-Woman, had forged complicated lives over millennia.

During the centuries preceding the colonial encounter (ca. A.D. 1200–1600) communities in northern Michigan developed an intricate regional tribal ritual system ensured on a monumental scale. That period saw marked cultural dynamism throughout the midcontinent, distinguished notably by the emergence of socially hierarchical, politically complex societies with numerous and sometimes massive monumental constructions, characterized as Mississippian traditions. The Mississippian world was a vast one. The impressive means of social, religious, and economic reproduction, control, and continental connections developed then are increasingly recognized and appreciated by archaeologists (for a small sample of such recent work, see Beck 2006; Blitz 1999; Brown 2004; Cobb and King 2005; Emerson 1997; Emerson et al. 2008; Kelly et al. 2008; Lankford 2006; Pauketat 2004, 2007; Peregrine and Lekson 2006; Schroeder 2004b; Blitz 2009 offers a quite thorough and recent summary of the current state of scholarship on the Mississippian). As these complex societies continue to receive intensive archaeological attention, the emerging knowledge helps deconstruct the idea that the pre-Columbian world was a land that time forgot occupied by pristine primitives or "people without history" (Wolf 1997 [1982]).

As discussed in the introduction, this idea emerged during the building of the Republic of the United States in the form of the "Mound Builder" myth. By promoting the theory that American Indians were incapable of constructing earthen monuments, this myth was used to help justify the territorial dispossession of American Indian lands. It is not just the complex societies of North America, however, that have something to teach us about the deep histories and complicated social systems of pre-Columbian times, embedded in the earthen constructions that still dot the landscape. The Late Prehistoric communities of the northern Great Lakes were not complex societies, yet they built, renewed, maintained, and used a suite of ceremonial monuments. Expanding our understandings of such noncomplex indigenous societies can also contribute to the deconstruction of static views of pre-Columbian times and help stop it from filling the "Savage Slot" for anthropology (see Cobb 2005; Trouillot 2003).

Summarizing: Regional Ritual Organization in the Northern Great Lakes, A.D. 1200–1600

During Late Prehistory (ca. A.D. 1200–1600) the coasts of the northern Great Lakes region saw economic shifts toward specialization in maize horticulture and fishing. These shifts were facilitated by social changes that made these activities dependable and significant. To ensure the success of maize horticulture and focused spawning fishing, coastal communities developed intensive local interactions and restricted ranges of movement. They acquired stronger senses of local territory and identity. As spatial proximity became increasingly important, coastal fisher-farmers began claiming and marking their territories and forming spatially restricted and regionally distinctive identities. The emergence of distinctive new ceramic stylistic traditions reflects the consolidation of coastal communities.

These shifts in territoriality and identity led groups to form distinct regional coastal tribal systems, which radically transformed the open, diffuse social and economic setting that had been in place since the Late Archaic period. Social alterity developed between communities on the coasts and inland, and the long-established foraging and freely mobile system was no longer sustainable in the northern Great Lakes. The milieu of Late Prehistory demanded creative social, economic, and ideological strategies from regional communities.

This period saw the development of a multifaceted regional system enacted through monumentalism (see Dillehay 2007). Late Prehistoric Anishinaabeg communities created rituals and constructed monuments with contrasting positions and roles in the landscape to facilitate local community coherence (mounds) and regional exchange (earthworks) in a constantly evolving cultural landscape. By creating permanent, meaningful, easily interpreted, consistent, and predictable contexts for the enactment of liturgical orders, constructed monuments conferred distinct advantages for facilitating intratribal and intertribal interaction.

Local Developments

The intensifying horticultural and fishing economies of the coasts of the Great Lakes changed social dynamics and encouraged closer local connections, resulting in the emergence of territorially exclusive tribal social systems. The interior High Plains has long been considered a "vacantscape"—a place with a limited resource profile used only by small groups from tribal communities along the coasts of the Great Lakes for hunting in the winter months. This book, however, presents various lines of evidence that show more activity/investment in this interior area than previously believed, suggesting that during Late Prehistory communities found themselves increasingly circumscribed to the inland where they had to develop new sustainable socioeconomic strategies.

The distribution of mounds and their correlation with inland lakes indicate a purposeful marking of interior resource zones, an investment of time and energy not expected from groups simply passing through. Communities seemed to begin using new resource zones in the interior, developing a more intensive and territorially restricted forager strategy of mobile rounds of seasonal subsistence focused on the most productive inland resources to compensate for reduced access to the coast. These inland resource zones include an array of waterscapes from Michigan's largest inland lake system (Houghton and Higgins) to the Dead Stream Swamp and the headwaters of the Muskegon, Manistee, and Au Sable rivers.

Ceramic evidence, while still accumulating, suggests that inland communities also made stylistic choices that differed from the strongly homogeneous coastal wares. One of these choices was the persistent use of earlier stylistic features on late interior vessels, most notably cord-marked exteriors, definitely confirmed by radiometric dating at the Chief White Bird site. While acknowledging that we do not currently have enough data to support the definition of a formal ceramic style produced by a late interior tribal system, I felt it important to contextualize the growing sense of distinct ceramic trends in the interior during Late Prehistory. Thus I refer to late ceramic vessels showing distinctive interior stylistic tendencies as "White Bird ware."

Lithic evidence from the Chief White Bird Site (20RO50) as well as raw material trends seen from late deposits at the Cut River Mounds (20RO1) indicate that groups using these interior sites lacked direct access to coastal raw materials. Interestingly, an aspect of local organization among circumscribed interior communities seems to have been the establishment of a preferred exchange axis with coastal communities to the southeast, in the Saginaw Bay area. Through these relationships, interior communities maintained some level of local access (albeit indirect) to coastal resources during the changes in the late period.

The least-cost paths running from sites in the interior High Plains converge at the Cut River Mounds (20RO1), located at the confluence of the Cut River and Houghton Lake (see chapter 6). These paths converge in a manner similar to those from Great Lakes coastal tribal territories, which provides additional support for the idea that the interior experienced developments complementary to those on the coasts. These included stronger local connections, increased reliance on local resources, and monumental investment in the landscape, all signifying some kind of locally inscribed, emergent tribal identity among interior communities. Extensive future work, producing ceramic collections comparable in size to those of coastal sites, will be needed to define this system formally.

While most activities in both coastal and inland areas occurred at the household level, intracommunity and intersocietal interaction offered critical economic and social advantages. Communities relied on social relationships and ritual events at two different types of ceremonial monuments to ensure these levels of interaction. Burial mounds formed panresidential, intratribal ceremonial centers; and earthwork enclosures were constructed to serve as intersocietal or intertribal aggregation centers between coastal and inland groups.

Intratribal Ceremonial Monuments

Late Prehistoric coastal and interior tribal groups both faced the challenges of claiming local resource zones and creating a sense of integration among previously unconnected and physically dispersed communities. Spatial modeling presented in chapter 3 shows that groups across coastal zones and the central interior High Plains used burial mounds to legitimize their claims to local resources (most notably inland lakes) in their territories. When territorialism was becoming pronounced in the region, inland and coastal groups both began marking with burial mounds previously unmarked local resource zones. While burial mounds had been built in the Great Lakes since the Middle Woodland (ca. A.D. 1–500/600), the data presented in chapter 4 reveal that during Late Prehistory mounds were built in a new fashion, in oval form and with an outline laid out like a map for construction. In the changing social, economic, and ideological milieu of Late Prehistory in the northern landscape, mounds were repurposed with a new significance and functionality. The evidence indicates that this new purpose was to serve as suprahousehold intratribal ceremonial monument centers.

In addition to claiming localized resources, these sacred burial monuments created hubs that demanded panresidential interaction because people had living responsibilities to these ancestral locales that they had to fulfill. Dispersed communities benefited by the social and economic resources of such periodic gatherings, including access to seasonally abundant resources marked by these constructions. These gatherings helped equalize the uncertainty of resource production inherent in each tribal community's defined territory and provided opportunities for groups to express their horizontal (segmental) differentiation from other tribal systems.

Burial mounds provided fixed and recognizable symbols across the northern Great Lakes region that asserted rights to resource hotspots and extended these rights over time, standing as a corporate claim even when local groups were not present. The sites of these sacred structures also provided distinct contexts for local tribal community aggregation. These intratribal monuments thus became critical tools for reducing resource uncertainty and increasing tribal integration in the social and economic sphere of Late Prehistory (A.D. 1200–1600).

Intertribal Ritual Gatherings, Monumentalism, and Macroregional Imbrication

The evidence presented here substantiates my proposal that inland and coastal communities invested time, energy, labor, and resources into the planning, design, construction, and maintenance of monumental ceremonial precincts in the form of earthwork complexes for large-scale intersocietal ritual events. Both inland and coastal groups occupied environments riddled with risk and uncertainty, making interaction and access to outside resources important. Periodic aggregations of groups from different settings provided opportunities for resource pooling and exchange as well as for establishing social contacts with other groups and gaining access to their resources. Through mutual participation in formal liturgical events at earthwork sites, coastal and inland Late Prehistoric communities in northern Michigan maintained a productive and macroregionally imbricated intertribal interaction system.

Numerous shared design features emerge across the northern enclosure complexes, including enclosure pairing, an association with mounds, and a connection to some kind of water feature (often a spring) while at the same time being removed from major resource zones, in neutral positions (see chapter 6). The detailed research at the Missaukee Earthworks presented in chapter 5 allows archaeologists to infer that these ritual centers involved spatially distinct, activity-specific stations outside the earthworks that were repetitively utilized as well as large clusters of cache pits used for storage of trade goods or provisions during ritual events. The open space inside the earthworks was the locus of distinct ritual action.

Comparisons of the ceramic collections available from other enclosure sites indicate a mixture of inland and coastal presence at the enclosures but show that the proportions varied in ways reflecting each enclosure's positioning in the landscape. The mobility GIS modeling (see chapter 6) suggested that these monument sites formed interconnected centers in a regional ritual circuit and confirmed trends seen in the ceramics. Although connected, these complexes still reflected their geographic positioning. That is, this ritual circuit was imbricated on a macroregional scale to provide a geographically coherent system for interaction between regional tribal communities (see the speculation in chapter 6 that this system was perhaps so planned out that the enclosures of one pair—South Flats and Mikado—were built on opposite Great Lakes coasts).

Given the amount of labor and energy required to construct and maintain this series of earthwork complexes and the long distances that groups traveled to reach these sites, it is clear that the ritual network was foundational in the social, economic, and ideological systems of Late Prehistory. The repetition of this design blueprint across the landscape suggests a common origin for the enclosure complexes and the spreading importance of the intertribal ritual practice they embodied.

The way in which elements of this regional ritual have shaped the historic and modern Midewiwin ceremonial adds support to this view. An ethnohistoric convergence between Bear's Journey with the Midé pack and the design of the Missaukee Earthworks (see chapter 5) suggests that these complexes were most likely designed and built as direct referents to Bear's Journey. The marked symbolic salience of these monuments both drew Late Prehistoric communities from considerable distances and made the monuments safe and accessible for ritual events. Embedding liturgy in these monuments gave material form to the immaterial ideals of shared public ritual, ensuring that it would occur regularly and without marked hostility or aggrandizement between territorially distinct groups. This ritual network anchored the regional organization of northern Michigan for centuries before it was interrupted by European contact (ca. A.D. 1600).

During Late Prehistory in the northern Great Lakes region, the formation of strong group identities helped both coastal and inland peoples to specialize, but only with ritual and ceremonial gatherings could they mutually benefit from their respective economic specializations. Far from being a place full of "simple" societies, the northern Great Lakes was a land occupied by dynamic groups who called themselves the Spontaneous People and developed a complicated and foundational regional ritual system in the centuries before contact. These people were part of the vast and fascinating world of North America before the first Europeans ever arrived.

Tribal and Monumental

Tribal communities in northern Michigan during the Late Prehistoric period (ca. A.D. 1200–1600) built, renewed, maintained, and used a suite of ceremonial monuments. These monuments were used to facilitate intra- and intertribal interaction and integration, creating a regional network that bound together groups with exclusive social and territorial boundaries. The present case raises some theoretical points that merit (re)emphasis.

By showing that monuments long considered an "important index of social complexity" (Sherratt 1990: 147) can be a routine aspect of tribal social systems, this case contributes to scholarship that is actively decoupling monuments and complexity in archaeology. It adds more evidence showing that organizational variables manifest in societies in different degrees and indicating how problematic it is to define societal types by a discrete and inflexible list of traits.

Intra- and intertribal interaction and integration are two critical aspects of all tribal systems (see chapter 1). When tribal systems construct and use monuments, it is in large part to fulfill these needs, because the construction of a monument confers distinct advantages for facilitating interaction. These processes of intra- and intertribal integration are sufficiently distinct to necessitate the production of monuments with contrasting scales, positions, and roles in the landscape.

Applying these general expectations to a specific case, I have investigated and interpreted the mounds and earthworks of Late Prehistoric northern Michigan in a new way that better fits the archaeological data. My work alters previous understandings of these built features and allows me to offer a working model of regional organization in northern Michigan that is not dependent on historical sources but stands alongside them (see below).

Enriching Frameworks for Studying Monuments in Nonhierarchical Societies

Work all over the world continues to show that nonhierarchical societies have perhaps not complex but complicated relationships with monuments: building, using, and reusing multiple ceremonial monuments to fill competing socioeconomic demands. Scholars have found that egalitarian societies from the Neolithic North Atlantic to Woodland North America routinely elaborated their built ritual landscapes without concurrent elaborations of their nonritual built landscapes such as permanent agricultural settlements, a development that would be expected if groups were shifting toward complexity (Clay 2009: 55). This book focuses on how monumentalism can directly further tribal social organization. This particular perspective serves as one means of enriching the frameworks that archaeologists can employ to analyze the dynamic ways in which monumentalism was used to order social worlds by egalitarian communities.

Because ceremonial monuments give material form to the immaterial social and moral order that liturgy expresses (Keane 2007: 109), I propose that they offer a highly effective means of obligating the enactment of both intratribal and intertribal interaction. Ritual order becomes political order. Public ritual creates connections (or unity) during events drawing together individuals whose daily lives rarely include such interaction; the monumental materialization of these cultural processes guarantees their continuation. When examining the constructed landscapes of "simple" societies, considering the processes of intra- and intertribal integration may help explain observed patterns and variations. The case study presented in this book shows that these processes are sufficiently distinct to produce monuments with contrasting scales, positions, and roles in the landscape. More simply put, monuments intended for use by a single community materialize differently from monuments intended for use by a broader population.

It is not unimportant that in the case presented here both types of ceremonial monuments emerged in a setting of territorialism and heightened social alterity. Local communities added intratribal monuments to Cut River, a site used for centuries, when the social scene shifted to a closed setting. In the emergent setting of strong tribal identities, demarcating local territory and staking a permanent claim to the Cut River's resource rights became critical. In turn, as the closed social setting emerged, groups decided to construct substantial "detached" intertribal ceremonial monument centers (the earthwork complexes) and develop a regionally imbricated ritual circuit. Before the closed social setting, ceremonial monuments were not used (they were not needed) to facilitate regional interaction. This situation is not just case specific but is also applicable at a more general level.

While the construction of a monument is one solution "to the often conflicting claims that subsistence and political demands pose" in tribal populations (DeBoer and Blitz 1991: 62), this case suggests that monument construction was a solution more often (or possibly even only) selected when tribal populations were living in a setting of pronounced territorialism, strong group identity with concurrent heightened social alterity, and exclusive social boundaries. Monuments require substantial labor and energy. In these settings the permanency, wide interpretability, formality, shared symbolism, and attractiveness of monuments conferred an advantage over a simply defined location for actualizing cultural processes. Thus tribal groups chose to construct them.

In this specific case, both intra- and intertribal monuments were constructed in forms that had widespread symbolic salience, another finding that carries implications for the general understanding of tribal monuments. The intratribal monuments of the Late Prehistoric period had a mortuary association, which I expected to be important. What was interesting, however, was that both coastal and inland groups used a long-established and well-recognized mortuary structure form, the burial mound, but altered it to be specific to the role of intratribal monument centers (the design layout and oval shape). This familiarized the center as well as distinguished it from previous constructions that were not the same kind of territorial/ social markers. Researchers may expect to find the incorporation but also alteration of previous symbolic forms to familiarize/legitimate and create a new interaction context as a common aspect of intratribal monuments cross-culturally.

The earthwork enclosures that served as intertribal ceremonial monuments were not just built in a widely recognized symbolical form but were monumental renditions of a foundational religious ceremonial element, Bear's Journey. The story of Bear's Journey has parallels to the built structures at Chaco Canyon, where symbolically potent architecture was built on an idealized scale at the largest ceremonial center; these structures were the "principal fact" of Chaco Canyon (Lekson 1999a: 21).

Researchers may expect detached intertribal monument centers to be constructed in forms that have fundamental ceremonial significance in the regional religious/ideological system. Through these forms, intertribal monument sites provide an even more palpable and formal context in which liturgy can vouchsafe interaction between dispersed and distinct communities unconnected by political hegemony.

Taking a tribal cultural process approach to monuments avoids a common pitfall: treating monuments in nonhierarchical societies as isolated features in the landscape, as the result of unusual and rarified events unrepresentative of the social system within which they were produced. Rather, the framework presented here offers one way to link monuments directly with the social, economic, and ideological contexts of the groups that constructed, maintained, and used them. I hope that this book may be useful for archaeologists working to decode the multilayered monumental landscapes left by egalitarian societies in other times and places.

Looking cursorily at two hotly debated sites in indigenous North America, Chaco Canyon and Poverty Point, I see openings for interpretive gains from applying this framework. Positioning Chaco Canyon as a "detached" intersocietal ceremonial center could help explain its small residential population (see Judge 1989; Mills 2002) and expand understandings of other constructions in the local region as well as broader hinterlands that may have filled complementary roles as intracommunity centers (see Adler and Wilshusen 1990; Lekson 1999a; Van Dyke 2004). Evaluating evidence from the Late Archaic Poverty Point site in Louisiana within my framework could resolve ongoing debates over whether it was a local monument center showing features expected for an intratribal center or a place made by and for dispersed (foreign) groups showing features expected for an intertribal center (see, for instance, Gibson 2007; Jackson 1991; Kidder 2002; Sassaman 2005). Evidence shows that monumental mound building had even deeper roots in the Poverty Point region (Louisiana and Mississippi), with a Middle Archaic mound tradition now well documented there (see Sassaman and Heckenberger 2004; Saunders 1994; Saunders and Allen 1994; Saunders et al. 2005). The framework presented in this book may be fruitful in expanding interpretations of these ancient constructions, which show variations in size and landscape distribution not yet fully understood (Saunders 1994: 133), and the trajectory of mound-building traditions practiced over millennia in this region by hunter-gatherer communities. Future research possibilities abound.

People with Their Own History

Late Prehistory had a dynamism that was significant in its own right and left a material record to be investigated and understood. The working model of regional organization presented throughout this book has emerged from this straightforward recognition and is not derived from or dependent on historical sources. The long-standing approach to understanding Late Prehistory in the Great Lakes has relied on generalized models of adaptations of historic American Indian communities as prototypes for the past. As noted in chapter 2, the facts of colonial encounter make the utility and the validity of using historically "known cultural adaptations to specific ecological settings" to project "back onto the prehistoric period" in order to "elucidate late prehistoric cultural patterns in the Upper Great Lakes Region" questionable (Fitting and Cleland 1969: 289). The ongoing reliance on historic communities hinders our ability to understand the actual interaction between precontact communities and postcontact communities and to understand how both are presented in the textual and material record.

We know that indigenous communities of the Great Lakes practiced survivance (see Vizenor 1998) during contact by being open and creative with their identity and their occupation of the landscape. The French Empire encountered people whose living "relationships" did not fit the European view of the world. American Indians had a way of relating to everything in the cosmos (Miller 2009: 27). The indigenous world was filled with interrelationships among humans, animals, plants, societies, the spirit world, and the land (Holm et al. 2003: 18). People were responsible for ensuring the well-being of all these elements in the cosmos, including their families and communities (Miller 2009: 28). The French created separate tribes from multiethnic Algonquian groups who could assume different ethnic and social identities as needed (Witgen 2007). American Indians filled these roles to further their exchange with the French, to maintain that vital "Middle Ground" (see White 1991), but these constructed historic "tribes" remained flexible identities for many years, consolidating only over the course of European colonization as these kinds of discrete entities gained weight with imperial powers. If homogeneous historic tribal groups were an imagined colonial ideal, archaeologists need to evaluate how much these inventions should impact our interpretation of the past. What do we deny precontact communities by imposing historically observed patterns onto them? What diversity might we obscure?

To continue to move our investigations of Late Prehistory forward, we must obtain material evidence and consider it complementary to historic sources. Privileging historic data generates inaccurately static views of the past, because it populates the pre-Columbian world with people whose history is that of those living hundreds of years later in a "Shatter Zone" (see Ethridge 2009), a postapocalyptic world (see Larson 2007). In Late Prehistory people undoubtedly made some choices similar to those made historically, but people also undoubtedly made choices that differed, perhaps radically, from historical observations. Ongoing archaeological research in Michigan, including the work presented here, is revealing discrepancies between the site record and historically observed cultural activities/adaptations that confirm this expectation.

To approach the complicated reality of the pre-Columbian past, we need to make connections among ethnohistory, archaeological sites, and living tribal communities in ways that avoid letting any one source of information obscure the importance of the others. By building a picture of the dynamic developments of Late Prehistory in this way, archaeology can provide a foundation for understanding the colonial encounter in the Great Lakes. Through detailed study of material remains, we can gain insight into the lives that produced them, understand more thoroughly what European contact disrupted, trace the trajectory of this contact, and better appreciate the diversity that persists in living tribal communities today.

Lessons from the Past

Contextualized studies of the past can help answer questions about historic developments as well as allow fuller appreciations of the trajectory of postcontact events. Let me illustrate by considering the ethnohistoric convergence between the earthworks and Bear's Journey (detailed in Howey and O'Shea 2006). Uncertainty about the antiquity of the Midewiwin is long-standing. Was it an indigenous, precontact development or a post–European contact nativistic development? Several early ethnographers who regarded it as indigenous pointed to reports in the *Jesuit Relations* of a cross seen by Father Jacques Marquette in the Mascouten-Miami village on Fox River in 1673 (Thwaites 1896–1901: vol. 59:103). They argued that this was a cross of the fourth degree of the Midewiwin (Hoffman 1891; Kinietz 1947). Working in the 1960s, ethnohistorian Harold Hickerson disputed this; from his own study of the *Jesuit Relations* he concluded that the cross was in fact Christian, because "never did any Jesuit in the western Great Lakes region mention a cross in any context other than with respect to his own activities or teachings" (Hickerson 1962: 418). Using additional historical evidence (e.g., the first definite mention of the Midewiwin in colonial accounts did not occur until 1714 in relation to the Potawatomis at Detroit: Hickerson 1963:76), Hickerson argued that "all indication is that the Midewiwin was developed at approximately the turn of the 18th century" (Hickerson 1962: 418). Although Hickerson's argument for a post–European contact origin of the Midewiwin has been widely accepted among Euro-American scholars (Aldenderfer 1993; Dewdney 1975; Schlesier 1990; Spindler 1978), many Ojibwas "consider his theories to be culturally arrogant as well as inaccurate" (Angel 2002: 68).

Establishing a link between Bear's Journey as represented in the Midé scrolls and sketchings and the Missaukee Earthworks site has important implications for understanding the Midé ceremony and its historical development. First and foremost, the earthworks demonstrate the antiquity of Bear's Journey and defeat the ethnohistorical argument that the ritual was a consequence of European contact and interaction with French Christian missionaries. The unambiguous dating of the earthworks to the pre-European era makes clear that the Midewiwin, or at least Bear's Journey, has precontact roots.

While the archaeology does not speak to the details of the Midé Lodge and its symbolism, the identification of this prehistoric layout of Bear's Journey provides an important starting point for understanding the development of the Midé ceremony as it evolved to accommodate new realities and needs during the contact era. Historical observations by outsiders report that the major function of the Midewiwin Society was serving as the Grand Medicine Society, a healing and medicinal ritual system. With the temporal depth offered by the archaeological data, we can now understand that what was essentially an account of creation rendered on a monumental scale (Bear's Journey) was transformed during the colonial encounter with the addition of an elaborated healing ceremony which over time became the core of the ritual.

This developmental sequence makes sense given the stresses encountered by Anishinaabeg communities in the Upper Great Lakes following European contact. As noted in chapter 2, early contact in the Upper Great Lakes was a world where massive losses of life resulted from epidemics of European-introduced diseases. Incorporating the healing ritual onto a foundational ritual system enabled the earlier practice to provide a level of familiarity as well as authority to the new, evolving postcontact practices. The pressing need for health and stability after contact was facilitated by this affiliation. This specific case emphasizes how important it is for archaeologists and ethnohistorians to consider the long-term history of ritual practices (cf. Brown 1997; Hall 1997; Marcus and Flannery 1994, 2004). While the meaning of rituals and symbols from differing practices cannot be assumed to remain the same, physical elements themselves frequently recur; their maintenance helps naturalize and legitimize evolving ritual practices.

Countering Colonial Legacies

Understanding and finding ways to show that American Indian history did not begin with Columbus is important for the field of anthropology but also carries implications well beyond the discipline. Researchers' theories often lead to beliefs held by the general public. We saw how powerful this connection can be when the "Mound Builder" theory of the origin of the midcontinent's earthen constructions (as made by a lost group of white people) was widely embraced in the early years of the development of the United States and actively used to dispossess Indian lands. As we approach the past, we must challenge the still powerful idea that Native North America before Columbus was populated by primordial, unchanging peoples or "people without history" (Wolf [1997] 1982). While the era of using this idea to dispossess Indian lands may be over, the legacies remain. We must stay aware of and focused on countering such colonial legacies by developing fresh appreciations of the deep histories embedded in the material evidence of the archaeological record. Archaeologists are both burdened and blessed with a responsibility not only to the people whose cultures we study but also to people living today. We can change inaccurate views of the past that still circulate. But if we continue to use post-Columbian observations to explain pre-Columbian pasts, we will perpetuate the belief that nothing dynamic or new happened before "true history." I humbly hope that this book will show readers just how much exciting knowledge stands to be lost when we let this happen and will motivate others to build upon my research by conducting their own.

Notes

Introduction

1. Andrew Jackson, Case for the Removal Act, First Annual Message to Congress, December 8, 1830 (emphasis added). Accessed online: http://www.mtholyoke.edu/acad/intrel/andrew.htm.

Chapter 2. Modeling Late Prehistory in the Northern Great Lakes

1. In many parts of the midcontinent, Late Woodland developments ended with the start of the Mississippian, Fort Ancient, and Oneota traditions (Schroeder 2004a: 318). In the northern Great Lakes, the Late Woodland continued after these changes circa A.D. 1000/1100; but to avoid confusion, some archaeologists use the term "Late Prehistoric" to refer generally to the period after circa A.D. 1000/1100. In this book I use this term for this temporal designation (Schroeder 2004a: 318). Some scholars have stopped using the term "Prehistory" (given the connotation that this was a time with no history) and now use the term "precontact" (see Schroeder 2004a: 318 for a clear explanation). The term "precontact," however, can still imply a level of staticness (see Hall and Silliman 2006 for a discussion of this). Neither term does justice to the dynamics of the period. In this book I use "Late Prehistory" (a term conventionally used in archaeology in Michigan) as the temporal designation. While this is not an ideal term, it is a descriptor that avoids confusion with earlier Late Woodland developments in other parts of the midcontinent and ties into the literature on the region.

2. This reflects an acculturative or adaptationist approach to technology. For instance, this kind of approach suggests that Native American peoples became aware that kettles would "let them be better Indians" because these items drastically increased their cooking efficiency, creating time for other activities (see Fitting 1976). Much work has shown that the acculturative model is flawed. It is clear that for decades after the introduction of kettles tribal communities used them for lots of things, but rarely for cooking (see Ehrhardt 2005 and Turgeon 1997 for details on the ways the kettle circulated and was used for symbolic purposes during early contact).

3. The review presented below is not exhaustive, and several other works provide details on the postcontact history of the region (see Cleland 1992; Clifton et al. 1986; Richter 1992; Richter and Merrell [eds.] 2003 [1987]; Tanner 1987; White 1991). Also, several nineteenth-century American Indian scholars wrote detailed histories of their own Great Lakes communities, including Simon Pokagon (Potawatomi) (1899), Kahgegagahbowh/George Copway (Mississauga Ojibwa) (1980 [1851]), Kahkewaquonaby/Peter Jones (Mississauga Ojibwa) (1861), Andrew J. Blackbird (Ottawa) (1887, 1897), and William W. Warren (Chippewa) (1984 [1885]).

4. The term "Algonquian" refers to speakers of one or more of the languages of the Algonquian family. As scholars like Carolyn Podruchny (2004: 694) have noted, this term covers peoples from a tremendous geographic range with concurrent tremendous cultural diversity and thus can be somewhat unsatisfying and awkward as a descriptor. Nevertheless, it remains useful when broadly discussing the indigenous space of the Northeast and Great Lakes (Brooks 2008). As described in the opening chapter, the Algonquian speakers

of the northern Great Lakes understood themselves as An-ish-in-aub-ag (Anishinaabeg). "Haudenosaunee" refers to the European-named Iroquois confederacy. In this book I use both historically imposed Western terms and indigenous terms for tribal communities.

5. As explicated by Gerald Vizenor (1998: 15), survivance, "in the sense of native surviv-ance, is more than survival, more than endurance or mere response; the stories of survivance are active presence."

Chapter 3. Monuments and Tribal Ritual Organization

1. Despite years of debate and scholarly work, no single synthesis of the appropriate way to use ceramic style to index social processes has been accepted across the discipline of archae-ology (see Deetz 1965; Hegmon 1992; Longacre 1966; Pollock 1983; Sackett 1985; Sinopoli 1991; Stark [ed.] 1998; Whallon 1968; Wiessner 1984; Wobst 1977). While debate contin-ues, ceramic style has been consistently shown to be an important indicator of social inter-action, social boundaries, and group identity in Late Woodland Michigan (Brashler 1981; Hambacher 1992; Holman 1978; Lovis 1973; Milner 1998; Stothers 1999).

2. In contrast, the work of Margaret B. Holman (1978) defining Pine River ware suggests that something more exclusive may have been occurring in the Mackinac Straits/Inland Waterway region during the early Late Woodland (ca. A.D. 600–1000).

3. This situation is very common at ritual centers. Documentation shows that groups go to particularly great lengths to acquire exotic raw materials for ritual artifacts (Helms 1993; see Spielmann 2002 for discussion of Hopewell ritual lithics made on materials from hun-dreds, even thousands, of kilometers away). The locations of preferred raw materials take on symbolic and social significance; in this process, the raw material can become as impor-tant as the mechanical function of the artifact itself (Bradley 2000: 90). Ritual artifacts made from preferred/exotic sources can come to be considered "pieces of places" by the producers and users of the artifacts (Bradley 2000: 88). Sites with a specialized use, such as ritual activ-ity, have been consistently documented throughout North America as having a wider range and greater number of highly exotic lithic materials than domestic use sites (Cameron 2001; Krakker 1997; Pugh 2001; Spielmann 2002; Winters 1984).

4. Local microenvironmental events and factors can create localized variation within larger ecosystems, however, and thus it is possible that micro lake-effect zones around this region's major inland lakes would have extended the growing season to allow for small-scale prehis-toric horticulture along these inland lakeshores. See Howey (2006: 50–55) for a detailed anal-ysis of National Oceanic and Atmospheric Administration (NOAA) weather records from the High Plains that suggests a micro lake-effect around Houghton Lake, the largest inland lake in Michigan. This raises the possibility that some years would have sufficient growing seasons. Nevertheless, while coastal communities had to consider fluctuations in productiv-ity of maize horticulture, anyone growing corn inland would have to consider fluctuations as a mere possibility. Maize could *not* have formed a major part of any local subsistence system during Late Prehistory.

5. Additionally, it should be noted that the evidence for both Late Archaic and historic occupation in this inland resource zone is a significant find in its own right. For the Late Archaic, most data come from sites in the Saginaw Valley (Lovis 1989; Lovis and Robertson 1989; Robertson et al. 1999). Thus the Meade's Bridge site (20RO5) holds the potential to alter current perspectives on Late Archaic occupation in the Great Lakes. In addition, while much has been written about Michigan during the historic period, very few archaeological sites from this time have been investigated (Cleland 1999). Those that have are large, well-documented sites, such as forts and missions (Cleland 1999). Hence Meade's Bridge (20RO5), as a Native American historic fur-trapping site, offers a unique chance to investigate Indian activities during the contact era in a context outside of large, European-dominated spaces.

Further, current models of historic resource procurement activities (including fur trapping) suggest that Michigan's Indian groups never traveled more than 80 miles upriver into the interior of the Lower Peninsula (cf. Tanner 1987). This historic fur-trapping site, more than 80 miles up the Muskegon River, could potentially alter such understandings.

6. Developing an accurate data set of earthen constructions in northern Michigan presents some challenges. Many of these sites were destroyed before they were ever reported, so this map presents an already reduced picture (Halsey 2003). Additionally, some mounds and earthworks were reported but have since been destroyed, and little is or can be known about them. Moreover, unreported sites may also exist. I digitized all sites to the quarter section level into GIS through consultation of three sources. First, U.S. Geological Survey (USGS) maps, which locate sites, were copied at the State Archaeologist's Office. Second, State Site Files were accessed at UMMA Great Lakes Range. Third, the *Archaeological Atlas of Michigan* (Hinsdale 1931) was also consulted. This last source was particularly important, as I tried to avoid counting double-reported sites in state site files. (All of Hinsdale's sites were assigned site numbers; as people reported new site numbers over the years, the same sites were often assigned another number. This seemed to be particularly common for earthworks.) My aim was to produce a data set of reported mounds and earthworks without duplication and include only constructions with some certainty of existence (as far as could be determined from available information in the site files). As work proceeded, each construction was assigned a level: certain, somewhat certain, somewhat uncertain, or uncertain. Those assigned the category "uncertain" were not included in this data set. The dating of mounds typically available was an estimate of broad cultural historical level: Middle Woodland or Late Woodland (which includes the period of interest in this study).

7. For a possible Hopewell-influenced mound in northern Michigan that has never been excavated, see the State Site File about the Kida Mounds (20BZ61) in Benzie County. The mounds were reported in these files as second in impressiveness only to Norton Mounds by Charles Cleland on a private visit.

8. But see John D. Speth (1966) on the Whorely Earthwork located in southern Michigan. He suggests that evidence does not support a fort interpretation. Likewise, Thomas Lee (1958) accepts the Parker Earthwork (a southern Ontario enclosure) as a fort, but it has features that complicate the picture, including burial mounds and light occupation debris.

9. In the process of eliminating reported enclosures that were clearly duplicates or did not exist based on my evaluation of the records and in-person site visits to their reported locales, I decided to leave out a reported pair of enclosures on Clam Lake (20AN11) that I am less confident existed. These enclosures were reported from an early historic reference but are not included in the Hinsdale atlas (1931). They might have been destroyed before Hinsdale made his atlas; but given that this vague reference was the only piece of information available, I decided not to include them. More information than this was available for all other enclosures. The pair of earthworks on Clam Lake, if real, would be interesting to consider, given their location in the Traverse Corridor.

10. Earthworks were commonly reported twice in State Site Files. This data set reflects my best attempt at an estimate of reported earthworks in these northern counties, without including duplicates, sites that probably never existed, and so on. During fieldwork in the region, I attempted to locate as many earthworks as possible to verify their existence. That information also informs this data set. I am aware of the presence of unreported earthworks on private property in Ogemaw County. I am working with a local amateur archaeologist who knows the landowners to try to gain access to these features; but as of now I cannot include them in this discussion. The potential to find more of these features even in this modern disturbed landscape is exciting.

Chapter 4. Staking Local Claims

1. Note that these excavations were explicitly done in a manner to avoid disturbing any interments in the mounds themselves but still be able to reveal the construction process and timing.

2. The combination of well-drained soils with the possibility of a micro lake-effect from Houghton Lake makes very small-scale horticulture a potential resource activity in this locale. While it could not have been a major economic activity of inland groups, it could indeed have been incorporated into the resource rounds. Long-time residents of the resort Bob and Carol Pennell have a photograph of the garden belonging to the previous owner of the Mounds resort, Mrs. Stoobey. In this garden, next to the smaller mound at the site, she grew corn completely organically (Pennell and Pennell, personal communication, 2004). This is an interesting possible explanation for the origin of the corn in these late features, but trade with the coasts is still the most parsimonious explanation.

3. Note that the landowner asked that no detailed information on this burial site in his yard be published, such as maps and photos.

4. Supplying an image was deemed inappropriate, given that this tool is a human remain. This item has been reported on the recently updated Native American Graves Protection and Repatriation Act (NAGPRA) roster at UMMA.

5. The faunal analysis was conducted by Amy Nicodemus, Great Lakes Range, UMMA. See Howey (2006: appendix C) for full tables.

6. An interesting hint supporting indirect trade arrangements as an important avenue of connection comes from a vessel recovered during work on a Late Prehistoric site in the Saginaw Valley. Several vessels were recovered, most of which fit with defined late coastal wares and even outside ceramic types (shell-tempering) (Sommer, personal communication, 2010). But one vessel did not fit with any currently defined Late Prehistoric ceramic styles. It has features that seem to be common for "White Bird ware" (a term to describe distinctive vessels recovered from late contexts in the interior), most notably a channel running along the lip (Sommer, personal communication, 2010).

7. Portions of this chapter were previously published as "Confounding Kinship: Regional Ritual Organization in Northern Michigan, AD 1200–1600," in *Ancient Complexities: New Perspectives in Pre-Columbian North America*, edited by Susan Alt, Foundations in Archaeological Inquiry (Salt Lake City: University of Utah Press, 2010).

Chapter 5. Coming Together

1. The mound near 20MA12 was not assigned a distinct site number; the mound south of the western enclosure, excavated by Greenman (1927b), was assigned site number 20MA10.

2. Indeed, Cleland and his crew cut their 1965 season short because the cultural debris was so light. His crew moved to test other sites, including the nearby Boven enclosures and the Skegemog Point village site (20GT8) in the Traverse Corridor.

3. The axe and remains are part of the NAGPRA inventory at UMMA; images are not shown because of the sacred nature of human remains and associated grave goods.

4. This boulder appears to be roughly 2 meters in circumference. Whether it was moved into the earthwork or already located there is not known. But I do think it would have been possible for the constructors of the enclosures to move the boulder into its centered position.

5. Before conducting this comparison, I assessed the possibility that significant differences between vessels from (1) the two separate enclosures and (2) the three outside activity stations confounded the pattern between inside and outside enclosure space. The ceramics from the two enclosures do not differ significantly in any decorative or functional variable. The ceramics from the three outside activity stations do not differ in any decorative variable.

They do differ in some functional attributes, but not in ways that negate the inside/outside comparison.

6. Highly exotic materials occur infrequently: one lithic flake of the highly exotic Mercer chert from 650 kilometers south in Ohio and three flakes of the even more exotic Indiana hornstone from 800 kilometers south in Indiana (Luedtke 1976; see fig. 3.2).

7. This table presents only materials found at all three lithic-producing stations because including the infrequently occurring exotics, Mercer and Indiana hornstone, made a statistical test of differences between the three stations invalid (too many cells under 5 to run a test).

8. Portions of this chapter were previously published as "Midewiwin Myths, Missaukee Earthworks: Living Traditions and Material Evidence in the Archaeologies of Religion" in *Religion, Archaeology, and the Material World*, edited by Lars Fogelin (Center for Archaeological Investigations, Occasional Paper No. 36; Carbondale: Southern Illinois University). Copyright 2008 by the Board of Trustees, Southern Illinois University.

Chapter 6. Pairs and Precincts

1. Site numbers referencing features of this complex are 20WX37, 20WX155 (Hardy Earthwork), 20WX39, 20WX103, and 20WX104. No professional archaeological work ever occurred at these enclosures, and the Hardy Earthwork is reported to have been destroyed. I did not locate these enclosures during fieldwork.

2. The various site numbers referencing the Mosquito Creek earthwork complex are 20MA19 (Boven enclosure), 20MA6 (the burial mound), 20MA7, 20MA8, 20MA9, 20MA53, and 20MA56.

3. Unfortunately, the scale and accuracy of the maps showing the locations of the enclosures and their orientation to each other are not reliable, because distances and orientation are hand-drawn relative to roads and other landmarks rather than physically measured and plotted.

4. I examined all extant ceramic collections from across the earthwork cluster, including private collections when possible. No sampling occurred; I looked at the entire research universe available at the time. Again, little systematic research has occurred at these sites. I hope to inspire others to revisit these sites, expand investigations and research, and in turn increase available assemblages.

5. All work was conducted with *ArcGIS* 9.1, an Environmental Systems Research Institute (ESRI) geographic information system.

6. In trying to understand connections between enclosures, I wanted to include all enclosures in the northern series. But to avoid forced robustness and patterning in the modeling, I included enclosures stringently, basing my decisions on definite existence rather than probable presence. Thus I did not include the Boon Earthworks. For the others, I included the location of the Boven Earthwork within the Mosquito Creek Earthworks (the only enclosure in the complex confirmed to exist); one location for the Walters-Linsenman enclosure (again the only enclosure in the pair confirmed); four locations for Rifle River enclosures (all known to exist and visited personally); and the location of Mikado. The other 23 sites selected are significant late sites in Michigan (ceramic type–defining sites like the Juntunen site, the Skegemog site, and Moccasin Bluff) or late sites where active fieldwork is occurring.

7. For the raw numbers of path length and cost, see Howey 2007: table 3.

8. A noteworthy survey of the Muskegon River drainage was conducted by Earl J. Prahl (1966), who reported only small winter hunting sites in the interior reaches of the watershed; this GIS work (as well as the work presented throughout this book) suggests that revisiting this watershed is worthwhile.

Works Cited

Ackerman, Robert E., and Lillian A. Ackerman
1973   "Ethnoarcheological Interpretations of Territoriality and Land Use in Southwestern Alaska." *Ethnohistory* 20(4): 315–34.

Adler, Michael A.
2002   "Negotiating the Village: Community Landscapes in the Late Pre-Historic American Southwest." In *Inscribed Landscapes: Marking and Making Place,* edited by Bruno David and Meredith Wilson, pp. 200–218. Honolulu: University of Hawaii Press.

Adler, Michael A., and Richard H. Wilshusen
1990   "Large-scale Integrative Facilities in Tribal Societies: Cross-cultural Examples and Southwestern U.S. Examples." *World Archaeology* 22(2): 133–46.

Albert, Dennis A.
1995   *Regional Landscape Ecosystems of Michigan, Minnesota, and Wisconsin: A Working Map and Classification.* Gen. Tech. Rep. NC-178. St. Paul: U.S. Department of Agriculture, Forest Service, North Central Forest Experiment Station. Northern Prairie Wildlife Research Center Online: http://www.npwrc.usgs.gov/resource/1998/rlandscp/rlandscp.htm (Version 03JUN98).

Albert, Dennis A., Shirley R. Denton, and Burton V. Barnes
1986   *Regional Landscape Ecosystems of Michigan.* Ann Arbor: School of Natural Resources University of Michigan.

Aldenderfer, M. S.
1993   "Ritual, Hierarchy, and Change in Foraging Societies." *Journal of Anthropological Archaeology* 12(1): 1–40.

Alt, Susan (editor)
2010   *Ancient Complexities: New Perspectives in Precolumbian North America.* Foundations in Archaeological Inquiry. Salt Lake City: University of Utah Press.

Anderson, Benedict
2006 [1983] *Imagined Communities.* Revised ed. London: Verso.

Andrefsky, William
1994   "Raw-Material Availability and the Organization of Technology." *American Antiquity* 59(1): 21–34.
1998   *Lithics: Macroscopic Approaches to Analysis.* Cambridge: Cambridge University Press.

Angel, Michael
2002   *Preserving the Sacred: Historical Perspectives on the Ojibwa Midewiwin.* Winnipeg: University of Manitoba Press.

Arnold, Jeanne E.
2000   "Revisiting Power, Labor Rights, and Kinship: Archaeology and Social Theory." In *Social Theory in Archaeology,* edited by Michael B. Schiffer, pp. 14–30. Foundations in Archaeological Inquiry. Salt Lake City: University of Utah Press.

Arnold, Jeanne E. (editor)
1996   *Emergent Complexity: The Evolution of Intermediate Societies.* Ann Arbor: International Monographs in Prehistory.

Ashmore, Wendy, and Arthur B. Knapp
1999   "Introduction." In *Archaeologies of Landscape: Contemporary Perspectives,* edited by Wendy Ashmore and Arthur B. Knapp, pp. 1–32. London: Blackwell Publishing.

Axtell, James
1997   *The Indians' New South: Cultural Change in the Colonial Southeast.* Baton Rouge: Louisiana State University Press.

Bailey, Reeve M., William C. Latta, and Gerald R. Smith
2004   *An Atlas of Michigan Fishes.* Ann Arbor: Museum of Zoology, University of Michigan.

Barker, Alexander W.
1999   "Chiefdoms and the Economics of Perversity." Ph.D. dissertation, University of Michigan, Ann Arbor.

Barnes, Burton V., and Warren H. Wagner
2004   *Michigan Trees: A Guide to the Trees of the Great Lakes Region.* Ann Arbor: University of Michigan Press.

Barrett, John C.
1994   *Fragments from Antiquity: An Archaeology of Social Life in Britain, 2900–1200 BC.* Oxford: Basil Blackwell.

Barrett, John C., Richard Bradley, and Martin Green (editors)
1991   *Landscape, Monuments and Society: The Prehistory of Cranborne Chase.* Cambridge: Cambridge University Press.

Barth, Fredrik
1967   "On the Study of Social Change." *American Anthropologist* 69(6): 661–69.

Basso, Keith H.
1996   *Wisdom Sits in Places: Landscape and Language among the Western Apache.* Albuquerque: University of New Mexico Press.

Beck, Robin
2006   "Persuasive Politics and Domination at Cahokia and Moundville." In *Leadership and Polity in Mississippian Society,* edited by Brian Butler and Paul Welch, pp. 19–42. Center for Archaeological Investigations, Occasional Paper No. 33. Carbondale: Southern Illinois University.

Beld, Scott
1993   "Site 20IA37 (Arthursburg Hill Earthworks), Lyons Township, Ionia County,
        Michigan." In *Lyons Township Archaeological Survey, S-92-313,* edited by S. Beld,
        pp. 3–82. Lansing, Mich.: Office of the State Archaeologist.
2004   Personal Communication. University of Michigan Museum of Anthropology.

Bell, Catherine M.
1992   *Ritual Theory, Ritual Practice.* New York: Oxford University Press.
1997   *Ritual: Perspectives and Dimensions.* New York: Oxford University Press.

Bell, Tyler, and Gary R. Lock
2000   "Topographic and Cultural Influences on Walking the Ridgeway in Later
        Prehistoric Times." In *Beyond the Map: Archaeology and Spatial Technologies,*
        edited by Gary Lock, pp. 85–100. Amsterdam: IOS Press, Amsterdam.

Bender, Barbara
1990   "The Dynamics of Nonhierarchical Societies." In *The Evolution of Political Systems:
        Sociopolitics in Small-scale Sedentary Societies,* edited by Steadman Upham, pp.
        247–63. Cambridge: Cambridge University Press.

Bender, Barbara, and Paul Aitken
1998   *Stonehenge: Making Space.* Oxford: Berg.

Bernardini, Wesley
2004   "Hopewell Geometric Earthworks: A Case Study in the Referential and
        Experiential Meaning of Monuments." *Journal of Anthropological Archaeology*
        23(3): 331–56.

Binford, Lewis R.
1979   "Organization and Formation Processes: Looking at Curated Technologies."
        Journal of Anthropological Research 35(3): 255–73.
1980   "Willow Smoke and Dogs' Tails: Hunter-Gatherer Settlement Systems and
        Archaeological Site Formation." *American Antiquity* 45(1): 4–20.

Binford, Lewis R., and George I. Quimby
1963   "Indian Sites and Chipped Stone Materials in the Northern Lake Michigan Area."
        Fieldiana 36: 277–307.

Bird-David, Nurit
1992   "Beyond 'The Original Affluent Society': A Culturalist Reformulation." *Current
        Anthropology* 33(1): 25–47.

Blackbird, Andrew J.
1887   *History of the Ottawa and Chippewa Indians of Michigan.* Ypsilanti, Mich.:
        Ypsilantian Job Printing House.
1897   *Complete Both Early and Late History of the Ottawa and Chippewa Indians of
        Michigan: A Grammar of Their Language, Personal and Family History of the
        Author.* Harbor Springs, Mich.: Babcock and Darling.

Blackhawk, Ned
2006   *Violence Over the Land: Indians and Empires in the Early American West.*
        Cambridge, Mass: Harvard University Press.

Blakeslee, Donald
1987   "John Rowzee Peyton and the Myth of the Mound Builders." *American Antiquity*
        52(4): 784–92.

2002   "Fractal Archaeology: Intra-Generational Cycles and the Matter of Scale, an Example from the Central Plains." In *The Archaeology of Tribal Societies,* edited by William A. Parkinson, pp. 173–99. Ann Arbor: International Monographs in Prehistory.

Blanton, Richard, Gary M. Feinman, Stephen A. Kowalewski, and Peter N. Peregrine
1996   "A Dual-Processual Theory for the Evolution of Mesoamerican Civilization." *Current Anthropology* 37(1): 1–14.

Blasingham, Emily
1956   "The Depopulation of Illinois, Part I." *Ethnohistory* 3(3): 193–224.

Blitz, John H.
1999   "Mississippian Chiefdoms and the Fission–Fusion Process." *American Antiquity* 64: 577–92.
2009   "New Perspectives in Mississippian Archaeology." *Journal of Archaeological Research* (published online August 21, 2009).

Blundell, Valda J.
1980   "Hunter-Gatherer Territoriality: Ideology and Behavior in Northwest Australia." *Ethnohistory* 27(2): 103–17.

Bourque, Bruce J.
1994   "Evidence for Prehistoric Trade on the Maritime Peninsula." In *Prehistoric Exchange Systems in North America,* edited by Timothy G. Baugh and Jonathon E. Ericson, pp. 23–46. New York: Plenum Press.

Bourque, Bruce J., and Ruth H. Whitehead
1985   "Tarrentines and the Introduction of European Trade Goods in the Gulf of Maine." *Ethnohistory* 32: 327–41.

Bradley, James W.
1987   *Evolution of the Onondaga Iroquois: Accommodating Change, 1500–1655.* Syracuse: Syracuse University Press.
2007   *Before Albany: An Archaeology of Native-Dutch Relations in the Capital Region, 1600–1664.* Albany: New York State Museum Bulletin.

Bradley, Richard
1998   *The Significance of Monuments: On the Shaping of Human Experience in Neolithic and Bronze Age Europe.* London: Routledge.
2000   *An Archaeology of Natural Places.* London: Routledge.
2002   "The Land, the Sky and the Scottish Stone Circle." In *Monuments and Landscape in Atlantic Europe: Perception and Society during the Neolithic and Early Bronze Age,* edited by Christopher Scarre, pp. 122–38. London: Routledge.

Brandão, Jose A., and William A. Starna
1996   "Treaties of 1701: A Triumph of Iroquois Diplomacy." *Ethnohistory* 43(2): 209–44.

Brandt, Kari L.
1996   "The Effects of Early Agriculture on Native North American Populations: Evidence from the Teeth and Skeleton." Ph.D. dissertation, University of Michigan, Ann Arbor.

Branstner, Susan
1992   "Tionontate Huron Occupation at the Marquette Mission." In *Calumet and Fleur-de-Lys: Archaeology of Indian and French Contact in the Midcontinent,* edited

by John A. Walthall and Thomas E. Emerson, pp. 177–201. Washington, D.C.:
Smithsonian Institution Press.

Brashler, Janet G.
1981   *Early Late Woodland Boundaries and Interaction: Indian Ceramics of Southern
        Lower Michigan.* East Lansing: Michigan State University Museum.

Brashler, Janet G., and Margaret. B. Holman
1985   "Late Woodland Continuity and Change in the Saginaw Valley of Michigan."
        Arctic Anthropology 22(2): 141–52.

Braun, David P., and Stephen Plog
1982   "Evolution of 'Tribal' Social Networks: Theory and Prehistoric North American
        Evidence." *American Antiquity* 47(3): 504–25.

Breck, James
2004   *Compilation of Databases on Michigan Lakes.* State of Michigan Department of
        Natural Resources, http://www.michigan.gov/documents/dnr/2004-2tr_362468_7.
        pdf.

Brooks, Lisa
2008   *The Common Pot: The Recovery of Native Space in the Northeast.* Minneapolis:
        University of Minnesota Press.

Brose, David S.
1971   "The Direct Historic Approach to Michigan Archaeology." *Ethnohistory* 18(1):
        51–61.
2001   "Introduction to Eastern North America at the Dawn of European Colonization."
        In *Societies in Eclipse: Archaeology of the Eastern Woodlands Indians, A.D. 1400–
        1700,* edited by David S. Brose, Robert C. J. Mainfort, and Wesley C. Cowan, pp.
        1–7. Washington, D.C.: Smithsonian Institution Press.

Brose, David S., and Michael Hambacher
1999   "The Middle Woodland in Northern Michigan." In *Retrieving Michigan's Buried
        Past: The Archaeology of the Great Lakes State,* edited by John R. Halsey and
        Michael D. Stafford, pp. 173–92. Bloomfield Hills, Mich.: Cranbrook Institute of
        Science.

Brose, David S., and N'omi Greber (editors)
1979   *Hopewell Archaeology.* Kent, Ohio: Kent State University Press.

Brose, David S., Robert C. J. Mainfort, and Wesley C. Cowan (editors)
2001   *Societies in Eclipse: Archaeology of the Eastern Woodlands Indians, A.D. 1400–1700.*
        Washington, D.C.: Smithsonian Institution Press.

Brown, James A.
1997   "The Archaeology of Ancient Religion in the Eastern Woodlands." *Annual Review
        of Anthropology* 26: 465–85.
2004   "The Cahokian Expression: Creating Court and Cult." In *Hero, Hawk, and Open
        Hand: American Indian Art of the Ancient Midwest and South,* edited by Robert V.
        Sharp, pp. 105–23. New Haven: Yale University Press.

Buikstra, Jane E., and Douglas K. Charles
1999   "Centering the Ancestors: Cemeteries, Mounds, and Sacred Landscapes of
        the Ancient North American Midcontinent." In *Archaeologies of Landscape:*

Contemporary Perspectives, edited by Wendy Ashmore and Arthur B. Knapp, pp. 201–28. London: Blackwell Publishing.

Burnett, Adam W., Matthew E. Kirby, Henry T. Mullins, and William P. Patterson
2003   "Increasing Great Lake–Effect Snowfall during the Twentieth Century: A Regional Response to Global Warming?" *Journal of Climate* 16(21): 3535–42.

Cameron, Catherine M.
2001   "Pink Chert, Projectile Points, and the Chacoan Regional System." *American Antiquity* 66(1): 79–101.

Cameron, Catherine M., and H. W. Toll
2001   "Deciphering the Organization of Production in Chaco Canyon." *American Antiquity* 66(1): 5–13.

Carlson, Roy L.
1994   "Trade and Exchange in Prehistoric British Columbia." In *Prehistoric Exchange Systems in North America,* edited by Timothy G. Baugh and Jonathon E. Ericson, pp. 307–62. New York: Plenum Press.

Carneiro, Robert
1987   "Cross-currents in the Theory of State Formation." *American Ethnologist* 14: 756–70.
2002   "The Tribal Village and Its Culture: An Evolutionary Stage in the History of Human Society." In *The Archaeology of Tribal Societies,* edited by William A. Parkinson, pp. 34–52. Ann Arbor: International Monographs in Prehistory.

Carr, Christopher, and D. T. Case (editors)
2005   *Gathering Hopewell: Society, Ritual, and Ritual Interaction.* New York: Kluwer Academic/Plenum Publishers.

Carruthers, Peter J.
1969   "The Mikado Earthwork 20AA5." Ph.D. dissertation, University of Calgary, Alberta, Canada.

Cashdan, Elizabeth A.
1983   "Territoriality among Human Foragers: Ecological Models and an Application to Four Bushman Groups." *Current Anthropology* 24(1): 47–55.

Cashdan, Elizabeth A. (editor)
1990   *Risk and Uncertainty in Tribal and Peasant Economies.* Westview Press, Boulder.

Chapman, Robert W.
1995   "Ten Years After: Megaliths, Mortuary Practices, and the Territorial Model." In *Regional Approaches to Mortuary Analysis,* edited by Lane A. Beck, pp. 29–51. New York: Plenum Press.
2003   *Archaeologies of Complexity.* London: Routledge.

Charles, Douglas K., and Jane E. Buikstra
2002   "Siting, Sighting and Citing the Dead." In *The Space and Place of Death,* vol. 11, edited by Helaine Silverman and David Small, pp. 13–26. Arlington, Va.: American Anthropological Association.

Childe, Vere Gordon
1950   "The Urban Revolution." *Town Planning Review* 21: 3–17.

Clark, Caven
1982   "Lithic Configurations and Raw Material Distribution at an Archaic Site in Central Lower Michigan." *Michigan Archaeologist* 28(4): 79–91.

Clay, R. Berle
1987   "Circles and Ovals: Two Types of Adena Space." *Southeastern Archaeology* 6: 46–56.
1998   "The Essential Features of Adena Ritual and their Implications." *Southeastern Archaeology* 17: 1–21.
2009   "Where Have All the Houses Gone? Webb's Adena House in Historical Context." *Southeastern Archaeology* 28: 29–63.

Cleland, Charles E.
1965   "Field Notes from 1965 Season at the Missaukee Earthworks." On file in the University of Michigan Museum of Anthropology Great Lakes Range.
1966   *The Prehistoric Animal Ecology and Ethnozoology of the Upper Great Lakes Region.* Anthropological Papers No. 29. Ann Arbor: University of Michigan Museum of Anthropology.
1982   "The Inland Shore Fishery of the Northern Great Lakes: Its Development and Importance in Prehistory." *American Antiquity* 47(4): 761–84.
1992   *Rites of Conquest: The History and Culture of Michigan's Native Americans.* Ann Arbor: University of Michigan Press.
1999   "Cultural Transformation: The Archaeology of Historic Indian Sites in Michigan, 1670–1940." In *Retrieving Michigan's Buried Past: The Archaeology of the Great Lakes State,* edited by John R. Halsey and Michael D. Stafford, pp. 244–48. Bloomfield Hills, Mich.: Cranbrook Institute of Science.

Clifton, James A.
1977   *The Prairie People: Continuity and Change in Potawatomi Indian Culture, 1665–1965.* Lawrence: Regents Press of Kansas.

Clifton, James A., James M. McClurken, and George Cornell
1986   *People of the Three Fires: The Ottawa, Potawatomi, and Ojibway of Michigan.* Grand Rapids, Mich.: Grand Rapids Inter-Tribal Council Publishing.

Cobb, Christopher
2005   "Archaeology and the 'Savage Slot': Displacement and Emplacement in the Premodern World." *American Anthropologist* 107(4): 563–74.

Cobb, Christopher, and Adam King
2005   "Re-Inventing Mississippian Tradition at Etowah, Georgia." *Journal of Archaeological Method and Theory* 12(3): 167–92.

Comer, P. J., D. A. Albert, H. A. Wells, B. L. Hart, J. B. Raab, D. L. Price, D. M. Kashian, R. A. Corner, and D. W. Scheun
1995   *Michigan's Native Landscape, as Interpreted from the General Land Office Surveys, 1816–1856.* Lansing: Michigan Natural Features Inventory (digital map).

Conkey, Margaret W.
1980   "The Identification of Prehistoric Hunter-Gatherer Aggregation Sites: The Case of Altamira." *Current Anthropology* 21(5): 609–30.

Conn, Steven
2004   *History's Shadow: Native Americans and Historical Consciousness in the Nineteenth Century.* Chicago: University of Chicago Press.

Copway, George
1980 [1851] *The Traditional History and Characteristic Sketches of the Ojibway Nation.*
        Boston: B. F. Mussey & Co.

Cornelius, Eldon S., and Harold W. Moll
1961   "The Walters-Linsenman Earthwork Site." *Totem Pole* 44(9).

Crawford, Gary W., David G. Smith, and Vandy E. Bowyer
1997   "Dating the Entry of Corn (*Zea mays*) into the Lower Great Lakes Region."
        American Antiquity 62(1): 112–19.

Crown, Patricia, and Jeffery Hurst
2009   "Evidence of Cacao Use in the Prehispanic American Southwest." *Proceedings of
        the National Academy of Science* 106(7): 2110–13.

Dancey, William S., and Paul J. Pacheco (editors)
1997   *Ohio Hopewell Community Organization.* Kent, Ohio: Kent State University Press.

Daniel, Glenda, and Jerry Sullivan
1981   *A Sierra Club Naturalist's Guide to the North Woods of Michigan, Wisconsin, and
        Minnesota.* San Francisco: Sierra Club Books.

DeBoer, Warren, and John H. Blitz
1991   "Ceremonial Centers of the Chachi." *Expedition* 33(1): 53–62.

Deetz, James
1965   *The Dynamics of Stylistic Change in Arikara Ceramics.* Urbana: University of
        Illinois Press.

Deloria, Phillip J.
1998   *Playing Indian.* New Haven: Yale University Press.

DeMarrais, Elizabeth, Timothy K. Earle, and Luis J. Castillo
1996   "Ideology, Materialization, and Power Strategies." *Current Anthropology* 37(1):
        15–31.

Densmore, Frances
1929   *Chippewa Customs.* Bulletin 86. Washington, D.C.: U.S. Govt. Printing Office.

Dewdney, Selwyn H.
1975   *The Sacred Scrolls of the Southern Ojibway.* Toronto: University of Toronto Press.

Dibble, Harold L., Utsav Schurmans, Radu P. Iovita, and Michael V. McLaughlin
2005   "The Measurement and Interpretation of Cortex in Lithic Assemblages." *American
        Antiquity* 70(3): 545–60.

Dietler, Michael, and Brian D. Hayden (editors)
2001   *Feasts: Archaeological and Ethnographic Perspectives on Food, Politics, and Power.*
        Washington, D.C.: Smithsonian Institution Press.

Dillehay, Tom D.
1990   "Mapuche Ceremonial Landscape, Social Recruitment and Resource Rights."
        World Archaeology 22(2): 223–41.
2007   *Monuments, Empires, and Resistance: The Araucanian Polity and Ritual Narratives.*
        Cambridge: Cambridge University Press.

Dowd, Gregory E.
2002   *War under Heaven: Pontiac, the Indian Nations, and the British Empire.* Baltimore:
        John Hopkins University Press.

Dunham, Sean B.

2000   "Cache Pits: Ethnohistory, Archaeology, and the Continuity of Tradition."
In *Interpretations of Native North American Life: Material Contributions to
Ethnohistory,* edited by Michael Nassaney and Eric S. Johnson, pp. 225–60.
Gainesville: University Press of Florida.

2009   "Nuts about Acorns: A Pilot Study on Acorn Use in Woodland Period Subsistence
in the Eastern Upper Peninsula of Michigan." *Wisconsin Archaeologist* 90: 113–30.

Durkheim, Emile

1976 [1912]   *The Elementary Forms of the Religious Life.* 2nd ed. London: Allen and Unwin.

Dustin, Fred

1932   *Report on the Indian Earthworks in Ogemaw County, Michigan.* Bloomfield Hills,
Mich.: Cranbrook Institute of Science.

1966   "Prehistoric Storage Pits in Saginaw County, Michigan." *Michigan Archaeologist*
14(1–2): 48–52.

DuVal, Kathleen

2006   *The Native Ground: Indians and Colonists in the Heart of the Continent.*
Philadelphia: University of Pennsylvania Press.

Dyson-Hudson, Rada, and Eric A. Smith

1978   "Human Territoriality: An Ecological Reassessment." *American Anthropologist*
80(1): 21–41.

Eagan, Kathryn

1990   "Paleoecology of the Bridgeport Area." In *The Bridgeport Township Site:
Archaeological Investigation at 20SA620, Saginaw County, Michigan,* edited by
John M. O'Shea and Michael Shott, pp. 11–20. Ann Arbor: University of Michigan
Museum of Anthropology.

Earle, Timothy K.

1997   *How Chiefs Come to Power: The Political Economy in Prehistory.* Stanford: Stanford
University Press.

Edmonds, Mark

1999   *Ancestral Geographies of the Neolithic: Landscapes, Monuments, and Memory.*
London: Routledge.

Edmunds, R. David

1978   *The Potawatomis, Keepers of the Fire.* Norman: University of Oklahoma Press.

Ehrhardt, Kathleen L.

2005   *European Metals in Native Hands: Rethinking the Dynamics of Technological
Change, 1640–1683.* Tuscaloosa: University of Alabama Press.

Eldridge, William H., Marc D. Bacigalipi, Ira R. Adelman, Loren M. Miller, and Anne R.
Kapuscinski.

2002   "Determination of Relative Survival of Two Stocked Walleye Populations and
Resident Natural-Origin Fish by Microsatellite DNA Parentage Assignment."
Canadian Journal of Fisheries and Aquatic Sciences 59(2): 282–91.

Emerson, Thomas E.

1997   *Cahokia and the Archaeology of Power.* Tuscaloosa: University of Alabama Press.

Emerson, Thomas E., Susan Alt, and Timothy R. Pauketat
2008   "Locating American Indian Religion at Cahokia and Beyond." In *Religion, Archaeology, and the Material World,* edited by Lars Fogelin, pp. 216–36. Occasional Paper No. 36. Carbondale, Ill.: Center for Archaeological Investigations.

Ethridge, Robbie
2003   *Creek Country: The Creek Country and Their World, 1796–1816.* Chapel Hill: University of North Carolina Press.
2009   "Introduction." In *Mapping the Mississippian Shatter Zone: The Colonial Indian Slave Trade and Regional Instability in the American South,* edited by Robbie Ethridge and Sheri Shuck-Hall, pp. 1–62. Lincoln: University of Nebraska Press.

Ethridge, Robbie, and Charles Hudson (editors)
2002   *The Transformation of the Southeastern Indians, 1540–1760.* Jackson: University Press of Mississippi.

Ewers, John C.
1988   *Indian Life on the Upper Missouri.* Norman: University of Oklahoma Press.

Feeley-Harnik, Gillian
2001   "The Ethnography of Creation: Lewis Henry Morgan and the American Beaver." In *Relative Values: Reconfiguring Kinship Studies,* edited by Sarah Franklin and Susan McKinnon, pp. 54–84. Durham, N.C.: Duke University Press.

Feinman, Gary M., Kent G. Lightfoot, and Steadman Upham
2000   "Political Hierarchies and Organizational Strategies in the Puebloan Southwest." *American Antiquity* 65(3): 449–70.

Feinman, Gary M., and Jill Neitzel
1984   "Too Many Types: An Overview of Sedentary Prestate Societies in the Americas." In *Advances in Archaeological Method and Theory,* vol. 7, pp. 39–102. New York: Academic Press.

Fenton, William N.
1998   *The Great Law and the Longhouse: A Political History of the Iroquois Confederacy.* Norman: University of Oklahoma Press.

Fitting, James E.
1966   "Archaeological Investigations of the Carolinian-Canadian Edge Area in Michigan." *Michigan Archaeologist* 12(4): 143–49.
1968   "The Spring Creek Site." In *Contributions to Michigan Archaeology,* edited by James E. Fitting, John R. Halsey, and H. Martin Wobst, pp. 1–78. Anthropological Papers No. 32. Ann Arbor: University of Michigan Museum of Anthropology.
1975   *The Archaeology of Michigan: A Guide to the Prehistory of the Great Lakes Region.* 2nd ed. Bloomfield Hills, Mich.: Cranbrook Institute of Science.
1976   "Patterns of Acculturation at the Straits of Mackinac." In *Cultural Change and Continuity: Essays in Honor of James Bennett Griffin,* edited by Charles E. Cleland, pp. 321–34. New York: Academic Press.

Fitting, James E. (editor)
1972   *The Schultz Site at Green Point, A Stratified Occupation Area in the Saginaw Valley of Michigan.* Memoirs No. 4. Ann Arbor: University of Michigan Museum of Anthropology.

Fitting, James E., and Charles E. Cleland
1969   "Late Prehistoric Settlement Patterns in the Upper Great Lakes." *Ethnohistory* 16(4): 289–302.

Fitzgerald, William R., Ruth H. Whitehead, James W. Bradley, and Laurier Turgeon
1993   "Late Sixteenth-Century Basque Banded Copper Kettles." *Historical Archaeology* 27(1): 44–57.

Ford, Richard I.
1972   "Barter, Gift, or Violence: An Analysis of Tewa Intertribal Exchange." In *Social Exchange and Interaction,* edited by Edward Wilmsen, pp. 21–45. Anthropological Papers No. 46. Ann Arbor: University of Michigan Museum of Anthropology.

Fortier, Jana
2001   "Sharing, Hoarding, and Theft: Exchange and Resistance in Forager-Farmer Relations." *Ethnology* 40(3): 193–211.

Fowles, Severin M.
2002   "From Social Type to Social Process: Placing 'Tribe' in a Historical Framework." In *The Archaeology of Tribal Societies,* edited by William A. Parkinson, pp. 13–33. Ann Arbor: International Monographs in Prehistory.
2009   "The Enshrined Pueblo: Villagescape and Cosmos in the Northern Rio Grande." *American Antiquity* 74(3): 448–66.

Fox, William A.
2009   "Events Seen from the North: The Iroquois Confederacy and Colonial Slavery." In *Mapping the Mississippian Shatter Zone: The Colonial Indian Slave Trade and Regional Instability in the American South,* edited by Robbie Ethridge and Sheri Shuck-Hall, pp. 63–80. Lincoln: University of Nebraska Press.

Fried, Morton H.
1966   "On the Concepts of 'Tribe' and 'Tribal Society.'" *Transactions of the New York Academy of Science Series II* 28(4): 527–40.
1967   *Evolution of Political Society.* New York: Random House.
1975   *The Notion of Tribe.* Menlo Park, Calif.: Cummings Publishing.

Gallivan, Martin D.
2003   *James River Chiefdoms: The Rise of Social Inequality in the Chesapeake.* Lincoln: University of Nebraska Press.
2007   "Powhatan's Werowocomoco: Constructing Place, Polity, and Personhood in the Chesapeake, C.E. 1200–C.E. 1609." *American Anthropologist* 1: 85–100.

Galloway, Patricia
1995   *Choctaw Genesis, 1500–1700.* Lincoln: University of Nebraska Press.
2002   "Colonial Period Transformations in the Mississippi Valley: Disintegration, Alliance, Confederation, Playoff." In *The Transformations of the Southeastern Indians, 1540–1760,* edited by Robbie Ethridge and Charles Hudson, pp. 225–48. Jackson: University Press of Mississippi.

Garland, Elizabeth B., and Scott Beld
1999   "The Early Woodland: Ceramics, Domesticated Plants, and Burial Mounds Foretell the Shape of the Future." In *Retrieving Michigan's Buried Past: The Archaeology of the Great Lakes State,* edited by John R. Halsey and Michael D. Stafford, pp. 125–46. Bloomfield Hills, Mich.: Cranbrook Institute of Science.

Gearing, Frederick O.
1958   "The Structural Poses of 18th Century Cherokee Villages." *American Anthropologist* 60: 1148–57.

Geertz, Clifford
1973   "Religion as a Cultural System." In *The Interpretation of Cultures,* pp. 87–125. New York: Basic Books.

Gibson, Jon
2007   "'Formed from the Earth at That Place': The Material Side of Community at Poverty Point." *American Antiquity* 72(3): 509–23.

Gnatkowski, Mike
2010   "Michigan's Best Bets for Ice-Fishing." *Game and Fish Magazine.*December 6, 2010. http://www.gameandfishmag.com/2010/12/06/fishing_icefishing-fishing_best_bets_ice-fishing_120610/2/.

Goldstein, Lynne G.
1981   "One-Dimensional Archaeology and Multi-dimensional People: Spatial Organization and Mortuary Analysis." In *The Archaeology of Death,* edited by Robert Chapman, Ian Kinnes, and Klavs Randsborg, pp. 53–69. Cambridge: Cambridge University Press.
1995   "Landscapes and Mortuary Practices: A Case for Regional Perspectives." In *Regional Approaches to Mortuary Analysis,* edited by Lane A. Beck, pp. 101–21. New York: Plenum Press.

Greber, N'omi
1979   "A Comparative Study of Site Morphology and Burial Patterns at Edwin Harness Mound and Seip Mounds 1 and 2." In *Hopewell Archaeology,* edited by David S. Brose and N'omi Greber, pp. 27–38. Kent, Ohio: Kent State University Press.

Greenman, Emerson F.
1926   "Field Notes from 1926 Season at the Missaukee Earthworks." On file in the University of Michigan Museum of Anthropology Great Lakes Range
1927a   "The Earthwork Inclosures of Michigan." Ph.D. dissertation, University of Michigan, Ann Arbor.
1927b   "Michigan Mounds, with Special Reference to Two in Missaukee County." *Michigan Academy of Science, Arts and Letters Papers* 7: 1–9.

Gregg, Susan (editor)
1991   *Between Bands and States.* Center for Archaeological Investigations, Occasional Paper No. 9. Carbondale: Southern Illinois University.

Griffin, James B., Richard E. Flanders, and Paul F. Titterington
1970   *The Burial Complexes of the Knight and Norton Mounds in Illinois and Michigan.* Ann Arbor: University of Michigan Museum of Anthropology.

Griffin, Patrick
2005   "Reconsidering the Ideological Origin of Indian Removal: The Case of the Big Bottom Massacre." In *The Center of a Great Empire: The Ohio Country in the Early American Republic,* edited by Andrew R. L. Cayton and Stuart D. Hobbs, pp. 11–35. Athens: Ohio University Press.

Grimes, Ronald L.
1982   *Beginnings in Ritual Studies.* Washington, D.C.: University Press of America.

Habeck, James R.
1960 "Winter Deer Activity in the White Cedar Swamps of Northern Wisconsin." *Ecology* 41(2): 327–33.

Hall, Martin, and Stephen W. Silliman
2006 "Introduction: Archaeology of the Modern World." In *Historical Archaeology*, edited by Martin Hall and Stephen W. Silliman, pp. 1–22. London: Blackwell Publishing.

Hall, Robert L.
1997 *An Archaeology of the Soul: North American Indian Belief and Ritual.* Urbana-Champaign: University of Illinois Press.

Halsey, John R.
2003 "Where Did All the Mounds Go? A Few Answers." Paper presented at the Annual Meeting of the Michigan Archaeological Society, East Lansing.

Halstead, Paul, and John O'Shea
1989 "Introduction: Cultural Responses to Risk and Uncertainty." In *Bad Year Economics: Cultural Responses to Risk and Uncertainty*, edited by Paul Halstead and John O'Shea, pp. 1–8. Cambridge: Cambridge University Press.

Hambacher, Michael
1992 "The Skegemog Point Site: Continuing Studies in the Cultural Dynamics of the Carolinian-Canadian Transition Zone." Ph.D. dissertation, Michigan State University, East Lansing.

Hambacher, Michael J., Margaret B. Holman, Kathryn C. Egan, and Beverley A. Smith
1995 "Camp, Cache and Carry: The Porter Creek South Site (20MN100) and Cache Pits at 20MN31 in the Manistee National Forest." *Michigan Archaeologist* 41(2): 47–94.

Harding, James H., and J. A. Holman
1997 *Michigan Turtles and Lizards: A Field Guide and Pocket Reference.* 2nd ed. East Lansing: Michigan State University.

Harpending, Henry C., and Herbert Davis
1977 "Some Implications for Hunter-Gatherer Ecology Derived from the Spatial Structure of Resources." *World Archaeology* 8(3): 275–86.

Hayden, Brian D.
1993 *Archaeology: The Science of Once and Future Things.* New York: W. H. Freeman and Co.

Heckenberger, Michael
2005 *The Ecology of Power: Culture, Place, and Personhood in the Southern Amazon, A.D. 1000–2000.* London: Routledge.

Hegmon, Michelle
1992 "Archaeological Research on Style." *Annual Review of Anthropology* 21: 517–36.

Hegmon, Michelle, Kelley Hays-Gilpin, Randall H. McGuire, Alison E. Rautman, and Sarah H. Schlanger
2000 "Changing Perceptions of Regional Interaction in the Prehistoric Southwest." In *Archaeology of Regional Interaction: Religion, Warfare, and Exchange across the American Southwest and Beyond*, pp. 1–21. Tempe: Arizona State University Press.

Helms, Mary W.
1993   *Craft and the Kingly Ideal: Art, Trade, and Power.* 1st ed. Austin: University of Texas Press.

Hickerson, Harold
1962   "Notes on the Post-Contact Origin of the Midewiwin." *Ethnohistory* 9(4): 404–23.
1963   "The Sociohistorical Significance of Two Chippewa Ceremonials." *American Anthropologist* 65(1): 67–85.
1966   "The Genesis of Bilaterality among Two Divisions of Chippewa." *American Anthropologist* 68(1): 1–26.
1970   *The Chippewa and Their Neighbors: A Study in Ethnohistory.* New York: Holt, Rinehart and Winston.

Hinderaker, Eric
1997   *Elusive Empires: Constructing Colonialism in the Ohio Valley, 1673–1800.* Cambridge: Cambridge University Press.

Hinsdale, Wilbert B.
1931   *Archaeological Atlas of Michigan.* Ann Arbor: University of Michigan Press.

Hodder, Ian
1984   "Burials, Houses, Women and Men in the European Neolithic." In *Ideology, Power and Prehistory,* edited by Daniel Miller and Christopher Tilley, pp. 51–68. Cambridge: Cambridge University Press.

Hoffman, William
1891   "The Midewiwin or 'Grand Medicine Society' of the Ojibwa." In *7th Annual Report of the Bureau of American Ethnology for the Years 1885–1886,* pp. 143–300. Washington, D.C.: Smithsonian Institution Press.

Holm, Tom, J. D. Pearson, and Ben Chavis
2003   "Peoplehood: A Model for the Extension of Sovereignty in American Indian Studies." *Wicazo Sa Review* 18(1): 7–24.

Holman, Margaret B.
1978   "The Settlement System of the Mackinac Phase." Ph.D. dissertation, Michigan State University, East Lansing.
1984   "Pine River Ware: Evidence for In Situ Development of the Late Woodland in the Straits of Mackinac Region." *Wisconsin Archeologist* 65: 32–48.

Holman, Margaret B., and Janet G. Brashler
1999   "Economics, Material Culture, and Trade in the Late Woodland Lower Peninsula of Michigan." In *Retrieving Michigan's Buried Past: The Archaeology of the Great Lakes State,* edited by John R. Halsey and Michael D. Stafford, pp. 212–20. Bloomfield Hills, Mich.: Cranbrook Institute of Science.

Holman, Margaret B., and Frank J. Krist
2001   "Late Woodland Storage and Mobility in Western Lower Michigan." *Wisconsin Archaeologist: Papers in Honor of Carol I Mason* 2: 7–32.

Holman, Margaret B., and William A. Lovis
2008   "The Social and Environmental Constraints on Mobility in the Late Prehistoric Upper Great Lakes Region." In *The Archaeology of Mobility: Old and New World Nomadism,* edited by H. Barnard and W. Wendrich, pp. 280–306. Los Angeles: Cotsen Institute of Archaeology, University of California.

Holtorf, Cornelius J.
1998 "The Life-Histories of Megaliths in Mecklenburg-Vorpommern (Germany)." *World Archaeology* 30(1): 23–38.

Houghten, M.
1990 "Late Archaic Lithics." Senior Honors thesis, University of Michigan, Ann Arbor.

Howey, Meghan C. L.
2006 "Ritual, Resources and Regional Organization in the Upper Great Lakes, A.D. 1200–1600." Ph.D. dissertation, University of Michigan, Ann Arbor.
2007 "Using Multicriteria Cost Surface Analysis to Explore Past Regional Landscapes: A Case Study of Ritual Activity and Social Interaction in Michigan, A.D. 1200–1600." *Journal of Archaeological Science* 34: 1830–46.

Howey, Meghan C. L., and John M. O'Shea
2006 "Bear's Journey and the Study of Ritual in Archaeology." *American Antiquity* 71(2): 261–82.
2009 "On Archaeology and the Study of Ritual: Considering Inadequacies in the Culture-History Approach and Quests for Internal 'Meaning.'" *American Antiquity* 74(1): 193–201.

Ingold, Tim
1993 "Temporality of the Landscape." *World Archaeology* 25(2): 152–74.
2000 *The Perception of the Environment: Essays on Livelihood, Dwelling and Skill.* London: Routledge.

Irwin, Sara
2004 "Liturgy Deconstructed." Master of Divinity thesis. General Seminary of the Episcopal Church, New York.

Jackson, H. Edwin
1991 "Trade Fair in Hunter-Gatherer Interaction: The Role of Intersocietal Trade in the Evolution of Poverty Point Culture." In *Between Bands and States,* edited by Susan Gregg, pp. 265–86. Center for Archaeological Investigations, Occasional Paper No. 9. Carbondale: Southern Illinois University.

Jaga, R., M. Novaline, A. Sundaram, and T. Natarajan
1993 "Wasteland Development Using Geographic Information System Techniques." *International Journal of Remote Sensing* 14: 3249–57.

Johansen, Kaspar L., Steffen T. Laursen, and Mads K. Holst
2004 "Spatial Patterns of Social Organization in the Early Bronze Age of South Scandinavia." *Journal of Anthropological Archaeology* 23(1): 33–55.

Johansen, Peter G.
2004 "Landscape, Monumental Architecture, and Ritual: A Reconsideration of the South Indian Ashmounds." *Journal of Anthropological Archaeology* 23(3): 309–30.

Johnson, Gregory A.
1982 "Organizational Structure and Scalar Stress." In *Theory and Explanation in Archaeology: The Southhampton Conference,* edited by Colin Renfrew, M. J. Rowlands, and B. A. Seagraves, pp. 389–421. New York: Academic Press.

Johnston, Basil
1990 *Ojibway Heritage.* Winnipeg, Manitoba, Canada: Bison Books.

Jones, Michael L., John K. Netto, Jason D. Stockwell, and Joseph B. Mion
2003   "Does the Value of Newly Accessible Spawning Habitat for Walleye (*Stizostedion vitreum*) Depend on Its Location Relative to Nursery Habitats?" *Canadian Journal of Fisheries and Aquatic Sciences* 60(12): 1527–39.

Jones, Peter
1861   *History of the Ojebway Indians; with Especial Reference to Their Conversion to Christianity.* London: A. W. Bennett.

Judge, W. James
1989   "Chaco Canyon—San Juan Basin." In *Dynamics of Southwest Prehistory,* edited by Linda S. Cordell and George J. Gumerman, pp. 209–61. Washington, D.C.: Smithsonian Institution Press.

Junker, Laura L.
1996   "Hunter-Gatherer Landscapes and Lowland Trade in the Prehispanic Philippines." *World Archaeology* 27(3): 389–410.
2002   "Economic Specialization and Inter-ethnic Trade between Foragers and Farmers in the Prehispanic Philippines." In *Forager-Traders in South and Southeast Asia,* edited by Kathleen Morrison and Laura Junker, pp. 203–41. Cambridge: Cambridge University Press.

Kashian, D. M., B. V. Barnes, and W. S. Walker
2003   "Landscape Ecosystems of Northern Lower Michigan and the Occurrence and Management of the Kirtland's Warbler." *Forest Science* 49(1): 140–59.

Katzenberg, M. Anne, Henry Schwarcz, Martin Knyf, and F. Jerome Melbye
1995   "Stable Isotope Evidence for Maize Horticulture and Paleodiet in Southern Ontario, Canada." *American Antiquity* 60(2): 335–50.

Keane, Webb
2007   *Christian Moderns: Freedom and Fetish in the Mission Encounter.* Berkeley: University of California Press.

Keen, Richard A.
1993   *Michigan Weather.* Helena, Mont.: American and World Geographic Pub.

Keener, Craig S.
1999   "An Ethnohistorical Analysis of Iroquois Assault Tactics Used against Fortified Settlements of the Northeast in the Seventeenth Century." *Ethnohistory* 46(4): 777–807.

Kelleher, Margaret M.
1985   "Liturgy: An Ecclesial Act of Meaning." *Worship* 59: 482–97.

Kelly, John E., James A. Brown, and Lucretia S. Kelly
2008   "The Context of Religion at Cahokia: The Mound 34 Case." In *Religion, Archaeology, and the Material World,* edited by Lars Fogelin, pp. 297–318. Occasional Paper No. 36. Carbondale Ill.: Center for Archaeological Investigations.

Kidder, Homer H.
1994 [1910]   *Ojibwa Narratives of Charles and Charlotte Kawbawgam and Jacques LePique, 1893–1895.* Detroit: Wayne State University Press.

Kidder, T. R.
2002   "Mapping Poverty Point." *American Antiquity* 67: 89–101.

Kingsley, Robert
1999   "The Middle Woodland Period in Southern Michigan." In *Retrieving Michigan's Buried Past: The Archaeology of the Great Lakes State,* edited by John R. Halsey and Michael D. Stafford, pp. 148–72. Bloomfield Hills, Mich.: Cranbrook Institute of Science.

Kinietz, W. Vernon
1940   *The Indians of the Western Great Lakes, 1615–1760.* Ann Arbor: University of Michigan Museum of Anthropology.
1947   *Chippewa Village: The Story of Katikitegon.* Bloomfield Hills, Mich.: Cranbrook Institute of Science.

Konkle, Maureen
2004   *Writing Indian Nations: Native Intellectuals and the Politics of Historiography, 1827–1863.* Chapel Hill: University of North Carolina Press.

Krakker, James
1997   "Biface Caches, Exchange, and Regulatory Systems in the Prehistoric Great Lakes Region." *Midcontinental Journal of Archaeology* 22(1): 1–41.
1999   "Late Woodland Settlement Patterns, Population, and Social Organization Viewed from Southern Michigan." In *Retrieving Michigan's Buried Past: The Archaeology of the Great Lakes State,* edited by John R. Halsey and Michael D. Stafford, pp. 228–43. Bloomfield, Mich.: Cranbrook Institute of Science.

Ladefoged, Thegn N., and Michael W. Graves
2000   "Evolutionary Theory and the Historical Development of Dry-Land Agriculture in North Kohala, Hawai'i." *American Antiquity* 65(3): 423–48.

Landes, Ruth
1968   *Ojibwa Religion and the Midéwiwin.* Madison: University of Wisconsin Press.

Lankford, George E.
2006   "Some Southwestern Influences in the Southeastern Ceremonial Complex." *Arkansas Archeologist* 45: 1–25.

Larson, Sidner
2007   "Following Multiple Perspectivism in James Welch's 'Winter in the Blood' and 'The Death of Jim Loney.'" *American Indian Quarterly* 31(4): 513–34.

Lee, Thomas
1958   "The Parker Earthwork, Corunna, Ontario." *Pennsylvania Archaeologist* 28: 5–32.

Leighly, John
1941   "Effect of the Great Lakes on the Annual March Temperature in Their Vicinity." *Papers of the Michigan Academy of Science, Arts, and Letters* 27: 377–414.

Lekson, Stephen
1999a   *The Chaco Meridian: Centers of Political Power in the Ancient Southwest.* Walnut Creek, Calif.: Altamira Press.
1999b   *Rude Stone Monuments: Monumental Architecture in Non-State Societies.* Rio Rancho, N.Mex.: SRI Foundation.
2000   "Architecture." In *Archaeology Southwest,* vol. 14 (1). Tucson: Center for Desert Archaeology Winter Update (edition dedicated to Chaco Project).
2009   *A History of the Ancient Southwest.* Santa Fe: School for Advanced Research Press.
2010   "The Good Gray Intermediate: Why Native Societies of North America Can't Be States." In *Ancient Complexities: New Perspectives in Precolumbian North America,*

edited by Susan Alt, pp. 177–82. Foundations in Archaeological Inquiry. Salt Lake City: University of Utah Press.

Lepper, Bradley
2004   "The Newark Earthworks: Monumental Geometry and Astronomy at a Hopewellian Pilgrimage Center." In *Hero, Hawk, and Open Hand: American Indian Art of the Ancient Midwest and South,* edited by Robert V. Sharp, pp. 73–82. New Haven: Yale University Press.

Liu, A. Q., and G. W. K. Moore
2004   "Lake-Effect Snowstorms over Southern Ontario, Canada, and Their Associated Synoptic-Scale Environment." *Monthly Weather Review* 132(11): 2595–2610.

Llobera, Marcos
2000   "Understanding Movement: A Pilot Model Towards the Sociology of Movement." In *Beyond the Map: Archaeology and Spatial Technologies,* edited by Gary Lock, pp. 65–84. Amsterdam: IOS Press.

Longacre, William A.
1966   "Changing Patterns of Social Integration: A Prehistoric Example from the American Southwest." *American Anthropologist* 68(1): 94–102.

Lovis, William A.
1973   "Late Woodland Cultural Dynamics in the Northern Lower Peninsula of Michigan." Ph.D. dissertation, Michigan State University, East Lansing.
1978   "A Numerical Taxonomic Analysis of Changing Woodland Site Location Strategies on an Interior Lake Chain." *Michigan Academician* 11(1): 39–48.
1985   "Seasonal Settlement Dynamics and the Role of the Fletcher Site in the Woodland Adaptations of the Saginaw Drainage Basin." *Arctic Anthropology* 22(2): 153–70.
1989   "History of Investigations at the Weber I (20SA581) and Weber II (20SA582) Sites and Field and Lab Procedures." In *Archaeological Investigation at the Weber I (20SA581) and Weber II (20SA582) Sites, Frankenmuth Township, Saginaw County, Michigan,* edited by William Lovis, pp. 1–40. Lansing: Michigan Department of Transportation.
1999   "The Middle Archaic: Learning to Live in the Woodlands." In *Retrieving Michigan's Buried Past: The Archaeology of the Great Lakes State,* edited by John R. Halsey and Michael D. Stafford, pp. 83–94. Bloomfield Hills, Mich.: Cranbrook Institute of Science.
2001   "Clay Effigy Representations of the Bear and Mishipishu: Algonquian Iconography from the Late Woodland Johnson Site, Northern Lower Michigan." *Midcontinental Journal of Archaeology* 26(1): 105–19.

Lovis, William A., and James A. Robertson
1989   "Rethinking the Archaic Chronology of the Saginaw Valley, Michigan." *Midcontinental Journal of Archaeology* 14(2): 226–60.

Lovis, William A., Randolph E. Donahue, and Margaret B. Holman
2005   "Long-Distance Logistic Mobility as an Organizing Principle among Northern Hunter-Gatherers: A Great Lakes Holocene Settlement System." *American Antiquity* 70(4): 669–93.

Low, Setha, and Lawrence-Zúñiga, Denise
2003   "Locating Culture." In *The Anthropology of Space and Place: Locating Culture,* edited by Setha Low and Denise Lawrence-Zúñiga, 1–48. Oxford: Blackwell.

Luedtke, Barbara E.
1976   "Lithic Material Distributions and Interaction Patterns during the Late Woodland Period in Michigan." Ph.D. dissertation, University of Michigan, Ann Arbor.

MACPRA (Michigan Anishinaabek Cultural Preservation and Repatriation Alliance)
2009   http://www.macpra.org/ (accessed fall 2009).

Mahoney, Nancy
2000   "Chaco World." In *Archaeology Southwest,* vol. 14 (1), Tucson: Center for Desert Archaeology Winter Update (edition dedicated to Chaco Project).
2001   "Monumental Architecture as Conspicuous Display in Chaco Canyon." In *Chaco Society and Polity: Papers from the 1999 Conference,* edited by Linda S. Cordell, W. James Judge, and June Piper, pp. 13–29. Albuquerque: New Mexico Archaeological Society.

Mallam, Clark
1976   "Mound Builders: An American Myth." *Journal of the Iowa Archaeological Society* 23: 145–75.

Malville, J. M., and Nancy J. Malville
2001   "Pilgrimage and Periodic Festivals as Processes of Social Integration in Chaco Canyon." *Kiva* 66(3): 327–44.

Mann, Barbara A.
2003   *Native Americans, Archaeologists, and the Mounds.* Washington, D.C.: Peter Lang.

Mann, Rob
2005   "Intruding on the Past: The Reuse of Ancient Earthen Mounds by Native Americans." *Southeastern Archaeology* 24(1): 1–10.

Marcus, Joyce
2008   "The Archaeological Evidence for Social Evolution." *Annual Review of Anthropology* 37: 251–66.

Marcus, Joyce, and Kent V. Flannery
1994   "Ancient Zapotec Ritual and Religion: An Application of the Direct Historical Approach." In *Ancient Mind: Elements of Cognitive Archaeology,* edited by Colin Renfrew and Ezra Zubrow, pp. 55–74. Cambridge: Cambridge University Press.
2004   "The Coevolution of Ritual and Society: New C14 Dates from Ancient Mexico." *Proceedings of the National Academy of Science* 101: 18257–61.

Marshall, James
1990   *Map of the Missaukee Earthworks (20MA11–12).* On file at University of Michigan Museum of Anthropology, Great Lakes Range.

Martin, Scott W. J.
2008   "Languages Past and Present: Archaeological Approaches to the Appearance of Northern Iroquoian Speakers in the Lower Great Lakes Region of North America." *American Antiquity* 73(3): 441–63.

Martin, Susan R.
1989   "Reconsideration of Aboriginal Fishing Strategies in the Northern Great Lakes Region." *American Antiquity* 54(3): 594–604.

Mauss, Marcel
1990 [1922]   *The Gift: Forms and Functions of Exchange in Archaic Societies.* London: Routledge.

McAllister, Paul

1999   "Upper Mississippian in Western Lower Michigan." In *Retrieving Michigan's Buried Past: The Archaeology of the Great Lakes State,* edited by John R. Halsey and Michael D. Stafford, pp. 254–64. Bloomfield Hills, Mich.: Cranbrook Institute of Science.

McCarthy, F. D.

1939   "'Trade' in Aboriginal Australia, and 'Trade' Relationships with Torres Strait, New Guinea and Malaya." *Oceania* 9: 405–39.

McClurken, James M.

1991   *Gah-baeh-Jhagwah-buk—The Way It Happened: A Visual Culture History of the Little Traverse Bay Bands of Odawa.* East Lansing: Michigan State University Museum.

McGuire, Randall H.

1997   "Why Have Archaeologists Thought the Real Indians Were Dead and What Can We Do about It?" In *Indians and Anthropologists: Vine Deloria Jr. and the Critique of Anthropology,* edited by Thomas Biolsi and Larry Zimmerman, pp. 63–91. Tucson: University of Arizona Press.

McIntosh, Susan K.

1999   "Pathways to Complexity: An African Perspective." In *Beyond Chiefdoms: Pathways to Complexity in Africa,* edited by Susan K. McIntosh, pp. 1–30. Cambridge: Cambridge University Press.

McPherron, Alan

1967   *The Juntunen Site and the Late Woodland Prehistory of the Upper Great Lakes Area.* Anthropological Papers No. 30. Ann Arbor: University of Michigan Museum of Anthropology.

MDNR (Michigan Department of Natural Resources)

2009   Michigan Department of Natural Resources http://www.michigan.gov/dnr (accessed fall 2009).

Mehta, Jayur M.

2008   "An Archaeological Study of Sweat Lodges in the Southeastern United States." Manuscript on file, Archaeology Division, Historic Preservation, Mississippi Department of Archives and History, Jackson.

Merrell, James H.

1989   *The Indians' New World: Catawbas and Their Neighbors from European Contact through the Era of Removal.* Chapel Hill: University of North Carolina Press.

Meyer, David, and Paul C. Thistle

1995   "Saskatchewan River Rendezvous Centers and Trading Posts: Continuity in a Cree Social Geography." *Ethnohistory* 42(3): 403–44.

Michigan CGI (Center for Geographic Information)

2006   Michigan Center for Geographic Information. http://www.michigan.gov/cgi (data downloaded spring 2006).

Miller, Susan A.

2008   "Native America Writes Back: The Origin of the Indigenous Paradigm in Historiography." *Wicazo Sa Review* 23(2): 9–28.

2009   "Native Historians Write Back: The Indigenous Paradigm in American Indian Historiography." *Wicazo Sa Review* 24(1): 25–45.

Mills, Barbara J.
2000   "Alternative Models, Alternative Strategies: Leadership in the Prehispanic Southwest." In *Alternative Leadership Strategies in the Prehispanic Southwest,* edited by Barbara J. Mills, pp. 3–18. Tucson: University of Arizona Press.
2002   "Recent Research on Chaco: Changing Views on Economy, Ritual, and Society." *Journal of Archaeological Research* 10(1): 65–117.

Milner, Claire M.
1998   "Ceramic Style, Social Differentiation, and Resource Uncertainty in the Late Prehistoric Upper Great Lakes." Ph.D. dissertation, University of Michigan, Ann Arbor.

Milner, Claire M., and John M. O'Shea
1998   "The Socioeconomic Role of Late Woodland Enclosures in Northern Lower Michigan." In *Ancient Earthen Enclosures of the Eastern Woodlands,* edited by Robert C. Mainfort and Lynne P. Sullivan, pp. 181–201. Gainesville: University Press of Florida.

Milner, George
2004   *The Moundbuilders: Ancient Peoples of Eastern North America.* London: Thames & Hudson.

Milner, George, and George Chaplin
2010   "Eastern North American Population at ca. AD 1500." *American Antiquity* 75: 707–26.

Milner, George, and Richard Jefferies
1998   "The Read Archaic Shell Midden in Kentucky." *Southeastern Archaeology* 17: 119–32.

Minc, Leah, and Kevin Smith
1989   "The Spirit of Survival: Cultural Responses to Resource Variability in North Alaska." In *Bad Year Economics: Cultural Responses to Risk and Uncertainty,* edited by Paul Halstead and John O'Shea, pp. 8–39. Cambridge: Cambridge University Press.

Moll, Harold W., Norman G. Moll, and Eldon S. Cornelius
1958   "Earthwork Enclosures in Ogemaw, Missaukee, and Alcona Counties, Michigan." *Totem Pole* 41(3).

Morgan, Lewis H.
1996 [1851]   *League of the Iroquois.* New York: Corinth Books.
1997 [1871]   *Systems of Consanguinity and Affinity of the Human Family.* Lincoln: University of Nebraska Press.

Morrison, Kathleen, and Laura Junker (editors)
2002   *Forager-Traders in South and Southeast Asia: Long-term Histories.* Cambridge: Cambridge University Press.

Neitzel, Jill E. (editor)
2003   *Pueblo Bonito: Center of the Chacoan World.* Washington, D.C.: Smithsonian Institution Press.

Nelson, Ben A.
2006   "Mesoamerican Objects and Symbols in Chaco Canyon Contexts." In *The Archaeology of Chaco Canyon: An Eleventh-Century Pueblo Regional Center*, edited by Stephen H. Lekson, pp. 339–71. Santa Fe: School for Advanced Research Press.

Norder, John W.
2003   "Marking Place and Creating Space in Northern Algonquian Landscapes: The Rock-Art of the Lake of the Woods Region, Ontario." Ph.D. dissertation, University of Michigan, Ann Arbor.

O'Brien, Jean M.
1997   *Dispossession by Degrees: Indian Land and Identity in Natick, Massachusetts, 1650–1790*. Cambridge: Cambridge University Press.

O'Gorman, Jodie A.
2007   "The Myth of Moccasin Bluff—Rethinking the Potawatomi Pattern." *Ethnohistory* 54(3): 373–406.

O'Gorman, Jodie A., and William A. Lovis
2006   "Before Removal: An Archaeological Perspective on the Southern Lake Michigan Basin." *Midcontinental Journal of Archaeology* (special issue: The Potawatomi Removal, edited by Mark Schurr) 31(1): 21–56.

O'Shea, John M.
2003   "Inland Foragers and the Adoption of Maize Agriculture in the Upper Great Lakes of North America." *Before Farming: The Archaeology of Old-World Hunter-Gatherers* 2(3): 1–21.

O'Shea, John M., and Alexander W. Barker
1996   "Measuring Social Complexity and Variation: A Categorical Imperative?" In *Emergent Complexity: The Evolution of Intermediate Societies*, edited by Jeanne E. Arnold, pp. 13–24. Ann Arbor: International Monographs in Prehistory.

O'Shea, John M., and Meghan C. L. Howey
2003   "Test Excavations on Papineau Mound (20AA17), Hubbard Lake, MI." On file at University of Michigan Museum of Anthropology, Great Lakes Range.

O'Shea, John M., and Claire M. Milner
2002   "Material Indicators of Territory, Identity, and Interaction in a Prehistoric Tribal System." In *The Archaeology of Tribal Societies*, edited by William A. Parkinson, pp. 200–226. Ann Arbor: International Monographs in Prehistory.

O'Shea, John M., and Michael Shott (editors)
1990   *The Bridgeport Township Site: Archaeological Investigation at 20SA620, Saginaw County, Michigan*. Ann Arbor: University of Michigan Museum of Anthropology.

Owens, D'Ann, and Brian D. Hayden
1997   "Prehistoric Rites of Passage: A Comparative Study of Transegalitarian Hunter-Gatherers." *Journal of Anthropological Archaeology* 16: 121–61.

Ozker, Doreen
1982   *An Early Woodland Community at the Schultz Site 20SA2 in the Saginaw Valley and the Nature of the Early Woodland Adaptation in the Great Lakes Region*. Ann Arbor: University of Michigan Museum of Anthropology.

Parker, Kathryn E.

1996   "Three Corn Kernels and a Hill of Beans: The Evidence for Prehistoric
        Horticulture in Michigan." In Investigating the Archaeological Record of the
        Great Lakes State: Essays in Honor of Elizabeth Baldwin Garland, edited
        by Margaret Holman, Janet G. Brashler, and Kathryn E. Parker, pp. 307–39.
        Kalamazoo: Western Michigan University.

Parker Pearson, Mike, Joshua Pollard, Colin Richards, Julian Thomas, Christopher Tilley,
        and Kate Welham

2006   "Stonehenge, Its River and Its Landscape: Unraveling the Mysteries of a Prehistoric
        Sacred Place." *Archäologischer Anzeiger* 1: 237–58.

Parkinson, William A.

1999   "The Social Organization of Early Copper Age Tribes on the Great Hungarian
        Plain." Ph.D. dissertation, University of Michigan, Ann Arbor.

2002a   "Integration, Interaction, and Tribal 'Cycling': The Transition to the Copper Age
        on the Great Hungarian Plain." In *The Archaeology of Tribal Societies,* edited by
        William A. Parkinson, pp. 391–438. Ann Arbor: International Monographs in
        Prehistory.

2002b   "Introduction: The Archaeology of Tribal Societies." In *The Archaeology of Tribal
        Societies,* edited by William A. Parkinson, pp. 1–12. Ann Arbor: International
        Monographs in Prehistory.

Parkinson, William A. (editor)

2002   *The Archaeology of Tribal Societies.* Ann Arbor: International Monographs in
        Prehistory.

Pauketat, Timothy R.

2004   *Ancient Cahokia and the Mississippians.* Cambridge: Cambridge University Press.

2007   *Chiefdoms and Other Archaeological Delusions.* Walnut Creek, Calif.: Altamira
        Press.

Paynter, Robert

1989   "Archaeology of Equality and Inequality." *Annual Review of Anthropology* 18:
        369–99.

Pearsall, D. R., B. V. Barnes, G. R. Zogg, M. Lapin, and R. R. Ring (editors)

1995   *Landscape Ecosystems of the University of Michigan Biological Station.* Ann Arbor:
        School of Natural Resources and Environment, University of Michigan.

Pennell, Bob, and Carol Pennell

2004   Personal Communication.

Peregrine, Peter N.

2001   "Matrilocality, Corporate Strategy, and the Organization of Production in the
        Chacoan World." *American Antiquity* 66: 36–46.

Peregrine, Peter N., and Stephen H. Lekson

2006   "Southeast, Southwest, Mexico: Continental Perspectives on Mississippian
        Polities." In *Leadership and Polity in Mississippian Societies,* edited by Brian Butler
        and Paul Welch, pp. 351–64. Occasional Papers No. 33. Carbondale, Ill.: Center for
        Archaeological Investigations.

Peterson, Nicolas

1975   "Hunter-Gatherer Territoriality: The Perspective from Australia." *American
        Anthropologist* 77(1): 53–68.

Pilling, Arnold
1968   "A Use of Historical Sources in Archaeology: An Indian Earthworks Near Mt. Clemens, Michigan." *Ethnohistory* 15(2): 152–202.

Podruchny, Carolyn
2004   "Werewolves and Windigos: Narratives of Cannibal Monsters in French-Canadian Voyageur Oral Tradition." *Ethnohistory* 51(4): 677–700.

Pokagon, Simon
1899   *O-gî-mäw-kw*e mit-i-gwä-kî (Queen of the Woods)*. Hartford, Mich.: C. H. Engle.

Pollard, Joshua
2008   "Deposition and Material Agency in the Early Neolithic of Southern Britain." In *Memory Work: Archaeologies of Material Practices,* edited by Barbara J. Mills and William H. Walker, pp. 41–60. Santa Fe: School for Advanced Research Press.

Pollock, Susan
1983   "Style and Information: An Analysis of Susiana Ceramics." *Journal of Anthropological Archaeology* 2(4): 354–90.

Potter, James
2000   "Pots, Parties, and Politics: Communal Feasting in the American Southwest." *American Antiquity* 65: 471–92.

Prahl, Earl J.
1966   "The Muskegon River Survey: 1965 and 1966." *Michigan Archaeologist* 12(4): 183–210.

Pugh, Daniel
2001   "Aker Site (23PL43): Lithic Economy and Ritual Aggregation among the Kansas City Hopewell." *Plains Anthropologist* 46(177): 269–82.

Quimby, George I.
1960   *Indian Life in the Upper Great Lakes: 11000 B.C. to A.D. 1800.* Chicago: University of Chicago Press.
1962   "A Year with a Chippewa Family, 1763–1764." *Ethnohistory* 9(3): 217–39.
1965   "An Indian Earthwork in Muskegon County, Michigan." *Michigan Archaeologist— Papers in Honor of Emerson F. Greenman* (edited by James E. Fitting) 11(3/4): 165–69.

Randall, Asa, and Ken Sassaman
2010   "(E)mergent Complexities during the Archaic in Northeast Florida." In *Ancient Complexities: New Perspectives in Precolumbian North America,* edited by Susan Alt, pp. 8–31. Foundations in Archaeological Inquiry. Salt Lake City: University of Utah Press.

Rappaport, Roy A.
1979   *Ecology, Meaning, and Religion.* Richmond, Calif.: North Atlantic Books.
1999   *Ritual and Religion in the Making of Humanity.* Cambridge: Cambridge University Press.

Renfrew, Colin
2001   "Production and Consumption in a Sacred Economy: The Material Correlates of High Devotional Expression at Chaco Canyon." *American Antiquity* 66(1): 14–25.

Richter, Daniel K.
1992   *The Ordeal of the Longhouse: The Peoples of the Iroquois League in the Era of European Colonization.* Chapel Hill: University of North Carolina Press.

Richter, Daniel K., and James H. Merrell (editors)
2003 [1987]   *Beyond the Covenant Chain: The Iroquois and Their Neighbors in Indian North America, 1600–1800.* State College: Pennsylvania State University Press.

Robertson, James A., William Lovis, and John R. Halsey
1999   "The Late Archaic: Hunter-Gatherers in an Uncertain Environment." In *Retrieving Michigan's Buried Past: The Archaeology of the Great Lakes State,* edited by John R. Halsey and Michael D. Stafford, pp. 95–124. Bloomfield Hills, Mich.: Cranbrook Institute of Science.

Ross, Lester A.
1985   "16th-Century Spanish Basque Coopering." *Historical Archaeology* 19: 1–31.

Rowley-Conwy, Peter A.
2001   "Time, Change and the Archaeology of Hunter-Gatherers: How Original Is the 'Original Affluent Society'?" In *Hunter Gatherers: An Interdisciplinary Perspective,* edited by Catherine Panter-Brick, Robert H. Layton, and Peter A. Rowley-Conwy, pp. 39–72. Cambridge: Cambridge University Press.

Sackett, James R.
1985   "Style and Ethnicity in the Kalahari: A Reply to Wiessner." *American Antiquity* 50: 154–59.

Sahlins, Marshall D.
1961   "The Segmentary Lineage: An Organization of Predatory Expansion." *American Anthropologist* 63(2): 322–45.
1968   *Tribesmen.* Englewood Cliffs: Prentice-Hall.

Sahlins, Marshall D., and Elman R. Service (editors)
1960   *Evolution and Culture.* Ann Arbor: University of Michigan Press.

Said, Edward W.
2003 [1978]   *Orientalism.* New York: Vintage Books.

Salisbury, Neil
1996   "The Indians' Old World: Native Americans and the Coming of Europeans." *William and Mary Quarterly* 3: 435–58.

Sassaman, Kenneth
2005   "Poverty Point as Structure, Event, Process." *Journal of Archaeological Method and Theory* 12(4): 335–64.

Sassaman, Kenneth, and Michael Heckenberger
2004   "Crossing the Symbolic Rubicon in the Southeast." In *Signs of Power: The Rise of Cultural Complexity in the Southeast,* edited by Jon L. Gibson and Phillip J. Carr, pp. 214–33. Tuscaloosa: University of Alabama Press.

Saunders, Joe, and Thurman Allen
1994   "Hedgepath Mounds: An Archaic Mound Complex in North-Central Louisiana." *American Antiquity* 59(3): 471–89.

Saunders, Joe W., Rolfe D. Mandel, C. Garth Sampson, Charles M. Allen, E. Thurman
        Allen, Daniel A. Bush, James K. Feathers, Kristen J. Gremillion, C. T. Hallmark, H.
        Edwin Jackson, Jay K. Johnson, Reca Jones, Roger T. Saucier, Gary L. Stringer, and
        Malcolm F. Vidrine
2005   "Watson Brake, A Middle Archaic Mound Complex in Northeast Louisiana."
        American Antiquity 70(4): 631–68.

Saunders, Rebecca
1994   "The Case for Archaic Period Mounds in Southeastern Louisiana." *Southeastern
        Archaeology* 13(2): 118–34.

Saxe, Arthur A.
1970   "Social Dimensions of Mortuary Practices." Ph.D. dissertation, University of
        Michigan, Ann Arbor.

Scarre, Christopher (editor)
2002   *Monuments and Landscape in Atlantic Europe: Perception and Society during the
        Neolithic and Early Bronze Age.* London: Routledge.

Schachner, Gregson
2001   "Ritual Control and Transformation in Middle-Range Societies: An Example from
        the American Southwest." *Journal of Anthropological Archaeology* 20(2): 168–94.

Schaetzl, Randall J., Bruce D. Knapp, and Scott A. Isard
2005   "Modeling Soil Temperatures and the Mesic-Frigid Boundary in the Central Great
        Lakes Region, 1951–2000." *Soil Science Society of America Journal* 69(6): 2033–41.

Schlesier, Karl H.
1990   "Rethinking the Midewiwin and the Plains Ceremonial Called the Sun Dance."
        Plains Anthropologist 35(127): 1–27.

Schneider, Robert
1942   "Report of Cleaning Out a Cache Pit." *Totem Pole* 10(1): 5.

Schroeder, Sissel
2004a   "Current Research on Late Pre-Contact Societies of the Midcontinental United
        States." *Journal of Archaeological Research* 12(4): 311–72.
2004b   "Power and Place: Agency, Ecology, and History in the American Bottom, Illinois."
        Antiquity 78: 812–27.

Schumacher, J. P.
1918   "Indian Remains in Door County." *Wisconsin Archaeologist* 16(4).

Service, Elman R.
1962   *Primitive Social Organization: An Evolutionary Perspective.* New York: Random
        House.
1968   "War and Our Contemporary Ancestors." In *The Anthropology of Armed Conflict
        and Aggression,* edited by Morton Fried, Marvin Harris, and Robert Murphy, pp.
        160–67. Garden City, N.Y.: Natural History Press.

Shepherd, Jeffery
2008   "At the Crossroads of Hualapai History, Memory, and American Colonization:
        Contesting Space and Place." *American Indian Quarterly* 32(1): 16–42.

Sherratt, Andrew G.
1990   "The Genesis of Megaliths: Monumentality, Ethnicity and Social Complexity in
        Neolithic North-West Europe." *World Archaeology* 22: 147–67.

Sherwood, Sarah, and T. R. Kidder
2011   "The DaVincis of Dirt: Geoarchaeological Perspectives on Native American Mound Building in the Mississippi River Basin." *Journal of Anthropological Archaeology* 30: 69–87.

Shott, Michael
1990   "Lithic Analysis." In *The Bridgeport Township Site: Archaeological Investigation at 20SA620, Saginaw County, Michigan,* edited by John M. O'Shea and Michael Shott, pp. 59–108. Ann Arbor: University of Michigan Museum of Anthropology.

Silliman, Steve
2009   "Change and Continuity, Practice and Memory: Native American Persistence in Colonial New England." *American Antiquity* 74(2): 211–30.

Silverberg, Robert
1968   *Mound Builders of Ancient America.* Greenwich: New York Graphic Society.

Sinopoli, Carla M.
1991   *Approaches to Archaeological Ceramics.* New York: Plenum Press.

Skibo, James M.
1992   *Pottery Function: A Use-Alteration Perspective.* New York: Plenum Press.

Smith, Beverley A.
1996   "Systems of Subsistence and Networks of Exchange in the Terminal Woodland and Early Historic Periods in the Upper Great Lakes." Ph.D. dissertation, Michigan State University, East Lansing.
2004   "The Gill Net's 'Native Country': The Inland Shore Fishery in the Northern Lake Michigan Basin." In *An Upper Great Lakes Archaeological Odyssey: Essays in Honor of Charles E. Cleland,* edited by William A. Lovis, pp. 64–84. Bloomfield Hills, Mich.: Cranbrook Institute of Science.

Smith, Denise H.
2001   "Rock Art and the Shape of the Landscape." In *Painters, Patrons, and Identity: Essays in Native American Art to Honor J. J. Brody,* edited by Joyce M. Szabo, pp. 211–40. Albuquerque: University of New Mexico Press.

Smith, Eric A., and Bruce Winterhalder (editors)
1992   *Evolutionary Ecology and Human Behavior.* New York: Aldine de Gruyter.

Snow, Dean
1994   *The Iroquois.* Oxford: Basil Blackwell.
2002   "The Dynamics of Ethnicity in Tribal Society: A Penobscot Case Study." In *The Archaeology of Tribal Societies,* edited by William A. Parkinson, pp. 97–108. Ann Arbor: International Monographs in Prehistory.

Sommer, Jeffery
2010   Personal Communication. Curator of Archaeology, Saginaw Castle Museum.

Spencer, Herbert
1851   *Social Statics: or, The Conditions Essential to Human Happiness Specified, and the First of Them Developed.* London: J. Chapman.
1857   "Progress: Its Law and Cause." *Westminster Review.* http://www.readbookonline. net/readOnLine/23352/ (accessed fall 2009).
1897   *The Principles of Sociology, 1876–96.* Vol. 3. New York: D. Appleton and Co.

Speth, John D.
1966   "The Whorley Earthwork." *Michigan Archaeologist* 12(4): 211–27.

Spielmann, Katherine A.
1983   "Late Prehistoric Exchange between the Southwest and Southern Plains." *Plains Anthropologist* 28(1): 257–72.
2002   "Feasting, Craft Specialization, and the Ritual Mode of Production in Small-Scale Societies." *American Anthropologist* 104(1): 195–207.

Spielmann, Katherine A. (editor)
1991   *Farmers, Hunters, and Colonists: Interaction between the Southwest and the Southern Plains.* Tucson: University of Arizona Press.

Spielmann, Katherine A., and James F. Eder
1994   "Hunters and Farmers: Then and Now." *Annual Review of Anthropology* (23): 303–23.

Spindler, Louise S.
1978   "Menominee." *Handbook of North American Indians* 15: 708–24.

Stark, Miriam T. (editor)
1998   *The Archaeology of Social Boundaries.* Washington, D.C.: Smithsonian Institution Press.

Steward, Julian H.
1955   *Theory of Culture Change: The Methodology of Multilinear Evolution.* Urbana: University of Illinois Press.

Stothers, David M.
1995   "'Michigan Owasco' and the Iroquois Co-tradition: Late Woodland Conflict, Conquest, and Cultural Realignment in the Western Lower Great Lakes." *Northeast Anthropology* (49): 5–41.
1999   "The Late Woodland Models for Cultural Development in Southern Michigan." In *Retrieving Michigan's Buried Past: The Archaeology of the Great Lakes State,* edited by John R. Halsey and Michael D. Stafford, pp. 194–211. Bloomfield Hills, Mich.: Cranbrook Institute of Science.

Stothers, David M., Timothy J. Abel, and Andrew M. Schneider
1998   "The Bear Fort Complex (33SA8): A Stratified Prehistoric-Protohistoric Sandusky Tradition Occupation Site." *Archaeology of Eastern North America* 26: 55–95.

Struever, Stuart
1964   "The Hopewell Interaction Sphere in Riverine-Western Great Lakes Culture History." In *Hopewellian Studies,* edited by J. R. Caldwell and R. L. Hall, pp. 85–106. Springfield: Illinois State Museum.

Tacha, T. C., A. Woolf, W. D. Klimstra, and K. F. Abraham
1991   "Migration Patterns of the Mississippi Valley Population of Canada Geese." *Journal of Wildlife Management* 55: 94–102.

Tacon, Paul
1999   "Identifying Ancient Sacred Landscapes in Australia: From Physical to Social." In *Archaeologies of Landscape: Contemporary Perspectives,* edited by Wendy Ashmore and Arthur B. Knapp, pp. 33–57. London: Blackwell Publishing.

Tambiah, Stanley J.
1985   *Culture, Thought, and Social Action: An Anthropological Perspective.* Cambridge, Mass.: Harvard University Press.

Tanner, Helen H.
1987   *Atlas of Great Lakes Indian History.* 1st ed. Norman: published for the Newberry Library by the University of Oklahoma Press.

Taussig, Michael
1993   *Mimesis and Alterity: A Particular History of the Senses.* London: Routledge.

Thomas, Cyrus
1894   "Report on the Mound Explorations of the Bureau of Ethnology." In *12th Annual Report of the Bureau of American Ethnology for the Years 1890–1891,* pp. 3–730. Washington, D.C.: Smithsonian Institution Press.

Thomas, David H.
2000   *Skull Wars: Kennewick Man, Archaeology and the Battle for Native American Identity.* New York: Basic Books.

Thomas, Julian
1999   *Understanding the Neolithic.* 2nd ed. London: Routledge.

Thwaites, Reuben G. (editor)
1896–1901 *The Jesuit Relations and Allied Documents: Travels and Explorations of the Jesuit Missionaries in New France, 1610–1791.* Vol. 59, Section 3. Cleveland: Burrows Brothers.

Tilley, Christopher Y.
1994   *A Phenomenology of Landscape: Places, Paths, and Monuments.* Oxford: Berg.

Toll, H. Wolcott
2001   "Making and Breaking Pots in the Chaco World." *American Antiquity* 66(1): 56–78.

Trelease, Allen W.
1960   *Indian Affairs in Colonial New York: The Seventeenth Century.* Ithaca: Cornell University Press.
1962   "Indian-White Contacts in Eastern North America: The Dutch in New Netherland." *Ethnohistory* 9(2): 137–46.

Trigger, Bruce G.
1987   *The Children of Aataentsic: A History of the Huron People to 1660.* Montreal: McGill-Queen's University Press.
1990a   "Maintaining Economic Equality in Opposition to Complexity: An Iroquoian Case Study." In *The Evolution of Political Systems: Sociopolitics in Small-Scale Sedentary Societies,* edited by Steadman Upham, pp. 119–46. Cambridge: Cambridge University Press.
1990b   "Monumental Architecture: A Thermodynamic Explanation of Symbolic Behaviour." *World Archaeology* 22(2): 119–32.

Trouillot, Michel-Rolph
2003   *Global Transformations: Anthropology and the Modern World.* New York: Palgrave Macmillan.

Turgeon, Laurier
1997   "The Tale of the Kettle: Odyssey of an Intercultural Object." *Ethnohistory* 44(1): 1–29.

Tylor, Edward B.
1870   *Researches into the Early History of Mankind and the Development of Civilization.* London: J. Murray.
1871   *Primitive Culture: Researches into the Development of Mythology, Philosophy, Religion.* Croydon: Gordon Press.

Upham, Steadman (editor)
1990   *The Evolution of Political Systems: Sociopolitics in Small-Scale Sedentary Societies.* Cambridge: Cambridge University Press.

Van Dyke, Ruth M.
2004   "Memory, Meaning, and Masonry: The Late Bonito Chacoan Landscape." *American Antiquity* 69(3): 413–31.
2008   *The Chaco Experience: Landscape and Ideology at the Center Place.* Santa Fe: School for Advanced Research Press.

Vehik, Susan C.
2002   "Conflict, Trade, and Political Development on the Southern Plains." *American Antiquity* 67(1): 37–64.

Vizenor, Gerald
1998   *Fugitive Poses: Native American Indian Scenes of Absence and Presence.* Lincoln: University of Nebraska Press.

Vreeland, F. M.
1924   "Site Finding Trip Field Notes." On file at Ann Arbor: University of Michigan Museum of Anthropology, Great Lakes Range.

Wagner, Mark J.
1998   "Some Think it Impossible to Civilize Them at All: Cultural Change and Continuity among the Early Nineteenth-Century Potawatomi." In *Studies in Culture Contact: Interaction, Culture Change, and Archaeology,* edited by James Cusick, pp. 430–56. Occasional Paper No. 25. Carbondale: Center for Archaeological Investigations, Southern Illinois University.

Walker, W. S., B. V. Barnes, and D. M. Kashian
2003   "Landscape Ecosystems of the Mack Lake Burn, Northern Lower Michigan, and the Occurrence of the Kirtland's Warbler." *Forest Science* 49(1): 119–39.

Wallace, Anthony F. C.
1970   *The Death and Rebirth of the Seneca.* New York: Knopf.

Wallis, Neill
2008   "Networks of History and Memory: Creating a Nexus of Social Identities in Woodland Period Mounds on the Lower St. Johns River, Florida." *Journal of Social Archaeology* 8(2): 236–71.

Warren, William W.
1984 [1885]   *History of the Ojibway People.* St. Paul: Minnesota Historical Society Press.

Watanabe, John M.
2007   "Ritual Economy and the Negotiation of Autarky and Interdependence in a Ritual Mode of Production." In *Mesoamerican Ritual Economy: Archaeological and Ethnological Perspectives,* edited by E. C. Wells and Karla L. Davis-Salazar, pp. 301–22. Boulder: University of Colorado Press.

Wesson, Cameron B.
2008   *Households and Hegemony: Early Creek Prestige Goods, Symbolic Capital, and Social Power.* Lincoln: University of Nebraska Press.

Whallon, Robert
1968   "Investigations of Late Prehistoric Social Organization in New York State." In *New Perspectives in Archaeology,* edited by Lewis R. Binford and Sally R. Binford, pp. 223–44. Chicago: Aldine Press.

White, Bruce M.
1999   "The Woman Who Married a Beaver: Trade Patterns and Gender Roles in the Ojibwa Fur Trade." *Ethnohistory* 46: 109–47.

White, Richard
1991   *The Middle Ground: Indians, Empires, and Republics in the Great Lakes Region, 1650–1815.* Cambridge: Cambridge University Press.

Whitley, Thomas, and Lacey Hicks
2001   "Using a Geographic Information Systems (GIS) Approach to Extract Potential Prehistoric and Historic Period Travel Corridors across a Portion of North Georgia." http://www.brockington.org/papers/SEAC2001-WhitleyandHicks.pdf (accessed fall 2007).

Wiessner, Polly
1982   "Risk, Reciprocity and Social Influences on !Kung San Economics." In *Politics and History in Band Societies,* edited by Eleanor Leacock and Richard B. Lee, pp. 61–84. Cambridge: Cambridge University Press,
1983   "Style and Social Information in Kalahari San Projectile Points." *American Antiquity* 48(2): 253–76.
1984   "Reconsidering the Behavioral Basis for Style: A Case Study among the Kalahari San." *Journal of Anthropological Archaeology* 3(3): 190–234.
2002   "Vines of Complexity: Egalitarian Structures and the Institutionalization of Inequality among the Enga." *Current Anthropology* 43(2): 233–69.

Wilkins, David E.
1997   *American Indian Sovereignty and the U.S. Supreme Court: The Masking of Justice.* Austin: University of Texas Press.

Windes, Thomas C.
1991   "The Prehistoric Road Network at Pueblo Alto, Chaco Canyon, New Mexico." In *Ancient Road Networks and Settlement Hierarchies in the New World,* edited by Charles Trombold, pp. 111–31. Cambridge: Cambridge University Press.

Winters, Howard
1984   "The Significance of Chert Procurement and Exchange in the Middle Woodland Traditions of the Illinois Area." In *Prehistoric Chert Exploitation: Studies from the Midcontinent,* edited by Brian Butler and Ernest May, pp. 3–21. Carbondale: Center for Archaeological Investigations, Southern Illinois University.

Witgen, Michael
2007   "The Rituals of Possession: Native Identity and the Invention of Empire in 17th Century Western North America." *Ethnohistory* 54(4): 639–68.

Wobst, H. M.
1977   "Stylistic Behavior and Information Exchange." In *For the Director: Research Essays in Honor of James B. Griffin,* edited by Charles E. Cleland, pp. 317–42. Anthropological Papers No. 61. Ann Arbor: University of Michigan Museum of Anthropology.

Wolf, Eric R.
1997 [1982]   *Europe and the People without History.* Los Angeles: University of California Press.
1999   *Envisioning Power: Ideologies of Dominance and Crisis.* Berkeley: University of California Press.

Wright, Gary A.
1966   "Eastern Edge Survey: 1965 Season." *Michigan Archaeologist* 12: 151–68.

Wright, Joshua
2007   "Organizational Principles of Khirigsuur Monuments in the Lower Egiin Gol Valley, Mongolia." *Journal of Anthropological Archaeology* 3: 350–65.

Yarnell, Richard A.
1964   *Aboriginal Relationships between Culture and Plant Life in the Upper Great Lakes Region.* Anthropological Papers No. 23. Ann Arbor: University of Michigan Museum of Anthropology.

Yerkes, Richard
2002   "Hopewell Tribes: A Study of Middle Woodland Social Organization in the Ohio Valley." In *The Archaeology of Tribal Societies,* edited by William A. Parkinson, pp. 227–45. Ann Arbor: International Monographs in Prehistory.

Yoffee, Norman
2001   "The Chaco 'Rituality' Revisited." In *Chaco Society and Polity: Papers from the 1999 Conference,* edited by Linda S. Cordell, W. James Judge, and June Piper, pp. 63–78. Special Publication 4. Albuquerque: New Mexico Archaeological Council.
2005   *Myths of the Archaic State: Evolution of the Earliest Cities, States and Civilizations.* Cambridge: Cambridge University Press.

Zurel, Richard
1999   "Earthwork Enclosure Sites in Michigan." In *Retrieving Michigan's Buried Past: The Archaeology of the Great Lakes State,* edited by John R. Halsey and Michael D. Stafford, pp. 244–48. Bloomfield Hills, Mich.: Cranbrook Institute of Science.

Index

All references to illustrations are in italic type.